AF285186

Statehood in the Altaic World

Proceedings of the 59th Annual Meeting of the
Permanent International Altaistic Conference
(PIAC),
Ardahan, Turkey, June 26–July 1, 2016

Edited by
Hartmut Walravens
Barbara Kellner-Heinkele
Oliver Corff

BoD

Bibliographische Information der Deutschen Nationalbibliothek:
Die Deutsche Nationalbibliothek verzeichnet diese Publikation in der
Deutschen Nationalbibliografie; detaillierte bibliographische Daten
sind im Internet über http://dnb.dnb.de abrufbar.

ISBN 9783752802634

Herstellung und Verlag:
BoD – Books on Demand, Norderstedt

To the memory of

Albina H. Girfanova (1957–2018),

a faithful PIAC contributor

Contents

Preface

Annual meetings of the PIAC tend to take place in towns and cities that offer an attractive setting for scholarly encounters. If we consider the towns where we have gathered, just in the last decade, we see a wide variety of academic specialties and local culture on display: 2010: St. Petersburg/Russian Federation; 2011 Bloomington, Indiana/ USA; 2012 Cluj-Napoca/Romania; 2013 Kocaeli/Turkey; 2014 Vladivostok/Russian Federation; 2015 Dunajská Streda/Slovakia; 2016 Ardahan/Turkey; and, 2017 Székesfehérvár/ Hungary.

The 2016 Annual Meeting of 2016 offered its participants from twelve countries a special treat as it took place at Ardahan University in the far northeast of Turkey, near the town of Ardahan, not far from the city of Kars. Ardahan University is a young university, founded only in 2008, its buildings perch on the slope of an undulating mountain range. The view in late June 2016 was of green meadows flush with flowers. A few kilometers further on towards the Turkish-Georgian border, a mountain pass (more than 3000 m high) still carried patches of snow. Some participants sniffed the air of Ardahan and were reminded of the unspoiled nature of other exceptional regions they had visited.

Ardahan University displayed an impressive ensemble of attractive architecture over a wide area – faculty buildings, rectorate, conference hall, library, student housing, indoor and outdoor sports facilities, guest house, and more sites still under construction, all threaded through with flower beds and fledgling trees.

The participants of the 59th Annual PIAC Meeting were most cordially welcomed by the President of the Meeting, Prof. Dr. Ramazan KORKMAZ, rector and founder of Ardahan University. Prof. Dr. Gürkan DOĞAN, the organizer of the meeting, made the participants feel at home and oversaw the smooth running of the program. The participants were delighted with the hospitality they experienced at the very comfortable Yenisey Guesthouse, the realm of Mrs Havva VANLI and her team.

On Monday, 27 June, the Opening Ceremony assembled PIAC participants and international delegates from the Caucasus University Association for a series of lectures on the present state of international reseach in Turkology. In the afternoon, PIAC participants engaged in the "Confessions" (reports on current individual research). The presentation of papers took place on Tuesday and Thursday, leaving Wednesday free for an excursion to the extraordinary ruins of the medieval city of Ani and for a tour of Kars. Participants also enjoyed the visit to the town of Ardahan with its special regional flair.

Participation in the Ardahan meeting was average in number which made the sessions more focussed and left time between sessions for intensive discussions and for making new acquaintances and connections, which, after all, is a major function of all conferences.

This volume presents a number of the papers presented at the Ardahan meeting. Other papers were published independently in academic journals elsewhere. However, the topics dealt with in the present volume reflect the thematic distribution of papers at the meeting. They ranged from problems of the Old Turkic inscriptions to language reform in contemporary Turkic-speaking republics. There were linguistic comparisons encompassing Turkic, Mongolian, Manchu, Japanese, Korean and Chinese, along with a consideration of philological problems of rare texts. In other words, there was a large variety of research approaches and proposed results, accompanied by lively discussions.

In the name of the participants of the 59th Annual Meeting of the PIAC, the editors wish to express their heartfelt thanks to Prof. Dr. Ramazan KORKMAZ and Prof. Dr. Gürkan DOĞAN and their team, for the wonderful hospitality extended to the PIAC participants at Ardahan University. The atmosphere of generous academic exchange they provided will remain a lasting memory for those who attended the meeting.

March 2018

Barbara Kellner-Heinkele

Bâbur's Affinity for Fabric

Christine BELL (Berlin)

ZAHIR-UD-DIN MUHAMMAD BÂBUR (14 February 1483–26 December 1530), the Central Asian conqueror known as the founder of the Moghul empire, remains compelling today through his memoirs spanning 37 years. Annette Susannah BEVERIDGE, the translator of the *Bâbur-nâma*, wrote "... what has kept interest in it alive through some four centuries is the autobiographic presentment of an arresting personality ...," that have "the rare distinction of being contemporary with the events it describes, is boyish [age 11] in his boyhood, grows with his growth, matures as he matured. Undulled by retrospect, it is a fresh and spontaneous recital of things just seen, heard or done." (BEVERIDGE 1922, p. xxxi).

Bâbur is known for having recorded details of his surroundings during his travels: flora and fauna, geological features, biographical details, etc. It was brought to my attention by Dr. Münevver TEKCAN, Istanbul that many textile references can also be found in the Bâbur-nâma. This led to the idea of extracting them and explaining their relevance. My particular interest is in material culture – specifically the field of textiles. "In today's world of readily obtained, mass-produced goods, textiles are taken for granted, ... but historically textiles were an investment of time and resources that retained value." (VOLLMER 2002, p. 4). To understand how important fabric is as an economic factor, we need only to consider the effort invested in producing cloth. Industrialization has made the production of fabric less time consuming and less expensive, but the investment of energy and technology in cloth and clothing remains high even today.

Although most of us wear clothing almost all of the time, its importance is often ignored in economics, history and literature; its value should not be underestimated. Clothing demonstrates the group you belong to, the tribe you're from, your wealth, status and social position. Aisa MARTINEZ, a curator for the Zayed National Museum

Project in Abu Dhabi, states that garments are "active participants in creating and fostering a sense of cultural identity.... (and are) a form of non-verbal communication defining our roles in society (through) a language of personal adornment."[1] Even in the midst of marauding, skirmishing and military setbacks Bâbur takes note of cloth and clothing and recorded its tangible presence over and over again.

To keep things brief, I'm only presenting those excerpts and foot-notes in the Bâbur-nâma, including untranslated expressions, that appear relevant to my field of interest. Some passages have been abridged. Those with content belonging to more than one subject area are repeated. I'm clarifying these passages by bringing a knowledge of textiles and the role they play into the never-ending discussion on the Bâbur-nâma. My comments and explanations are included in brackets to differentiate from Beveridge's in parentheses.

Comments on Cloth
Costly textiles were traditionally a highly desirable commodity in Central Asia, that were appreciated as symbols of political power and prestige. From the beginning of their rule, Bâbur's nomadic ancestors went to great lengths to obtain luxury textiles and to control the sources. The elite of the 15th century were very much in contact with the major centers of Persianate Timurid culture. They were attuned to the concept of portable or wearable wealth; silk had a value that could be applied to the payment of taxes, war indemnity, bestowed as a tribute, used in rituals or as a burial offering. Cloth was collected as booty and clothing was valuable enough to present as a gift. On a local level, spinning wool and weaving cloth either for domestic use or as a cottage industry were ubiquitous in Bâbur's time. Aside from its aesthetic appeal, cloth was easily transportable and had long played a vital role in the highly profitable trade with China for the swift and slender, long-necked horses of Central Asia. Horses were especially crucial for the Chinese military that was sometimes forced to import

---

1   CAMPBELL 2016, p. 30. From a talk by the Arabian dress specialist at an event of the Textile Society of Boston's Museum of Fine Arts.

them from very distant places. "The presentation of an average horse by a Mongol [for selling to Chinese soldiers] required a bolt of high-quality silk, eight bolts of coarse silk and a cash payment equal to an additional two bolts of coarse silk." (WEATHERFORD 2010, p. 224).

Cloth was mentioned in the Bâbur-nâma in general terms numerous times without being specific but is almost certainly wool. White cloth appears several times; it clearly originates in Hindustan and almost certainly refers to cotton.

(Sec. I, page 129) "When we were near Nûndâk, a servant of KHUSRAU SHÂH brought me one set of nine horses and one of nine pieces of cloth." [Beveridge explains that the Turks and Mughûls customarily made gifts in sets of nines – *toquz*. The "auspicious" number 9 appears in the next excerpt in a different context.]

(I, 155) " ... the standards were acclaimed in Mughûl fashion. The Khân dismounted and nine standards were set up in front of him. A Mughûl tied a long strip of white cloth to the thighbone of a cow and took the other end in his hand. Three other long strips of white cloth were tied to the staves of three of the (nine) standards, just below the yak-tails, and their other ends were brought for the Khân to stand on one and for me and Sl. Muh. Khânika to stand each on one of the two others. The Mughûl who had hold of the strip of cloth fastened to the cow's leg, then said something in Mughûl while he looked at the standards and made signs towards them."[2]

---

2 ["Bâbur and his army saluting the standards" derives from an epic event depicted in a Bâbur-nâma painted circa 1589. Bâbur salutes the yak-tail standards on the left. Members of the royal military band blow trumpets and one, mounted on a camel at the upper right, beats a large drum. Three of the standards are loosely wrapped with strips of white cloth – probably cotton – and one is fastened to the leg of the cow on the lower left.]

Figure 1. Bâbur holding a bowl of fermented mare's milk (*kumis*) salutes the yak-tail standards.

(**I, 160**) "... in the old fashion, they had hung, on the left side, a haversack (*chantâi*) and an outer bag, ...". [*A tâsh chantâi* is a haversack – literally a sack of oats – and probably refers to a sturdy bag, of wool cloth, used for carrying rations.]

(**I, 202**) "Down to Kabul every year come 7, 8, or 10,000 horses and up to it, from Hindustan, come every year caravans of 10, 15 or 20,000 heads-of-houses, bringing slaves, white cloth, sugar-candy, refined and common sugars, and aromatic roots."

(**I, 233**) "Much white cloth fell into (their) hands." [This cloth clearly originated in Hindustan and probably refers to fine cotton muslin from Dhaka.]

(**I, 234**) "Our foragers went from there into the hills, destroyed the 'Îsa-khail *sangur* and came back with sheep, herds and cloth." [This cloth is probably of domestic productions and refers to wool.]

(**I, 235**) "Some of our men, riding light, reached villages of the Plain in the afternoon, raided a few, and brought back flocks, cloth and horses bred for trade."

(**I, 235**) "During our stay there, the foragers brought in from villages in the Plain, masses of sheep and cattle, and, from Afghân traders met on the roads, white cloths, aromatic roots, sugars, tîpûchâqs [the swift and slender, long-necked horses of Central Asia], and horses bred for trade."

(**I, 237**) "Cloth and things of the baggage fell to our men."

(**I, 237**) "He having driven the enemy off, other soldiers went over who returned with cloth and droves [herds of animals] of various sorts."

(I, 238) "Our men, by perpetually gallopping off on raids, had knocked up their horses; usually what they took, cattle mostly, was not worth the gallop; sometimes indeed in the Plain there had been sheep, sometimes one sort of cloth or other, but, the Plain left behind, nothing was had but cattle."

(I, 338-339) "The goods of the elder and younger (Arghun) brethren had been kept in separate treasuries; out of each had come chest upon chest, bale upon bale of stuffs [fabric of undistinguished quality] and clothes-in-wear (*artmâq*), sack upon sack of white tankas [small silver coins]."

(II, 631) "Before food all the sultans, khans, grandees, and amirs brought gifts of red, of white, of black, of cloth and various other goods. They poured the red and white on a carpet I had ordered spread, and side by side with the gold and silver piled plenishing [furnishings], white cotton piece-cloth [lengths of fabric] and purses of money."

Comments on fibers

Cotton

Although varieties of wild cotton could be found on several continents, India is generally believed to have first cultivated it. Greek historian Herodotus mentions Indian cotton in the 5th century BCE as "a wool exceeding in beauty and goodness that of sheep." Arab merchants reportedly brought cotton cloth to Europe as early as 800 A.D. By 1500, cotton was generally known throughout the world.

Gossypium arboreum, native to the Indus valley region, provided a source of fiber that was cheap and readily available since ancient times. Cotton became widespread during the Indus Valley Civilization, a Bronze Age civilization (3300–1300 BCE) extending from what today is northeast Afghanistan to Pakistan and northwest India. Its presence is probably responsible for the proficiency of spinning and weaving in ancient India.

Indus cotton provided the raw material for an industry that developed fabrication methods that were so sophisticated that they continued to be used long after the industrialization of the textile industry in Europe. It remains a major Indian export up to the present day. Bengali spinners developed the techniques to prepare and spin fibers from varieties of *Gossypium herbaceum* creating an incredibly fine thread that made their woven cotton unique. This fabric later became associated with the power and elegance of the Mughal court (ISLAM 2016 p. 30–31). This fabled muslin was made of the very lightest of fibers spun into thread and woven into an airy cloth that bears no resemblance to the machine-milled cotton we know under this name today[3].

In addition to the fineness and delicacy of the fabric, Indian textiles were also noted for their brilliant colours and prints. Indian craftsmen learned early on the secrets of mordants and dyes and how to manipulate them to create colorful textiles. The craftsmen managed to protect their knowlege of the complex techniques of cotton dyeing and printing secret from the rest of the world until the 17th century.

Cotton in its natural state is ivory, or pale green, red or brown and demands bleaching to make it white. It absorbs moisture and retains dye well, is strong and easy to launder and most importantly – it is comfortable. That's why it is still a favorite fiber today, used in 65% of all fabric produced for clothing and home furnishings.
Cotton fiber is mentioned in the Bâbur-nâma twice, muslin once:

(I, 67) "Such however was the discipline of our army that an order to restore everything having been given, the first watch of the next day had not passed before nothing, not a tag [scrap] of cotton, not a broken needle's point, remained in the possession of any man of the force, all was back with its owners."

(I, 380) "Do no hurt or harm to the flocks and herds, nor even to their cotton-ends [fragments] and broken needles."

---

3   Muslin from Hindustan was known at that time by such poetic names as *abrawan* (flowing water), *shabnam* (evening dew), *tanzeb* (flowing water)...

(II, 632) "On KUCHUM KHAN's envoy and on HASAN CHALABI's younger brother were bestowed silken head-wear and gold-embroidered surtouts [long outer robes] of fine muslin [fine Hindustani cotton], with suitable dresses of honour."

Silk (silken)

Sericulture was widely known in Bâbur's time, but silk was probably mostly imported from China via trade routes through the Himalayas. In the Bâbur-nâma the term "silk" is only found in relation to yardage or coats. The expression "silken" is mentioned in connection with clothing – especially headwear – but also in regards to furnishings. This usage may refer to a fabric known as "*sufi*" derived from the Persian word *musuffa*, meaning pure or – in this case – lawful. Sufi refers to a law that forbids orthodox Muslims from wearing silk unless mixed with cotton. (TORTORA & JOHNSON 2013 pp. 597–600).

(I, 70) "He had many gold and silver drinking cups and utensils, much silken plenishing [furnishings] and countless tîpuchâq horses" [the swift and slender, long-necked horses of Central Asian].

(I, 258) "He [Sultan HUSAIN MÎRZÂ] was slant-eyed and lion-bodied, being slender from the waist downwards. Even when old and white-bearded, he wore silken garments of fine red and green."[4]

(I, 338) "Excellent tîpûchâqs, strings and strings of he-camels, she-camels, and mules, bearing saddle-bags of silken stuffs and cloth, -- tents of scarlet [cloth] and velvet[5], all sorts of awnings, every kind of work-shop, ass-load after ass-load of chests."

---

4   Madder has a long history as a reliable red dye; a colorfast green dye didn't exist until the 1920's. In this case indigo-dyed yarn was probably overdyed with a yellow dyestuff before weaving, making green fabric a costly endeavor.

5   Velvet has a soft pile of an intense hue thus draping in a distinctive manner making it desirable for clothing and suitable for furnishings. Weaving it is labour-intensive, time-consuming and requires sophisticated looms. Two face-to-face lengths of fabric connected by an extra set of warp yarns are woven simultaneously and then sliced apart. The resulting fabric that absorbs and

(II, 632) "On Kuchum Khan's envoy and on Hasan Chalabi's younger brother were bestowed silken head-wear and gold-embroidered sur-touts [long outer robes] of fine muslin, with suitable dresses of honour."

Wool (woolen) and felt

Wool has been providing warmth and shelter for at least 6000 years. It affects such aspects of our lives as the domestication of sheep and the development of looms that were closely connected to the rise of industrialization. If the connection in the Western world with wool runs deep, we must understand how much more deeply ingrained it is in Central Asia's history, lifestyle and trade. "Wool" can found several times in the Bâbur-nâma, usually in connection with items of clothing or tents, but also metaphorically. In Central Asia fabric made of wool from sheep, yaks, goats or camels was probably so widespread that the word "cloth" most likely means wool.

Although felt is not often mentioned in the Bâbur-nâma, it was surely ubiquitous. Felt is thought to be the most ancient form of fabric known to mankind, predating looms. It is speculated that the unique natural properties of wool – the scales coating each fiber interlock irreversibly under the influence of heat, friction and moisture – was noticed by early man who discovered naturally felted wool on the inside of hides used in shoes.

White felt (just as white cotton or silk) is the most time consuming to produce. The lightest natural color of felt is yellowish and demands intensive bleaching to render it white, making it the most expensive of its kind.

Wool is a natural insulator that retains an ideal balance of moist-ure. It can soak up to as much as 30% of its weight in moisture

---

reflects light and can also accomodate 3-D designs. It isn't precisely known where and when velvet originated, but it existed as early as the Ming Dynasty. Recent tomb discoveries date silk velvet in China to about the 2nd century (KUHN 2012, p. 401). Although velvet today is woven with many different fibers, in Bâbur's time it was certainly made of silk.

without feeling wet. This is a result of its natural crimp that prevents wool fibers from laying flat.

(I, 20 & 21) "YÛNAS Khân went amongst them and took to wife AÎSÂN-DAULAT BEGÎM, the daughter of their chief, 'ALÎ-SHÎR BEG. They then seated him and her on one and the same white felt and raised him to the Khânship." [Beveridge reported that a primitive custom *khân kûtârdîlâr* was to lift the Khân-designate off the ground. This phrase became metaphorical for the inauguration of a khan.]

(I, 188) "So destitute were we that we had but two tents (*châdâr*) amongst us; my own used to be pitched for my mother, and they set an *âlâchuq* at each stage for me to sit in." [The term *chador* is known today as a tent-like garment; in Turkish the *alacık* is a felt-covered round tent of the nomads, a *yurt*.]

(I, 239) "After passing Chûtîâlî, my own felt-tent [*yurt*] had to be left from want of baggage-beasts. One night at that time, it rained so much, that water stood knee-deep in my tent (*châdâr*); I watched the night out till dawn, uncomfortably sitting on a pile of blankets." [According to Beveridge, Bâbur's felt-tent was "a *khar-gâh*, a folding tent on lattice frame-work". Turkish karagâh however means military headquarters. Perhaps the reference is to the tent's function and not descriptive.]

(II, 572) "The absurd Hindus, knowing their position perilous, *dispersed like carded wool before the wind, and like moths scattered abroad*." [This is a quote from the Koran.]

(II, 678) "We laid them in the folds of a woolen throne-carpet, put this on the throne and on it piled blankets." [This refers to pages of the Bâbur's autobiography scattered during an unexpected flood and is apparently related to one of the lacunae.]

Comments on clothing

Clothes play an important role in the Bâbur-nâma and are mentioned repeatedly. As we know clothing is worn in almost all human societies. Apparel depends on social and geographic considerations while providing a protective barrier between the skin and the environment. Central Asia was under nomadic Mongolian influence as of the middle of the 13th century. Costumes were well adapted to the climatic and environmental conditions of life on the steppe and the pastoral activities of nomads. Design elements and terms evolving from this period still prevail in Central Asia today.

One of the most basic aspects of a nomadic life is riding. By the age of 5 to 6 every child had his or her own horse. Trousers worn under layers of clothing were topped by either a hip-long jacket or a knee-long coat with an overlap and sometimes lined with fur. A wide variety of headgear with protective flaps and brims also served to identify clans and groups. Typical weapontry also was adapted to local conditions; cattle rustling was widespread and horse stealing especially popular as a rite-of-passage among young men. (URAY-KŐHALMI 1989 pp. 48.)

In wide-open spaces proficiency with the bow was of particular importance. The development of bows and quivers demonstrate innovations to make them easier and faster in usage. Nomad warriors avoided hand-to-hand fighting. Their strength lay in surprise attacks and fake flight. Their tactics of warfare were those of light cavalry and their protective quilted clothing with sparse metallic fittings reflected this. (URAY-KŐHALMI 1989 pp. 49–50.)

Nomads in Central Asia occupied an area between two garment-making traditions; both of which reflect the optimal use of available materials. In forested areas of the north, animal hides provided the raw materials for clothing. The physical dimensions of hides and cloth differ, having an impact on garment construction. Hide is limited by the size and shape of the animal and requires reinforcement and piecing. To the south, sedentary populations developed weaving and cloth became the basis of garment construction. Woven fabric depends on the width of the loom resulting in garments with straight seams and rectangular shapes.

Whenever materials from one culture are adopted by another culture to make clothing, concessions are inevitable. Sometimes traditional construction methods are so entrenched that they are retained regardless of economic considerations. Whatever the reason, as cloth became more widespread, it impacted the cut of traditional garments of the steppe (VOLLMER 2002, p. 35–36).

"Strategies for garment construction vary but demonstrate re-markable consistency within geographic regions and among ethnic and linguistic groups" (VOLLMER 2002, p. 143–144). This is for-tunate, as not many actual garments or even textiles are in existence from this period and region. The garments that survive almost all come from tombs; they generally reveal more about material and weaves, designs and colors, than about cut. As was often the case with clothing, most surviving garments were altered at some time and usually belonged to members of the higher levels of society. Style is quite another matter; it is influenced by taste, status or rank. A very important aspect of costume is the autocratic intentions of rulers and their influence on it as well as its use to promote ethnic identity for further political ambitions (VOLLMER 1980, p. 30). Regulations, terms and even styles of garments were decreed.[6]

Manuscript illustrations and drawings by artists working in courtly ateliers between 1400–1500 A.D. provide excellent details of clothing in the essential features of cut, although one should probably disregard an imaginative use of color and patterns (*Encyclopædia Ira-nica, online*).

If we accept that animal hides or homespun fibers and the width of handwoven cloth determine the design of a culture's garments, we

---

6 During Bâbur's reign the hem of the *jâmah* was straight cut and had open side seams that resulted in drooping corners on each side of the body. Bâbur's grandson AKBAR (1556–1605) decreed that such minor sartorial details as the hem of the jâmah be redesigned and renamed during his realm. He decreed that the skirt should be cut in such a way as to eliminate these unaesthetic drooping corners and is therefore responsible for the rounded hems that prevail today.

must also understand the reverence they display for even the smallest piece of material. Historically manufacturing cloth or curing leather was labor intensive and time consuming; imported yardage was an expensive luxury. An accommodating fit and the construction of garments that made the utmost use of fabric was almost always of economic interest (VOLLMER 2002, p. 143).

An important aspect of clothing that I chose not to pursue in this paper is the *khilcat-i-khâsa* and the *bâsh-ayâqin*. This formal presentation of sets of clothing (robes of honor and head-to-foot) by rulers and victors to dignitaries, allies and subjects is mentioned 40 times in the Bâbur-nâma.

(I, 258) "He [Sultan HUSAIN Mîrzâ] was slant-eyed and lion-bodied, being slender from the waist downwards. Even when old and white-bearded, he wore silken garments of fine red and green."

Figure 2. Genghis Khan and three of his four sons. Illustration from a 15th-century *Jami' al-tawarikh* manuscript[7]

---

7   The *Jāmi' al-tawārīkh*, is a work of literature and history, produced in the Mongol Ilkhanate in Persia. Written by RASHID AL-DIN HAMADANI (1247–1318) at the start of the 14th century, the breadth of coverage of the work has caused it to be

Mongol men's clothing of Bâbur's time

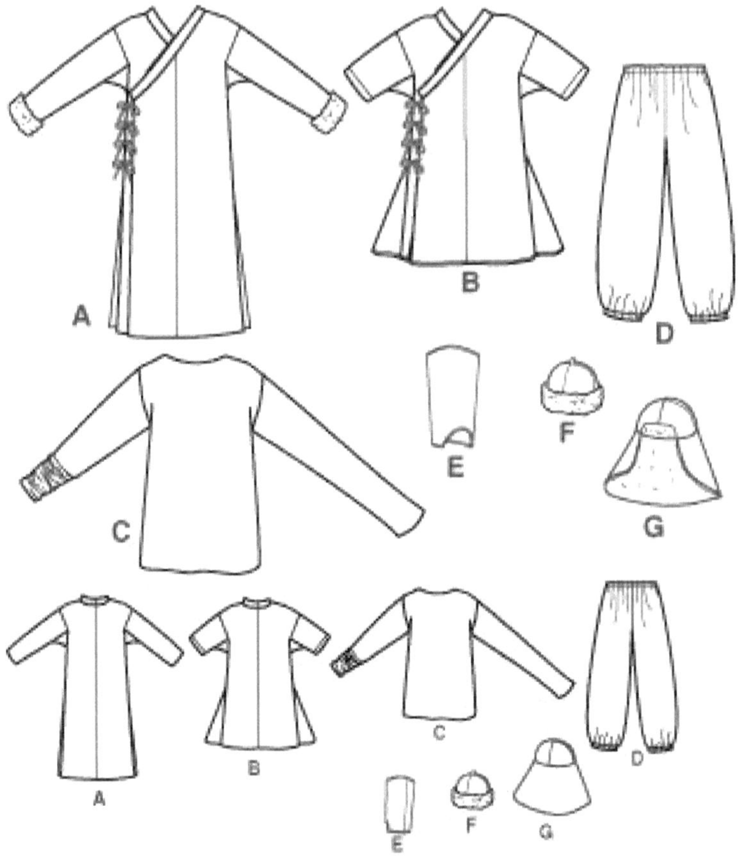

Figure 3. Some traditional Mongolian men's garments – front and back views

(I, 338–339) "The goods of the elder and younger (Arghun) brethren had been kept in separate treasuries; out of each had come chest upon

---

called "the first world history".

chest, bale upon bale of stuffs [undistinguished fabric] and clothes-in-wear (artmâq), sack upon sack of white tankas."

Men's daily wear in Bâbur's time was comprised of 4 basic items of clothing:

A. a knee to ankle-length surcoat (*jâmah*) with over-long sleeves;
B. a shorter version of the surcoat (*nîmcha*) having shorter sleeves;
C. an undershirt (*kûnglâk*) with over-long sleeves;
D. trousers (*pai-jama*) with a drawstring waist;
E. a conical hat of felt or;
F. a fur trimmed skullcap (*börk*) or;
G. a skullcap or helmet with protective flaps of leather, felt or padded fabric.

Additional items of clothing not included in this illustration are:

1. the *jabbah* a sleeveless, ankle-length surcoat with a center-front opening;
2. the *chapan* a simple T-shaped, ankle-length coat with an over-lapping front opening for everyday use. Underwear, meaning a loin-cloth, and footwear completed the costume.[8]

Comments on headwear (*Bâshîq*)

It is a logical assumption that Turkic headgear evolved, from the practical leather, fur and felt helmets with protective flaps and brims that were preferred by nomads leading an active life on horseback, along with the spread of Turkic culture from Northeast Asia west-wards. Historical sources describe royal headgear in leather, fur or fabric as being decorated with metallic thread and ornaments. Textile hats with protective flaps (see Fig. 3 G), coverings and brims as well as helmets and coronets with metallic parts ultimately gave way to the Islamic turban wrapped around a tall cap. (ESIN 1970, p. 72).

(II, 632) "On Kuchum Khan's envoy and on Hasan Chalabi's younger brother were bestowed silken head-wear and gold-embroidered

---

8   Some difficulties arose in translating terms for clothing in the Bâbur-nâma. The Beveridge translation of the Bâbur-nâma generally kept to the Timurid terms but confusion arose when items were translated from Persian.

surtouts [outer robes] of fine muslin [delicate cotton from Hindustan], with suitable dresses of honour."

Figure 4. This idealized illustration (ca. 1605) of Bâbur on a hunting excursion provides generally accurate details of clothing of his time.

Börk/bûrkî (**cap**)

Börk (bûrkî) is a Turkish generic word for cap of so many styles that is usually qualified with an adjective (see Fig. 3 F). It appears that the börk of Central Asia had a brim but the Muslim Türkmens of the Near East wore a brimless börk, that could also serve as the base around which a turban was wound (ESIN 1970, p. 74). In many illustrations of that time and region, men are depicted wearing turbans or armored headgear of leather and metal. Tall felt or fur hats can occasionally be identified (see Fig. 3 E.) as well as hats that can be identified as the tall, 4-sided, brimmed Kyrgyz felt *kalpak (qalpaq)* that is still popular in Central Asia today.

(**I, 150**) "QASIM Beg said, with much insistance, 'As these men are going, send something special of your own wear by them to JAHANGIR Mirza.' I sent my ermine cap [*âs bûrk*]." [This bestowal of a hat owned – and worn – by Bâbur was a designation of honour and status.]

(**I, 167**) "I had on the cap of my helm; TAMBAL chopped so violently at my head that it lost all feeling under the blow. A large wound was made on my head, though not a thread of the cap was cut." [According to Beveridge the *dûwûlgha bûrkî* is the sturdy soft cap worn under the iron helmet. It would have been padded and quilted for insulation as well as for comfort.]

(**I, 175**) "Next I shot at a man running away along the ramparts, adjusting for his cap against the battlements; he left his cap nailed on the wall and went off, gathering his turban-sash together in his hand." [This cap – a *börk* – served as the base for his turban. To trick onlookers he left his cap in an exposed place and left taking his sash with him.]

(**I, 258**) "He used to wear either the black lambskin cap (*qarâqûzi bûrk*) or the *qâlpâq* ..." [The high-crowned, 4-sided kalpak worn by men in Central Asia is made of felt or sheepskin. The brim can be turned up all the way around. A kalpak keeps the head warm in winter and shades the eyes during summer. In the Turkic cultures of Central Asia they taper to resemble a mountain, in Turkey they are more cylindrical.]

(I, 396) "...TAMBAL chopped at my head. It was wonderful! The (under)-cap of my helm was on my head; not a thread of it was cut, but on the head itself was a very bad wound." [In this skirmish Bâbur had no time to put on his armour, not even his helmet; just a quilted undercap, the *dûwûlgha bûrkî*, to protect him.]

Mughûl bûrk (Moghul cap)

Redhouse reportedly translates the term *bûrk* (börk) – as a generic Turkish word for hat or cap, and describes it as being tall and of felt. An adjective used to qualify the Mughûl cap (*muftûl* or *mûftûnlûq*) has been understood to mean, solid, twisted or gold-embroidered.[9] The sturdy crowns of Mongolian caps of felt or fabric are often reinforced by lines of quilting sometimes with metallic threads. A princely börk was apparently distinguished from other börks through its height (ESIN 1970, p. 73).

(I, 14–15): "In the heats and except in his Court, he [Bâbur's father UMAR SHAIKH MÎRZÂ] generally wore the Mughûl cap." [Wearing a cap instead of a turban is an indication of Umar Shaikh Mîrzâ's preference for comfort and a certain disregard of rank.]

(I, 160) "All his men had adorned themselves in Mughûl fashion. There they were in Mughûl caps (bûrk); long coats of Chinese satin, broidered with stitchery, Mughûl quivers and saddles of green shagreen-leather, and Mughûl horses adorned in a unique fashion."

---

9 THACKSTON speculates that this tall Mongolian cap was decorated with a twisted appliqué or braid. Knowledge of textile techniques indicate that a "twisted" appliqué not possible; twisted braid is more plausible.

Figure 5. Detail from "Bâbur and Humayun receive a courtier"
showing a man wearing a turban wrapped around a tall, quilted velvet
or felt *bûrk*.

[It is not clear what Mughûl fashion means, perhaps it refers to the quilted coats and hats of Chinese brocade. Shagreen is untanned leather with a pebbly finish that provides a good grip.][10]

(**I, 179**) "Some men have gone along that road, led by one wearing a Mughûl cap; there is no going that way."

Turban

It is safe to assume that *turban*s originally were utilitarian: worn around the waist, flung over the shoulder or loosely wrapped around the head as protection from the sun or to bind up hair; it could be used in transporting property, to carry young or weak animals, or to kneel on for prayer.

Although the turban is of pre-Islamic origin, it came in Islamic times to distinguish first the Arab from the non-Arab and then the Muslim from the non-Muslim. According to certain traditions, when Adam descended to earth, a turban was placed on his head as a substitute for the crown he had worn in paradise thus paving the way for the association of turbans with crowns (*Encyclopædia Iranica*, *online*).

As the turban became emblematic with the spread of Islam, originally having a clerical character and later as Islamic royal headgear, its use became increasingly obligatory in court; the bûrk was relegated to military garments. (ESIN 1970, p. 131). Muslim men of Central Asia often shaved their heads and covered them with various types of skullcaps with and without brims. When a turban was worn, a sash was wrapped around a brimless cap and this ensemble was treated as a single unit. It was not unusual to take off the cap wrapped with its

---

10 Shagreen in Central Asia was traditionally prepared by trampling seeds into the damped rawhide of a horse. When the skin was dry the seeds were removed leaving scars on the surface of the leather. Today shagreen is commonly made of the skins of Southeast Asian stingrays (probably the pearled ray, *Hypolophus sephen*) and is known as sharkskin. (*Wikipedia, online*). This may predate the Central Asian shagreen.

Figure 6. Various Moghul turban styles

twisted sash, place it in on a shelf and don a simple cap for wear at home.

A turban came to symbolise authority. They indicated a man's wealth and social standing. The longer (larger) a turban was, the greater the authority of the person wearing it. Turbans differed in the style of wrapping and the fabric from which they were made; plain white muslin was commonly used and was probably imported from the Indian subcontinent.

The portraits we have of Bâbur were painted after his death; a. contempory rendition of him is yet unknown but he is generally shown with a book in his hand and wearing an elaborately twisted and decorated turban wrapped around a pointed, pleated cap. Although few *kavuk* have survived to the present day, a portrait of MEHMED II "Fatih" (reigned 1444–1446 & 1451–1481) was portrayed in ca 1480 wearing this headgear (ATASOY 2012, p. 33).

In the collection of the Topkapı a *kavuk* is described as being made of paper mache and wood. REDHOUSE translates *kavuk* as a quilted turban, a rather unsatisfactory explanation as the kavuk is clearly the quilted undercap around which a turban is wrapped. Perhaps kavuk came in time to mean an ensemble including both items.[11] The word turban appears seven times in the Bâbur-nâma.

Figure 7. 16th century Ottoman turban with a pleated red velvet *kavuk*

---

11 It is interesting to note that the Persion *kulâh* – just as the Turkish *börk* – appears to be a generic word for caps of so many styles that they are virtually always qualified with adjectives.

(I, 14-15) "He [UMAR SHAIKH Mîrzâ] was not choice in dress or food. He wound his turban in a fold (dastar-pech); all turbans were in four folds (*chār-pech*) in those days people wore them without twisting and let the ends hang down." [In this case Umar Shaikh Mîrzâ apparently folded a sash once lengthwise, wrapped around his skullcap and tucked in the ends, although the fashion of the time was to wrap the untwisted sash four times around the cap and leave the ends hanging free.][12]

(I, 33) "He [Sl. AHMAD Mirza] had very pleasing manners. As was the fashion in those days, he wound his turban in four folds and brought the end forward over his brows."

(I, 70) "He had many gold and silver drinking cups and utensils, much silken plenishing [furnishings] and countless tîpuchâq horses. He now lost everything. He hurled himself in his flight down a mountain track, leading to a precipitous fall. He himself got down the fall, with great difficulty, but many of his men perished there." [He purportedly escaped from the precipice by tying turban-sashes together and letting himself down.]

(I, 101) "On that day, Page KHALIL, the turban-twister, went well forward and got his hand into the work." [Wrapping turbans was a task that required skill. Often the turban with the undercap were removed and stored together.]

(I, 175) "Next I shot at a man running away along the ramparts, adjusting for his cap against the battlements; he left his cap nailed on the wall and went off, gathering his turban-sash together in his hand." [He hung the cap worn under his turban on the wall and ran off with the sash.]

---

12 According to the *Encyclopedia Iranica* a meaning was eventually assigned to every twist of the sash as it "generated additional light in the heart of the wearer". Therefore the number of twists became important.

(I, 258) "He used to wear either the black lambskin cap (*qarâ-qûzi bûrk*) or the *qalpaq*, but on a Feast-day would sometimes set up a little three-fold turban, wound broad and badly, stick a heron's plume in it and so go to Prayers." [He preferred wearing traditional Central Asian caps on a daily basis, but put a badly-twisted turban on for prayers and Islamic holidays.]

(I, 409) "I bestowed on him a turban twisted for myself, and also a head-to-foot (*bâsh-ayâq*)."

Kûnglâk (undershirt or vest)

In many illustrations a garment worn next to the skin can be seen at the neck of the jâmah (Fig. 3, C.). The opening was rounded, usually undyed and sometimes appears to be quilted. This is the straight-cut *kûnglâk* (undershirt) found throughout most of Central Asia. It was pulled on over the head and generally closed on the right shoulder. It is constructed of rectangular pieces of fabric without tucks or darts but with gussets under the arms to provide freedom of movement.

(I, 171) "Drowsy with sleep, he gets into his vest (kûnglâk), goes out, with five or six of his men, charges the enemy and drives them out with blow upon blow."

(I, 175) "As we came opposite the Gate, we saw Shaikh BAYAZID, wearing his pull-over shirt above his vest, coming in with three or four horsemen."

Jâmah (coat)

Jâmah in the Bâbur-nâma is translated variably as a tunic, shirt or a coat. In Bâbur's time it demonstrates its nomadic background and practicality in an active outdoor life. This garment, usually with a waist seam and flaring skirt, was undoubtedly derived from animal-hide prototypes. Although few jâmah from Bâbur's time have survived, a wealth of artistic evidence allows us to identify this garment and the gradual changes in its design throughout his era (VOLLMER 2002, p. 42).

Figure 8. The Portrait of Ottoman Sultan MEHMED the Conqueror by
İtalian painter Gentile BELLINI, 1480.

Essentially it is a knee-to-ankle-length garment with over-long, tapered sleeves that created folds at the wrist and could be pulled down to cover the hand. The close-fitting bodice has a distinctive crossover front that provided additional warmth and protection for a horseman. Fabric ties – 10 to 15 cm in length – descending under the right arm keep the jâmah bodice closed. These were placed to allow easy access to a sword belted on the left side of the body and a dagger or a quiver of arrows on the right. The sleeves feature a gusset in the armpit to allow a snug fit without compromising mobility. The crossover front of the bodice was often used as a pocket.

To prevent it from bunching at the waist when riding jâmahs generally had either a gathered or pleated "skirt" that was attached to the bodice by a seam usually hidden under a sash or belt. The front bottom corners of the jâmah could be tucked into the belt to provide freedom of movement.

Unlined coats were called *yaktâî jâmah*; two-fold ones *du-tahi jâma* [presumably meaning lined]. See Fig. 3 and 9.

(I, 14) "He [Umar Shaikh Mîrzâ] used to wear his tunic [jâmah] so very tight that to fasten the strings he had to draw his belly in and, if he let himself out after tying them, they often tore away. He was not choice in dress or food." [Umar Shaikh Mîrzâ was apparently disinterested in appearance but liked food; the fashion of the time was for the tunic to be worn tight – his jâmah did not properly accomodate his belly.]

(I, 104) "If we had them seized and stripped bare, where would be the wrong? and this especially because they might be going about before our very eyes, riding our horses, wearing our coats [jâmah? chapan?], eating our sheep. Who could put up with that?"

(I, 166) "It was my habit to lie down, even in times of peace, in my tunic [jâmah]; up I got instanter, put on sword and quiver and mounted."

Figure 9. Mongolian silk *deel* (jâmah) 13th–14th century, Inner
Mongolia

MONGOL COAT
(JAMA)

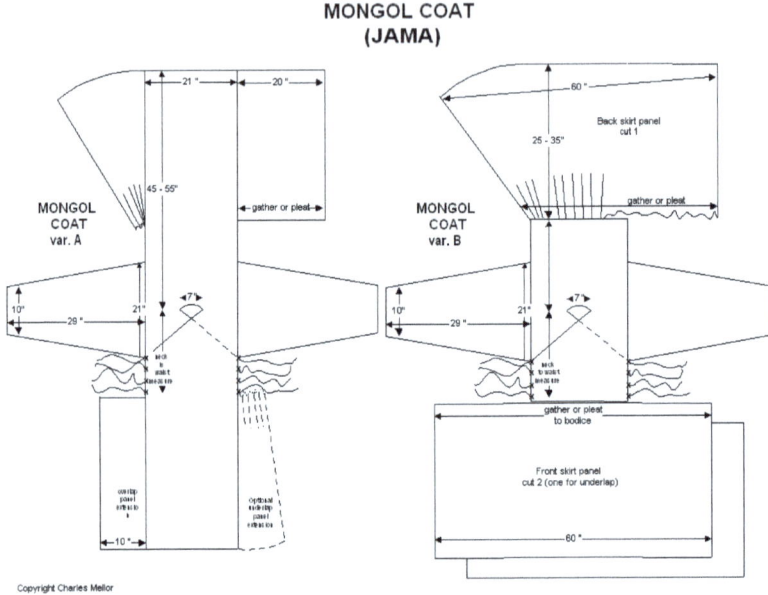

Copyright Charles Mellor

Figure 10. Pattern schemes for two differing styles of *jâmah*

(I, 180) "Each of us putting a loaf into the breast of his tunic [the crossover above the waist sash was often used as a pocket] we went quickly up the rise, tethered our horses there in the open valley and went to higher ground, each to keep watch."

(II, 642) "In congratulation on the birth of HUMAYUN's son and KAMRAN's marriage, Mulla TABRIZ and Mirza Beg TAGHAL were sent with gifts to each Mirza of 10,000 *shâhrukhis*, a coat I had worn, and a belt with clasps." [This bestowal of a jâmah worn by Bâbur was a special honour.]

(II, 652) "After the meal, he and his sons were dressed in unlined coats (*yaktâî jâmah*) ... " [According to Beveridge the *yaktâî* or one-fold coat is an unlined coat in contrast to the *du-tahi* or two-fold coat; it follows that the du-tahi is a lined coat.]

Figure 11. 17th cent. illustration showing Isfandiyâr killing two lions.

This brilliantly colored image from FIRDAUSI's *Shahname* shows details of Central-Asian traditional clothing that have remained much the same for centuries. ISFANDIYÂR is wearing a long-sleeved mauve jâmah with a green lining under a red nîmcha over his yellow pai-jâmas. He has tucked the front corners of his jâmah and nîmcha into his belt to have more freedom of movement. He is wearing a greenish sash under his leather belt and has a shield on his back. He appears to be wearing heeled shoes – Persian style – for riding. He is wending a sword, wearing a dagger in his belt and has a quiver of arrows at his waist. On his head he wears a princely helmet with chain mail covering one ear and that continues around the back of the head to the other one. His helmet sports an aigrete with black and white plumes.

Nîmcha (jacket)

The *nîmcha* of Bâbur's time was a jacket much the same as the jâmah but shorter and having cap sleeves that extended beyond the shoulders and ended above the elbow. It sometimes appears to have a center front opening instead of the jâmah's usual crossover. This jacket was worn over the jâmah and transformed the appearance of it through a contrasting color, fabric or insignia thus also providing an indicator of rank or status. Its functional role was to provide an extra layer of insulation and protection while retaining the ease of movement convenient on horseback (VOLLMER 2002, p. 48–49). A sash and/or sword belt was worn with it. (See Fig. 3 B).[13]

Period illustrations show the popularity of this garment as the outer layer of clothing worn daily by soldiers and hunters[14]. The front opening of a military nîmcha can be decorated with vertical rows of horizontal braid ending with "knots" made of braid[15] opposite loops of

---

13 A popular layered look was achieved by wearing this shorter nîmcha with short sleeves over the jâmah, tucking it into the trousers (*pai-jama*) or wearing it unsashed and open in the front.

14 The expression nîmcha survives today. It has been used at least since the XIX century in Uzbekistan to describe knee-long sleeveless jackets worn by women.

15 In Central Asian "buttons" were generally "knots" created from fabric. Vertical rows of horizontal braid with knots and corresponding loops were often indicated in the auspicious number 9 or 18. These closures became so fashionable in

braid on the other. These provide additional protection for the torso and were popular with light-armed cavalry instead of heavy armor. (See Fig. 11) This costume proved very practical for troops on reconnaissance in advance of the army, harassing enemy skirmishers, raiding for fodder and pursuing fleeing troops. This style of jacket survives even today in the regimental clothing of light-horsemen such as in modern "hussar" uniforms.

(II, 642) "Through Mullâ BIHISHTI were sent to Hind-âl an inlaid dagger with belt, an inlaid ink-stand, a stool worked in mother-o'pearl, a tunic and a girdle *[tak-band]*, together with the alphabet of the Bâburî script and fragments written in that script." [According to BEVERIDGE's footnotes, the tunic is a nîmcha; the takband is a silk or wollen girdle with a "hook & eye" fastening, but maybe a buckle is meant.]

(II, 652) "After the meal, he and his sons were dressed in unlined coats *(yaktâî jâmah)* and short tunics *(nîmcha)*."

Jabbah (surtout)

The Arabic *jubba*, or Turkish *cübbe* is an ankle-length outer garment resembling an open coat, somtimes sleeveless or long sleeved. It often has the same knot & loop closing as the nîmcha but this was definitely a fashion statement as this garment doesn't lend itself horseback riding.

Beveridge used *surtout* to describe a garment longer than the nîmcha but having a similar cut. The French term derives from *sur* 'over' + *tout* 'everything' that came into use in the late 17th century to describe a double-breasted, knee-length coat. It is impossible to know exactly what item of clothing is meant in the Bâbur-nâma but is likely to have been an ankle-length sleeveless garment with a center-front opening worn over an ankle-length jâmah. (See Bâbur's clothing in

---

Ottoman times that almost every Sultan is portrayed wearing garments using this front closure.

Fig. 4) This robe could be lined or trimmed with fur; decorated with gold embroidery, braid, or pearls; and is made of wool, silk, or cotton.

(II, 631-632) "After the chief of the food had been set out, Khwâja 'ABDU'SH-SHAHÎD and Khwaja KALAN were made to put on surtouts (*jabbah*) [16] of fine muslin, spotted with gold-embroidery, and suitable dresses of honour, and those headed by Mullâ FARRÛKH and HÂFIZ had jackets [nîmcha?] put on them. On Kûchûm Khân's envoy and on Hasan Chalabi's younger brother were bestowed silken head-wear [turbans?] and gold-embroidered surtouts of fine muslin, with suitable dresses of honour. Gold-embroidered jackets and silk coats were presented to the envoys of ABÛ-SA'ID SL. (Aûzbeg), of Mihr-bân Khânim and her son Pulâd Sl., and of Shâh HASAN (Arghûn)."

Chapan (lined surcoat)

The *ubiquitous* robe of Central Asia, the simple T-shaped *chapan* with its overlapping front opening, has basically remained unchanged for centuries. It quite probably evolved as an auxiliary garment suited to camp-based and herding activities (VOLLMER 2002, p. 49). Artistic evidence shows that this item of outerwear is cut much like the nîmcha but it is longer; ranging somewhere below the knee to above the ankle. It is worn over the jâmah and is lined and sometimes quilted. The cut of this garment is generally the same for both men and women, but a man's chapan generally had a narrow stand-up collar in addition to a front tie closing.

Chapans often have decorative edging on the front opening, as well as along the hem and the sleeves as they are thought to ward off evil spirits. Both chapan and *postin* have vents in the lower side seams for ease of movement. Worn by both nomads and settled people, chapans were lined for summer wear and padded and quilted for warmth in the

---

16 BEVERIDGE wrote that both scribes and translators were puzzled here, but as the gifts were presented in Agra they would probably be Indian. A *jabbah* of fine muslin with gold-embroidery was almost certainly Indian, where a ankle-length, but long-sleeved garment is still known today as a jabbah.

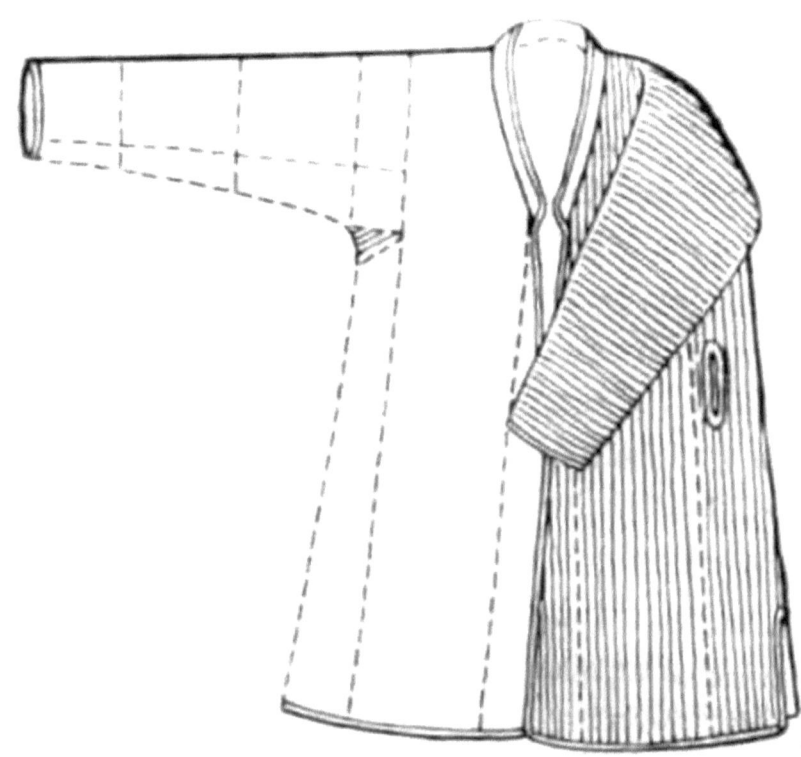

Figure 12. T-shaped chapan from Central Asia

winter. The sleeves are generally longer than the hands, to provide warmth (gloves weren't in use) or to conceal them (MELLER 2013, p. 36)[17].

---

17 Bâbur is said to have worn caftans thus providing us with the oldest documentation of this garment. There are no references in the Beveridge translation of the Bâbur-nâma to directly support this. But caftans have a long history in the traditional dress of Central Asia as well as in the Middle East. The origin of the word *kaftan* derives from the Arabic or Turkish (qaftan), Persian (khaftan) or maybe the Russian (kaftán). As far as the shape and construction of the caftan, it

(I, 187) "Those who, hoping in me, went with me into exile, were, small and great, between 2 and 300; they were almost all on foot, had walking-staves in their hands, brogues on their feet, and long coats on their shoulders. ...." [The long coat is identified in the Bâbur-nâma as being a *chapan*, an ordinary quilted outer garment of Central Asia that is still worn today.]

(I, 400) "To Malik Shāh Mansūr was given a long silk coat [probably a chapan] and an under-coat with its buttons [probably a jâmah with fabric knots – buttons as we know them were not much in use in the 16th century]; to one of the other chiefs was given a coat with silk sleeves [maybe a chapan] and to six others silk coats [chapan?]. To all leave to go was granted."

Kîpîng/kipik (rain-cloak: see Fig. 13)
(I, 389) "We dismounted in Kaldah-kahar. That day too it rained amazingly; people with rain-cloaks (*kîpîng*) were in the same case as those who had none!" [ERSKINE explains in a footnote that the root of the work *kip* means dry. The kîpîng or *kipik* is a kind of cloak covered with wool – in this case obviously soaked.]

Postîn/pustin/tûn (sheepskin coat: see Fig. 16)
The first textile term in the Bâbur-nâma occurs just 9 pages into Bâbur's description of Farghâna. This occurs when a mountain stream is compared to the embroidered front of a lambskin coat. The postîn (variously shortened to *tûn*) is a long, bulky sheepskin overcoat with the tanned leather outside. Long wollen fleece is exposed on all open edges; the front opening looking rather like a waterfall. Such shearling coats are known in Central Asia today and still bear the same name in Kyrgyzstan. Embroidery and colorful edging along the front opening

---

is closely related to the Central Asian *chapan* (it is speculated that the term is a variant of caftan). This garment is mentioned in Bâbur's memoirs several times.

Figure 13. Mongol rider in rainwear.

were traditionally thought to provide talismanic protection. A postin required 6–8 sheepskins making them initially an expensive garment. This term appears seven times in the Bâbur-nâma.[18]

---

18 Neither BEVERIDGE nor THACKSTON were sufficiently acquainted with clothing.

(I, 10–11) "Kasan has excellent air and beautiful little gardens. As these gardens all lie along the bed of the torrent people call them the 'fine front of the coat': postîn pesh b:r:h." [19]

(I, 181): "They found a worn, coarse sheepskin coat (*postin*) and brought it to me; I put it on."

(I, 203–204): "Even in the heats, one cannot sleep. ... at night without a fur-coat." [The coat is identified as a *pûstîn* made of sheepskin. The wide range in temperature in Kabul during a 24-hour period is well-known.]

(I, 302) "Muzaffar Mîrzâ gave me a sword-belt, a lambskin surtout [probably a postîn], and a grey tîpuchâq."

(I, 371): "We allowed him to leave after putting a coat (tûn) on him and after writing orders with threats to the Yusuf-zal."

(I, 398): "At Khwaja Hasan, 'ABDU'L-LAH, in his drunkenness, threw himself into water just as he was in his *tûn aûfrâghi*." [This possibly means with his long coat out-spread.]

(I, 413): "The Dilazak Afghans entreated pardon for them; we gave it and set the captured free, fixed their tribute at 4000 sheep, gave coats (tûn) to their chiefs, appointed and sent out collectors."

---

terms of Central Asia and didn't recognize when the shortened form for this sheepskin coat was used (*tûn* or *ton* is the contracted form of *postin* still in use in Central Asia today).

19 In the BEVERIDGE translation 7(!) footnotes provide much speculation by experts as to the correct translation of this obscure phrase apparently denoting lambskins. I would have to agree with BEVERIDGE "(h) . . . but would not the flowery border of a mountain stream prompt rather a phrase bespeaking ornament and beauty than one expressing warmth and textile softness? If the phrase might be read as postin pesh perd, what adorns the front of a coat, or as postin pesh bar rah, the fine front of the coat, the phrase would recall the gay embroidered front of some leathern postins." THACKSTON puts forth yet an another suggestion "the fleece before the lamb", that makes it clear that he doesn't know what a postîn is.

(I, 423): "Opposite Nûr-gal (Rock-village) an old man begged from those on the rafts; every-one gave him something, coat (tûn), turban, bathing-cloth and so on, so he took a good deal away."

Châr-qâb (cloud collar; see Fig. 14)

In BEVERIDGE's translation of the Bâbur-nâma two differing opinions for this item were brought forth. It was identified either as a garment or as a shawl bestowed as a mark of rank. In any case, *châr* is 4 in Persian and this item is clearly woven or embroidered in gold. Thackston had more recent sources allowing him to identify it as the popular 4-cornered cloud collar often to be seen in Timurid paintings associated with Central Asian Turkic rulers (THACKSTON, 2002, p. 512).

(I, 304) "In such matters he had no match. At the end of the party he gave me an enamelled waist-dagger, a *châr-qâb*, and a tîpûchâq."

(II, 527-8) "At this party there were bestowed on Humâyûn a chârqâb, a sword-belt, a tîpûchâq horse with saddle mounted in gold; on Chîn-tîmur Sultân, Mahdî Khwâja and Muhammad Sl. Mîrzâ chârqâbs, sword-belts and dagger-belts; and to the begs and braves, to each according to his rank, were given sword-belts, dagger-belts, and dresses of honour, ..." [In the following list eight items of purpet over-garments probably count as the dresses of honour; additionally 51 lengths of purpet[20] were bestowed.]

---

20 The word *purpet* occurs several times; the text indicates that clothing as well as yardage. Perpet (a.k.a. perpetuano or petuna) is probably meant. It was a light, but sturdy, glossy twilled woolen cloth often mentioned in the 17th and early 18th centuries as an export from England however it is highly unlikely that material mentioned in the Bâbur-nâma originated there. In the 15th century the production of woolen fabric, especially in the cooler regions like Kashmir, was just as sophisticated as in Europe. "Purpet" was probably used by Beveridge to indicate a durable woolen cloth having similar qualities as an English fabric manufactured at a later date.

Figure 14. An ink drawing of Sultan HUSAIN MÎRZÂ wearing a cloud collar (ca. 1500–1525).[21]

---

21 This is one of the few illustrations that probably existed during Babur's lifetime being presumably an actual portrait of Sultan Husain Mîrzâ. It shows him wearing a Chinese-inspired cloud collar. The long sleeves of his jâmah can be seen under a long nîmcha. He is wearing a dagger and chopsticks on a belt with metal fittings. He has a handkerchief on his right knee. His turban is elegantly twisted and sports an aigrette, an upright tuft of feathers fastened to his turban.

Jîba (quilted corselet)

This garment is worn under a coat-of-mail. It is a close-fitting stuffed and quilted corselet onto which four plates of mail are attached.

(I, 195) "In this camp all the armour (jîba) of Khusrau Shâh's armoury (*jîba-khana?*) was shared out. There may have been as many as 7 to 800 coats-of-mail (*joshan*) and horse accoutrements (*kûhah*) [horse-mail with accoutrements] . . ."

(I, 315 & 316) "I had my cuirass on [close-fitting defensive armor for covering the upper body originally made of leather worn over the jiba] but had not fastened the *gharîcha* nor had I put on my helm." [ERSKINE explains that the gharîcha are the four plates of mail made to cover the back, front and sides of the torso.]

(I, 396) "I was just in my jîba; Tambal and another were standing like gate-wards in front of his array; I came face to face with Tambal, shot an arrow striking his helm; shot another aiming at the attachment of his shield; they shot one through my leg; ..." [BEVERIDGE explained that Bâbur was not yet dressed for fighting. He was wearing his jiba but the four plates of mail were not yet attached to it]

Kamr-bund (belt/sash) & tak-band (girdle)

Kamr-bund is a combination of 2 Persian words that literally mean waistband. Cummerband entered the English vocabulary from India as early as 1616. Although this word appears in the Bâbur-nâma, it is not defined. In illustrations of the period two different pieces of apparel are shown around the waist: decorative sashes worn over the jâmah and sword or tunic belts worn on the hips over the jâmah or nîmcha. Sashes were embellished in various ways, most likely woven, block-printed, or tie-dyed. Servants and courtiers in a hunting party are shown wearing shorter and plainer sashes. The *tak-band/tak-bundq* is explained as being a silk or woolen girdle fastening with a clasp, here meant to be worn over a nîmcha (see Fig. 14). It could also be the sword belt.

(**I, 156**) "That day some-one stole the gold clasp (*qulâb*) of my girdle."

(**I, 298**) "Qasim Beg, as he was my well-wisher and held my reputation as his own, gave my girdle a tug; ... "

(**II, 642**) "Through Mullâ Bihishti were sent to Hind-âl an inlaid dagger with belt, an inlaid ink-stand, a stool worked in mother-o'pearl, a tunic and a girdle, together with the alphabet of the Bâburi script and fragments written in that script." [According to Beveridge the takband is a silk or woolen girdle fastened with a "hook and eye".]

Footwear
This is the only mention in the Bâbur-nâma regarding footwear. Bâbur is not as interested in footwear as in fabric.

Chârûq (brogues)
(**II, 187, 1**): "Those who, hoping in me, went with me into exile, were, small and great, between 2 and 300; they were almost all on foot, had walking-staves in their hands, brogues on their feet, and long coats (*chapan*) on their shoulders. ..." [These rough shoes of untanned leather, are formed like moccasins with the leather drawn up around the foot. SHAW reported that they were worn by Kyrgyz mountaineers and caravan men.]

Miscellaneous clothing terms

Fûta (bathing-cloth)
(I, 275, 1) "Fully accepting this flattery, he put his *fûta* (bathing-cloth) round his neck and gave thanks." [According to MACCULLOCH's *Bengali Household Stories* this indicates among Muslims and Hindus obedience and submission.]

(**II, 327, 2**) "Believing these words, he put his bathing-cloth round his neck and gave thanks."

(II, 423, 3): "Opposite Nûr-gal (Rock-village) an old man begged from those on the rafts; every-one gave him something, coat (tûn), turban, bathing-cloth and so on, so he took a good deal away."

Lung/dhoti (breechcloth)
(II, 519) "Peasants and people of low standing go about naked. They tie on a thing called *lungûtâ* a decency-clout which hangs two spans below the navel. From the tie of this pendant decency-clout, another clout is passed between the thighs and made fast behind. Women also tie on a cloth (*lung*), one-half of which goes round the waist, the other is thrown over the head." [The *dhoti* is still known by this name in India, the women appear to have been wearing saris.]

Trades and tradesmen
Textile trades, as can be determined by references to them in the Bâbur-nâma, were of importance. A tunic-weaver's work was time consuming and therefore expensive. A needlemaker was a skilled professional who could demand high prices for his wares; the English pin money is indicative of how expensive needles and pins once were. A bleaching ground was necessary for preparing fabric for dyeing. Having a town gate named after a trade, either is an indication in the community of the importance of these trades or of the bad odors that prevailed there.

(I, 72–73) "Of the town-rabble, were brought in Diwana, the tunic-weaver and Kâlqâshûq, headlong leaders both, in brawl and tumult; they were ordered to death with torture in blood-retaliation for our foot-soldiers, killed at the Lovers' Cave."

(I, 143) "I, as the reserve, went to the spot, without anxiety about the Bleaching-ground and Needle-makers' Gates."

(I, 143) "There, opposite the space between the Needle-makers' and Bleaching-ground Gates, the enemy had posted 7 or 800 good men in ambush, having with them 24 or 25 ladders so wide that two or three could mount abreast."

(I, 143) "In the Needle-makers' Gate was posted Qarâ (Black) Barlâs, in the Bleaching-ground Gate, Qûtlûq Khwâja Kûkûldâsh with Sherîm Taghâî and his brethren, older and younger."

Furnishings

Carpets
(II, 629) "I went to Sl. Muhammad Bakhshî's house. After spreading a carpet, he brought gifts."

(II, 631) "They poured the red and white on a carpet I had ordered spread, and side by side with the gold and silver piled plenishing, white cotton piece-cloth and purses of money."

(II, 678) "We laid them in the folds of a woollen throne-carpet, put this on the throne and on it piled blankets."

Table-cloth
The following use of the expression tablecloth more likely means a ground cloth, as tables weren't generally in use at that time.

(I, 44) "This year I began to abstain from all doubtful food, my obedience extended even to the knife, the spoon and the table-cloth; also the after-midnight Prayer was less neglected."

(I, 132) "I seemed to go out to give him honourable meeting; he came in and seated himself; people seemed to lay a table-cloth before him, apparently without sufficient care and, on account of this, something seemed to come into his Highness Khwâja's mind."

(II, 542) "Again and again my heart rose; after retching two or three times I was near vomiting on the table-cloth."

Tents (see Fig. 15)

Tents are very important for armies, even today. A tent – first and foremost – provides shelter. The hallmark of a tent is its mobility made possible by designs sound enough to stand the test of time. Wall tents – still the preference of the military loosely follow the form of the yurt in maximizing indoor space.

In the Bâbur-nâma tents are mentioned more than 40 times including tents of different fabric, names and purposes: i.e. for audiences, women and storage. They came in different sizes and styles. Some of the "tents" were made of felt and lattice and today would likely be termed yurts.

A following selection of excerpts shows how tents were used and constructed, and clarifies their general importance. The following illustration provides a modest impression of the many different styles and kinds of tents in use in Central Asia somewhat later than in Bâbur's time.

(I, 54) "I waited on The Khân in the garden Haidar *Kûkûldâsh* had made outside Shâhrukhiya. He was seated in a large four-doored tent set up in the middle of it. Having entered the tent, I knelt three times, he for his part, rising to do me honour."

(I, 70) "Khusrau Shâh, for his part, did him good service, such service indeed, such kindness with horses and camels, tents and pavilions and warlike equipment of all sorts, both for himself and those with him , ... "

(I, 142) "For convenience in this I took up quarters in the middle of the town, in tents pitched on the roof of Aûlûgh Beg Mîrzâ's College."

Figure 15. Detail from "Da'ud Receives a Robe of Honor from
Mun'im Khan"

(I, 169) "This time I got even nearer perhaps, and he ran out as far as the end of the tent-ropes. ... 'You are talked about as a hero, my young brother!' took my arm and led me into his tent. The tents pitched were rather small and through his having grown up in an out-of-the-way place, he let the one he sat in be neglected; it was like a raider's, melons, grapes, saddlery, every sort of thing, in his sitting-tent."

(I, 188) "So destitute were we that we had but two tents (*chādar*) amongst us; my own used to be pitched for my mother, and they set an *âlâchâq* at each stage for me to sit in." [The term *chador* is known today as a tent-like garment; in Turkish the *alacık* is a felt-covered round tent of the nomads.]

(I, 239) "After passing Chûtîâlî, my own felt-tent had to be left from want of baggage-beasts. One night at that time, it rained so much, that water stood knee-deep in my tent (*châdâr*); I watched the night out till dawn, uncomfortably sitting on a pile of blankets."

(I, 264) "He had Qandahar given to him and, as was fitting with this, a daughter of Aûlûgh Beg Mîrzâ, (Bega Begîm), was set aside for him; when she went to Herl, Sl. Husain Mîrzâ made a splendid feast, setting up a great *châr-tâq* for it." [The châr-tâq appears to be a large tent rising into 4 domes or having 4 porches.]

(I, 298) "Four divans (*tûshuk*) had been placed in the tent. Always in the Mîrzâ's tents one side was like a gate-way and at the edge of this gate-way he always sat." [Stacks of mattresses were arranged here into 4 divans.]

(I, 319) "Muhammad Husain Mîrza in his terror having run away into Khânîm's bedding-room and got himself fastened up in a bundle of bedding,[22] we appointed Mirim Dîwân with other begs of the fort, to take control in those dwellings, capture, and bring him in."

---

22 THACKSTON explains that the Mirza ran away to the *tôshâkkhana*, but he does not translate. Meant is the mattress tent in which bedding was stored – he wrapped

(I, 338) "Excellent tîpûchâqs, strings and strings of he-camels, she-camels, and mules, bearing saddle-bags of silken stuffs and cloth, -- tents of scarlet (cloth) and velvet, all sorts of awnings, every kind of work-shop, ass-load after ass-load of chests."

(I, 400) "The party was held in a smallish tent in which I sometimes sat, in the Plane-tree garden south-east of the Picture-hall."

(I, 401) "We rose from it at the Bed-time Prayer when a move was made to the great tent where again there was drinking."

(I, 416) "Much rain fell; most of the begs and the household came into my tent, outside the Bâgh-i-kalân."

(II, 584) "Tents were set up on a stone platform made on the n.e. side of the Garden-of-victory which is now being laid out at Sîkrî, and in them the Feast was held."

(II, 678) " ... such a storm burst, in the inside of a moment, from the up-piled clouds of the Rainy-season, and such a stiff gale rose, that few tents were left standing. I was in the Audience-tent, about to write; before I could collect papers and sections, the tent came down, with its porch, right on my head. The *tûngluq* went to pieces.[23]"

---

himself up in a bedding sack. Tôshâk (tûshuk) refers to the narrow mattresses of Central Asia that are stacked during the day creating a divan and spread out on the floor during the night for sleeping; the storage tent took its name from them.

23 This opening – explained by BEVERIDGE as a flap in the roof of the tent – allows light and air to enter and smoke to leave. The word and because it "went to pieces" gives the impression that in fact the Central Asian *tunduk* – the wooden frame at the top of the yurt is being described. It is covered by a flap serving the functions described.

Figure 16. Postîn or tûn – sheepskin coat
From *Huang Qing zhigongtu*. Album. Ms.

Conclusions

I have searched the Beveridge translation of the Bâbur-nâma and compiled chronologically quotes on textile terms including fibers, clothing and furnishing. Although Bâbur was known for taking a keen interest in his surroundings and faithfully records i.e. geography, local flora and fauna, this is the first time that his interest in textiles and clothing, which far surpassed the attention given by other rulers to such matters, has been catalogued and analysed.

One very important aspect of clothing mentioned in the Bâbur-nâma is too complex and includes too much data to pursue here. This is the explanation of and distinction between the *khilcat-i-khâsa* (robes of honour mentioned 26 times) and the *bâsh-ayâqin* in Persian – *sar-u-pâ* (head-to-foot mentioned 14 times). These sets of clothing, awarded in the Turkic tradition to dignitaries, worthy subjects in recognition of a service rendered or in acknowledgement of a military and/or political alliance or role, should be compiled and analysed in depth. What exactly the distinction is, what the sets of clothing include and to whom they were presented could easily be the subject of another paper on Bâbur and his affinity for fabric.

Bibliography

ATASOY, Nurhan (2012): *Portraits and caftans of the Ottoman sultans*. New York: Assouline. 127 pp.

BEVERIDGE, Annette Susannah (1922): *The Bâbur-nâma in English*. Hertford: Stephen Austin. 880 pp.

CAMPBELL, Kay Hardy (2016): The gown that steals your heart. *Aramco World* Vol. 67, No 2. p. 22–33.

Encyclopaedia Iranica. Clothing ix. In the Mongol and Timurid periods. Online *<http://www.iranicaonline.org/articles/clothing-ix>*

ESIN, Emel: Bedük börk. The iconography of Turkish honorific headgears. *Proceedings of the IXth meeting of the Permanent*

International Altaistic Conference 1966 (1970). Naples: Istituto Universitario Orientale, Seminario di Turcologia, p. 71–138.

ISLAM, Khademul (2016): Our story of Dhaka muslin. *Aramco World* Vol. 67, No 3. p. 26–33.

KUHN, Dieter (Ed.) (2012): *Chinese silks.* New Haven, CN: Yale University Press. 571 pp.

LENZ, Thomas W.; Glenn D. LOWRY (1989): *Timur and the princely vision: Persian art and culture in the fifteeth century.* Los Angeles: L. A. Museum of Art. 393 pp.

MELLER, Susan (2013): *Silk and cotton. Textiles from the Central Asia that was.* New York: Abrams. 335 pp.

Shagreen. *Wikipedia, the free encyclopedia.* Online < http://www.wikipedia>

THACKSTON, Wheeler M. (2002): *The Baburnama: Memoirs of Babur, Prince and Emperor* translated, edited and annotated by Wheeler M. Thackston. New York: Modern Library Paperback Edition. 554 pp.

TORTORA, Phyllis G. & Ingrid JOHNSON (2013): *The Fairchild Books dictionary of textiles.* New York: Bloomsbury. 736 pp.

URAY-KŐHALMI, Käthe (1989): Das zentralasiatische Kultursyndrom. *Die Mongolen.* Herausgeber Heissig, Walther & Claudius Müller. Innsbruck: Pinguin Verlag, p. 47–51.

VOLLMER, John E. (1980): *Five colours of the universe: Symbolism in clothes and fabrics of the Ch'ing Dynasty (1644–1911).* Edmonton, Alberta: The Edmonton Art Gallery. 72 pp.

VOLLMER, John E. (2002): *Ruling from the dragon throne: costume from the Qing dynasty (1644-1911).* Berkeley, CA: Ten Speed Press. 161 pp.

WEATHERFORD, Jack (2010): *The secret history of the Mongol queens. How the daughters of Genghis Khan rescued his empire.* New York: Boardway Paperbacks. 317 pp.

List of illustrations

Figure 1. Detail from "Bâbur and his army saluting the standards". Courtesy of the British Museum (Museum number 1948,1009,0.71)

Figure 2. Genghis Khan and three of his four sons. Illustration from a 15th-century *Jami' al-tawarikh* manuscript. <Pinterest.com>

Figure 3. Modern pattern for traditional Mongolian men's garments. Simplicity Men Costumes and Hat 3772, <PatternReview.com>

Figure 4. This idealized illustration (ca 1605) of Bâbur hunting is courtesy of Berlin's Museum of Islamic Art, Inv.-Nr. I. 4593 fol. 49

Figure 5. Detail from "Bâbur and Humayun receive a courtier", attributed to Farrukh Beg. From a Bâbur-nâma, Lahore, 1589. Courtesy of Arthur M. Sackler Gallery, Smithsonian Institution. S1986.230

Figure 6. Moghul turban styles. See costume of Mughal period. <www.josbd.com>

Figure 7. Külah. Courtesy of <Bilddatenbank.khm.at>

Figure 8. The Portrait of Ottoman Sultan Mehmed the Conqueror by Italian painter Gentile Bellini, 1480. Courtesy of National Gallery, London.

Figure 9. Mongolian silk deel (jâmah) 13th–14th century, Inner Mongolia <Pinterest.com >

Figure 10. Mongol jamah by Charles Mellor, see Mongolian coat variations <Pinterest.com >

Figure 11. Isfandiyâr killing two lions. From Firdausî's *Shahname*. Beginning of 17th century. Courtesy of Staatsbibliothek zu Berlin. Oriental Dept., Ms. or. fol. 4251, f. 476r

Figure 12. T-shaped *chapan* from Central Asia, see chapan pattern <Pinterest. com>

Figure 13. Mongol rider. Yuan dynasty, China; on silk. Courtesy of Artnet International.

Figure 14. An ink drawing of Sultan Husain Mîrzâ wearing a cloud collar (ca 1500–1525). Courtesy of the Harvard University Art Museums, Arthur M. Sackler Museum. 1958.59

Figure 15. Detail from "Da'ud receives a Robe of Honor from Mun'im Khan". Attributed to Hiranand (ca 1596–1600). Courtesy of the Freer and Sackler Galleries. F 1952.31

Figure 16. Postîn or tûn – sheepskin coat. From *Huang Qing zhigongtu* 皇清 職貢圖. Album (1789). Courtesy of Bibliothèque nationale de France, Paris, Réserve b 7 (formerly Imperial Palace Collection, Peking).

A Boundless Homeland:
Terminology of Territorial Administration, Areas and Peoples in the Qing Empire

Oliver CORFF (Berlin)

Introduction

In 1644 the Manju rulers toppled the last Ming emperor and officially established the Qing dynasty. They successfully managed to govern a country with a population bigger than their own by two orders of magnitude, spread over a vast and diverse territory, and alien to them in many aspects, not least in language and matters of civil administration. During the first half of the Qing dynasty, which can be understood as ending with the death of the Qianlong emperor, there were serious attempts to create a structure which, in modern terminology, can be called a multi-ethnic state under unified and central rule. During the same time, the Qing Empire also had to acquaint itself with the existence of foreign powers.[1] One part of these efforts was the creation of an administrative terminology across the most important languages of the empire, including Manju, Tibetan, Mongolian, Turki and Chinese. Though the terminology is not always fully coherent when compared between these languages, this terminology nonetheless reveals the imperial world outlook of the Qing central state.

---

1   A rich body of literature deals with the numerous political challenges of the Qing state with regard to domestic and international relations. The nature of relations with non-Han nationalities varied widely. There were traditional tributaries 'inherited' from the Ming, like Korea, the Mongols, Jurchen and Tibetans, non-tributary trading countries and truly foreign countries dispatching embassies to the Court. See J. K. FAIRBANK and S. Y. TÊNG: "On the Ch'ing tributary system." *Harvard Journal of Asiatic Studies* 6.1941, pp. 135–246; Nicola di COSMO: "Qing colonial administration in Inner Asia." *The International History Review* 20.1998:2, pp. 287–309; Dittmar SCHORKOWITZ, CHIA Ning (eds.): *Managing frontiers in Qing China*. Leiden: Brill 2017.

Research efforts have been undertaken to collect the terminology of titles and official ranks in a systematic manner and to view them in a broader historical perspective. Most notable is Pavel POUCHA's *Rang und Titel bei den Völkern des mongolischen Raums im Laufe der Jahrhunderte*. This work contains an extensive survey of terminology as found in Chinese historical records (perused in Russian translation), the *Secret History of the Mongols*, the Mongolian chronicle *Sir-a tuγuji*, the Yuan Code, the Manju dictionaries which HAUER consulted for his *Handwörterbuch*, and finally the *Pentaglot*, a dictionary in five languages which marks the culmination point of Manju multilingual lexicography. This dictionary features 18671 lemmata in the following languages: Manju, Tibetan, Mongolian, Turki and Chinese. One would expect that the critical terminology is unified across all five languages, but this is evidently not the case; there are notable differences between individual languages in the rendering of ethnonyms, territorial administrative units as well as ranks and titles.

Ethnonyms: Names of Tibet and the Tibetans

The names used for Tibet and the Tibetans in various languages show differences not only in the adaptation of a given ethnonym to the phonology of a given language. In fact, within the very same language, we can observe different ethnonyms, depending on whether the ethnicity, the region or the language is of primary interest.

Tibetan can be ma. *tubet,* mo. *töbed* and tu. *tübet* (which meets naive expectations), however in Tibetan the autochthonous name tib. *bod* is used, whereas Chinese uses 番 *fān*, an ancient generic term for the ethnic minorities in the far west of China, sometimes translated as "[western] barbarian". An example for this combination is the name of the Tibetan mainah [4854.2]: *tubet kiongguhe* / *bod-kyi-khyim-bya.* / *töbed toti* / *tübet ǧōng tūtī* / 番鸜鵒 (*fān qú yù*) .[2]

2 All examples from the Pentaglot are given in the following order: [*xxxx.y*] *entry*, where the four digits *xxxx* stand for the page of the Beijing print edition of 1957, and *y* stands for the column on that page. The critical edition (CORFF et al.:2013) as well as all index volumes (CORFF et al.:2014) use this numbering scheme throughout. In this paper, the five members of a full language tupel (*entry*) are

Another name is introduced when the area, rather than the ethnicity, stands in the focus of the lemma. Besides the regional name *Zang* the ethnonym Tangut is introduced. In Manju, *wargi zang*, lit. "Western Zang", stands for the region, to which, offering further information, the ethnonyms ma. *tanggût monggo* are added. In Tibetan, the entry can be analyzed as follows: The Tibetans (equivalent for Tangut) tib. *bod,* and Mongolians tib. *hor,* of tib. *dbus-gtsang* ("Central [sic] Zang"). Turki simply uses the term "right wing" (or rather: "right hand") for the region. The full entry reads: [0307.1] *wargi zang ni tanggût monggo / dbus-gtsang-gi-bod-hor. / baraɣun ǰuu-yin tangɣud mongɣul / ōng qōl≠nīng tānggūt mōngġāl /* 西藏唐古特蒙古 (*xī zàng tánggǔtè ménggǔ*).

Tangut stands for Tibetan if the language is in focus. The Tibetan school is named [2834.4] *tanggût tacikû / bod-kyi-slob-grwa. / töbed-ün surɣaɣuli / tāng·ġūt maktab /* 唐古特學 (*tánggǔtè xué*) .

However, if the writing system is concerned, in Tibetan the name is not what could be naively inferred from the other languages: [3159.2] *tanggût hergenehe suje / lanytsa-ma. / töbed üsügtü torɣ≠a / tübet xaṭ·līk tavār /* 西番字緞 (*xī fān zìr duàn*), "silk brocade with Tibetan letters".

The parallel use of different terms for region, ethnicity and language can also be observed for other ethnonyms, e.g. the Mongolians. The name is basically stable in Manju (*monggo*), Mongolian (*mongɣul*) and Chinese (蒙古 *ménggǔ*), but in Tibetan we find both *sog* and *hor* while Turki offers *mōngġāl* and *qālmāq*. We will see at a later point that different naming conventions of region, inhabitants and language play an important role for the concept of statehood of the Qing empire.

---

given in the order of the book, i.e. Manju-Tibetan-Mongolian-Turki-Chinese. For the sake of brevity, labels (ma., tib., mo., tu. and chin.) are not used to mark individual languages in full examples; they are only used when terms in individual languages are discussed.

Terminology for administrative divisions

A first glance at the terminology used for everything related to
territorial administration seems to indicate that this terminology was
more or less completely accepted from Chinese and introduced in the
languages of the Qing empire in an unmodified form. A closer look
reveals that the situation is a bit more complex. We have to differentiate between local administration levels (everything below
provincial level) and higher levels, i. e. provincial level and above. On
the level which matters to the empire as a whole, territorial concepts
referring to the bigger portions of the territory are expressed in a
manner which reflects a totally different perception of areas, regions
and ethnicities.

Lower-level adminstrative divisions: ma. *fu, jeo, hiyan*

The Manju lexicon of the Pentaglot for things related to administrative terminology below provincial level demonstrates, with the exception of Tibetan, a consistent use of the terms ma. *fu, jeo* and *hiyan* as
in composite names of official positions. These are Chinese loans
from 府 (*fǔ*, seat of a local government, often translated as "prefecture"), 州 (*zhōu*, equally translated as "prefecture"), and 縣 (*xiàn*,
"county"). While ma. *fu, jeo* and *hiyan* form composite terms in the
Pentaglot, there is no single entry in this dictionary[3] for the name of
the territorial unit: these three words cannot be found as individual
entries.

   If we summarize the picture found in entries like [0374.2] *fu-i
aliha hafan / yul-bdag-blon. / fü-yin erkilegsen tüsimel / fü≠nīng
ūzūrlāgān bīg / 府尹 (fú yǐn)*, [0375.4] *jeo-i saraci / gling-mkhar-
shes-dpon. / zèü-yin medegči / ğū°≠nīng ħakimī / 知州 (zhī zhōu)* and
[0376.3] *hiyan-i saraci / mkhar-chung-shes-dpon. / hiyan-u medegči /
șiyan≠nīng ħakimī / 知縣 (zhī xiàn)*:

---

3   This observation is not exclusive to the Pentaglot as the majority of Qing dynasty
    multilingual dictionaries have evolved from a common ancestor. For a tabular
    overview of the history of Qing multilingual dictionaries, see CORFF et al.: 2013,
    p. xxiv.

Unit	Manju	Tibetan	Mongolian	Turki	Chinese
fu	*fu*	*yul*	*fü*	*fū*	府 *fŭ*
jeo	*jeo*	*gling, gling-mkhar*	*zeü*	*ğū*	州 *zhōu*
hiyan	*hiyan*	*mkhar, mkhar-chung*	*hiyan*	*şiyan*	縣 *xiàn*

Tibetan is the notable exception to the other three non-Chinese languages; it uses *yul* for 府 *fŭ, gling* and *gling-mkhar* for 州 *zhōu,* as well as *mkhar* and *mkhar-chung* for 縣 *xiàn.* Originally, the Tibetan term *yul* stands for a region, *gling* refers to the area of a monastery, whereas *gling-mkhar* refers to a fortified palace or stronghold, and *mkhar-chung* literally is a small stronghold.

Higher-Level Administrative Divisions: *golo (sheng)* and related terms

In contrast to the local-level administrative divisions, the terminology used for the highest administrative divisions, i.e. the provinces, is native to each language as entry [2715.4] *golo / zhing-sa. / muǰi / yūrt* / 省 (*shěng*) shows. With the exception of Turki, the Manju, Tibetan and Mongolian terms are functionally equivalent. Turki *yūrt* denotes both "province" (as in entry [2715.4]) and "country" as in 0730.4: *tāšqārqï yūrt≠nīng kitābī* "book in foreign script". It appears that the Turki scribes did not differentiate between "province" and "country", as long as it was far away (*tāšqārqï:* "outer"; the dimension of distance or remoteness is subject of the next paragraph). Turki makes use of another term for the "remote provinces" in entry [0373.2]: *tālā≠nīng bīgī* / 外省官員 (*wàishěng guānyuán*): "provincial official", with *tālā* evidently being a Mongolian calque: "steppe". A third Turki word can be observed in entry [4565.2]: *goloi beise / zhing-dpon. / muǰi-yin noyad / ãymāq bey·şä* / 諸侯 (*zhū hóu*); here, Turki uses yet another Mongolian calque: *ãymāq,* from mo. *ayimaɣ* "[administrative] area".

Far, far away – the Periphery [of the Empire]
Perceived distance from the centre of the empire appears as another
territorial entity concept in entries [2783.4] and [2784.2]: ma. *goro*,
"far [away]", "outer" is the root of *goroki* and *gorokingge*, as in entry
[2783.4]: *goroki be bilure bolgobure fiyenten* / *kha-lo-'dren-pa'i-*
gling-. / *qoladakin-i nomuqadqaqu ariɣudqaqu keltes* / *yirāq·dāqɪ≠nī*
āṣrāydūġān ārīġ·lātādūġān čučūq / 柔遠清吏司 (*róuyuǎn qīnglìsī*),
"department of the 理藩院 Lifan Yuan [Ministry ruling the Outer
Provinces[4]] for dealing with Mongolian affairs", and entry [2784.2]:
gorokingge be tohorombure bolgobure fiyenten / *ring-mgron-gling-.* /
qoladakin-i toquniɣulqu ariɣudqaqu keltes / *yirāq·dāqī āṣarātādūġān*
ārīġ·lātādūġān čučūq / 徠遠清吏司 (*láiyuǎn qīnglìsī*), "department of
the Lifan Yuan for dealing [among other tasks] with islamic peoples
of Hami and Turfan" (founded in year 26 of Qianlong, or 1761).

gurun and 國 guó
While the terminology for local administration levels is founded on
Chinese origins across the majority of languages, the term used for

---

4   For a detailed discussion of the unique rôle of the Lifan Yuan enabling the
     Manjus to deal with Inner Asian peoples see CHIA Ning: "The Lifanyuan and the
     Inner Asian rituals in the early Qing (1644–1795)." *Late Imperial China* 14.1993,
     pp. 60–92. The Lifan Yuan is known in Western literature under several names
     (cf. Chia, p. 61): "Barbarian Control Office" or "Court of Colonial Affairs", both
     of which are reasonably adequate interpretations of the Lifan Yuan mission;
     however, these renderings do not reflect the meaning of the original Manju name
     Tulergi golo be dasara jurgan, "Ministry ruling the Outer Provinces." The
     Pentaglot records this institution under entry [2782.4]: *tulergi golo be dasara*
     jurgan / *phyi'i-sog-po'i-khrims-grwa.* / *ɣadaɣadu mongɣul-un törü-yi ǰasaqu*
     yabudal-un yamun / *tālā·dāqï yūrt≠nī yaṣāy·dūġān ǧūrġān* 理藩院 (*lǐfān yuàn*).
     The various translations of this name are revealing examples of perception: Both
     Tibetan and Mongolian translations emphasize Outer Mongolia as subject of the
     Lifan Yuan's activities, whereas Turki simply refers to the "Province in the
     Steppe", using the term of Mongolian origin *tālā*. Chinese 藩 *fān*, "fence,
     boundary, outlying border" refers, by extension of this meaning, to anything
     "foreign", "non-Han", "Barbarian", without specific reference to Mongolian or
     Tibetan, but is usually understood as Tibetan. Compare section "Ethnonyms:
     Names of Tibet and the Tibetans", above.

"nation" or "state" is native to each language, with the exception of one official title in Chinese. The basic word form is [2713.3] *gurun / yul-ljongs-sam-srid. / ulus / īqlīm /* 國 *(guó).* The usage of this word is consistent in all five languages if the state as an entity is dealt with: [0257.2] *gurun be dalire janggin / srid-srung-dmag-dpon. / ulus-un tüsiy≠e ǰanggi / īqlīm≠nī tūrāydūǧān ǧang·gī /* 鎮國將軍 *(zhènguó jiāngjun).* Only Chinese uses the Manju term *gurun* (固倫 *gùlún):* [0262.2] *gurun-i gungju / srid-kyi-kong-jo. / ulus-un güngǰü / īqlīm≠nīng xānīgä·ṣī /* 固倫公主 *(gùlún gōngzhǔ),* "Imperial Princess", but three non-Chinese languages (except for Turki) all use the Chinese word for "princess": 公主 *gōngzhǔ.*

Yet, when not the state as such but a given country is meant, then Tibetan omits the qualifier *srid* and just gives the name of the nationality, as in [2831.3] *solho gurun-i kuren / ka-lingga'i-ra-ba. / solungyus ulus-un küriy≠e / gaōlī īqlīm≠nīng xānä /* 高麗館 *(Gāolì guǎn)* "Residence of the Korean Embassy".

Foreign countries: Russia

The Pentaglot mentions only a few truly foreign countries, either vassal states or sovereign countries. Russia is the earliest nation which established foreign relations with Qing China in a formal manner, and thus it is no wonder that it is mentioned in the Pentaglot in more contexts than other foreign countries. With one Tibetan exception, the name for Russia is rendered according to its Mongol-/Manju form *oros* which is also reproduced in Chinese: 俄羅斯 *éluósī.* The word is a reflection of the root *ros-,* but an initial vowel "o" is added as native Mongolian and Manju do not accept an initial "r". We thus find [0303.4] *oros niru / rgya-ser-mda'. / orus sumu / ōrūṣ ṣūmūn /* 俄羅斯佐領 *(éluósī zuólǐng)* "Russian company [using Russian prisoners of war]", [2832.1] *oros kuren / o-ro-su'i-ra-ba. / orus-un küriy≠e / ōrūṣ xānä /* 俄羅斯館 *(éluósī guǎn)* "Residence of the Russian Embassy" [2832.2] *oros bithei kuren / o-ro-su'i-yi-ge'i-grwa. / orus bičig-ün küriy≠e / ōrūṣ xaṭ·xānä /* 俄羅斯文館 *(éluósī wén guǎn)* "Russian Language Office", [4705.4] *oros tacikû / o-ro-su'i-slob-*

grwa. / *orus surɣaɣuli* / *ōrūṣ maktab* / 俄羅斯學 (*éluósī xúe*) "Russian
School [in Peking]".

Foreign countries other than Russia
Other countries mentioned in the Pentaglot include Korea, Ryukyu,
Holland and India. There were permanent Korean and Ryukyu
establishments in Peking, as [2831.3] *solho gurun-i kuren* / *ka-
lingga'i-ra-ba.* / *solungyus ulus-un küriyᴇe* / *gaōlī īqlīm≠nīng xānä* /
高麗館 (*gāolì guǎn*) and [2831.4] *lio kio gurun-i kuren* / *li'u-khyi'u-
ra-ba.* / *liu kiu ulus-un küriyᴇe* / *lyū čyū īqlīm≠nīng xānä* / 琉球館
(*liúqiú guǎn*) indicate. Holland and India are only known by the
exchange of diplomatic gifts, especially swords, of which the Pentaglot mentions two: [4639.1] *ho lan gurun-i loho* / *he-lan-gyi-ba-dan.*
/ *qo' lan ulus-un ildü* / *xōlān īqlīm≠nīng qılīnč* / 賀蘭刀 (*hèlán dāo*),
"sword from Holland" and [4637.3] *enetkek hergengge loho* / *dpa'-
dam-lanytsa-ma.* / *enedkeg-ün üsügtü ildü* / *änet·kek ħurūf·lūq qılīnč* /
梵字刀 (*fàn zì dāo*), "sword with Indian inscription".

Interpretation of terminology in context
The different usage of terminology on different levels of administration allows several interpretations. On the local level, Chinese
terminology is introduced on an "as is" basis, leading to the assumption that the Manju rulers simply continued the administrative
tradition of Han Chinese areas as it had been done before, without
much interference in or disruption of the existing order. Three of the
non-Han languages of the Pentaglot strictly follow the Chinese naming conventions, only Tibetan attempts to offer native Tibetan terms,
which, at closer look, are descriptive translations, probably without
match in previous Tibetan territorial administration.

On a higher level, there is a distinction of "traditional" and "remote" provinces. The provinces can be grouped into two categories:
a) ancient provinces of the Ming, inhabited by Han Chinese, and b)
the remote areas, inhabited by non-Han peoples, conquered by and
integrated into the Qing Empire. While the former provinces are
simply named "province" in four of the five languages of the Penta-

glot, only the Turki name *yūrt* – as a technical term – is non-specific and can, in other contexts, also be interpreted as "region", "homeland" or even "country". In contrast, the remote areas are not yet integrated into the civilian administration of the Qing Empire (in the case of Xinjiang ("New Territory"), this happened as late as in the 1880s); they are not classified as province but rather primarily perceived by their remoteness; hence the Manju name component *goro-,* the Mongolian name component *qola-* and the Chinese word 遠 *yuǎn.* The Lifan Yuan, the special institution created for the administration of the remote non-Han peoples, carries the connotation of remoteness and border in its name: *tulergi golo be dasara jurgan,* "Ministry ruling the Outer Provinces", while at the same time highlighting the fact that these areas and the peoples living there are part of the Empire and by no means to be considered as truly foreign or alien.

These three layers of territorial administration cover both Han and non-Han peoples, different languages and religions, as well as different human geographies (compare the Turki usage of *tālā*), all subject to the Qing Emperor.

True foreign nations are not part of the Empire; they have permanent delegations and embassies in Peking or exchange diplomatic gifts with the Court. The Pentaglot mentions only a few countries, notably Russia, Korea, Ryukyu, Holland and India, thus reflecting the reality of international relations at the end of Qianlong's reign; at that time, those nations that would enter the political stage of China in the 19th century, like France, were largely unknown, or, as in the case of the United Kingdom, the first significant interaction with the Court happened after the compilation of the Qing multilingual dictionaries.[5]

The core question: What is a state?

The terminology used for the territorial administration of the Qing multi-ethnic state reveals an interesting fact. With the exception of

---

5   Strictly speaking, the MACARTNEY Embassy (1793) happened before the draft of the Pentaglot was completed, but as the structure and lexicon of the Qing multilingual dictionaries had been defined many years earlier and left unchanged ever since, the United Kingdom did not make it into the list of keywords.

traditional Han-inhabited areas, for which Chinese terminology is adopted in a fairly uniform manner, the names of the largest administrative units, together with peoples and languages of these areas, are used in a rather incoherent manner across various languages of the Pentaglot. Some peoples even have more than one name in one given language, like the Mongolians in Tibetan (*sog* and *hor*) or Turki (*mōnggāl* and *qālmāq*). In Mongolian, these names stand for two different Mongolian ethnicities, a distinction which is blurred in Turki usage.

Yet, despite these apparent incoherencies, there is a common concept behind the naming conventions of the five languages for administrative units and ethnicities. First of all, at the level of the Empire, there is only a boundless and potentially infinite territory. There are not really well-determined boundaries, only regions close or remote (ma. *tulergi*, *goro*, but compare Chinese 外) when seen from the capital. At this level of perception, there is no link between Empire and Nation. Rather, the territory of the Empire is home to many nations (Manjus, Tibetans, Mongolians, Turkis and Chinese) perceiving each other partially as inhabitants of regions (cf. ma. *wargi dzang,* Western Dzang), partially as different tribes (Turki *mōnggāl* and *qālmāq*), always within the framework of the Empire. Truly foreign countries do exist, but not on an equal footing, nor do they pose a significant challenge to the Empire. The names of administrative units below provincial level reflect a local, not a unified central administrative perspective covering all regions and nations; the ruling order of the Empire is an amalgam of a central ideal and locally adapted administration.

If we were to apply the elements of the state as understood in the framework of modern public law, we would find that the constituents of the state: the territory, the people and the ruling order, are not – at least in the case of the Qing Empire – necessarily of an identical origin. According to Georg JELLINEK's theory,[6] these three con-

---

6   Georg JELLINEK (1851–1911), a public lawyer, introduced the concept of the three constituent elements of the state: Territory, people and rule. Known in German as the "Drei-Elementen-Lehre", this concept is explored in detail in the

stituents are the essential elements of the state. Yet, while western understanding tends to assume a union between these three elements (e.g. "the German people on German soil with native [German] rule"), the Qing empire demonstrated that any perceived unified identity of these three elements was by no means conditional for successfully running an empire: An essentially alien nation, the Manju, conquered and ruled a Chinese population by a ruling order without Ming or Manju precedent, encompassing territories, peoples and languages of the most diverse nature. Yet, despite these challenging facts, the Manju rulers undoubtedly succeeded in forging an empire many traits of which have survived into modern times.

Literature

CHIA Ning: "The Lifanyuan and the Inner Asian rituals in the early Qing (1644–1795)." *Late Imperial China* 14.1993:1, pp. 60–92.

CORFF, Oliver, Kyoko MAEZONO, Wolfgang LIPP, Dorjpalam DORJ, Görööchin GERELMAA, Aysima MIRSULTAN, Réka STÜBER, Byambajav TÖWSHINTÖGS, Xieyan LI (ed.): *Auf kaiserlichen Befehl erstelltes Wörterbuch des Manjurischen in fünf Sprachen. "Fünfsprachenspiegel". Systematisch angeordneter Wortschatz auf Manjurisch, Tibetisch, Mongolisch, Turki und Chinesisch. Vollständige romanisierte und revidierte Ausgabe mit textkritischen Anmerkungen, deutschen Erläuterungen und Indizes.* Wiesbaden: Harrassowitz 2013. ISBN 978-3-447-06970-0.

COSMO, Nicola di: "Kirghiz nomads on the Qing frontier: tribute, trade, or gift exchange?" In: COSMO, Nicola di and Don J. WYATT: *Political frontiers, ethnic boundaries, and human geographies in*

---

chapter "The legal position of the elements of the state", in *Allgemeine Staatslehre. Das Recht des modernen Staates*. 2. durchges. und verm. Aufl. Berlin: Häring 1905, pp. 381–393 (1. Das Staatsgebiet, "Territory of the State"), pp. 393–413 (2. Das Staatsvolk, "People of State"), and pp. 413–420 (3. Die Staatsgewalt, "Rule and Order of the State").

Chinese history. London and New York: RoutledgeCourzon 2003. ISBN 0-7007-1464-2, pp. 351–372.

Cosmo, Nicola di: "Qing colonial administration in Inner Asia." *The International History Review* 20.1998:2, pp. 287–309.

Fairbank, J. K.; S. Y. Têng: "On the Ch'ing tributary system." *Harvard Journal of Asiatic Studies* 6.1941:2, pp. 135–246.

Jellinek, Georg: *Allgemeine Staatslehre. Das Recht des modernen Staates.* 2. durchges. und verm. Aufl. Berlin: Häring 1905.

Nawiasky, Hans: *Allgemeine Rechtslehre als System der rechtlichen Grundbegriffe.* Einsiedeln: Benziger 1941.

Poucha, Pavel: "Rang und Titel bei den Völkern des mongolischen Raums im Laufe der Jahrhunderte." In: *Proceedings of the Ninth Meeting of the PIAC.* (Istituto Universitario Orientale, Seminario di Turcologia, Naples 1970), pp. 169–258.

Schorkowitz, Dittmar and Chia Ning (eds.): *Managing frontiers in Qing China. The Lifanyuan and Libu revisited.* Leiden: Brill 2017.

Denis Sinor (1916–2011) and Altaic Studies

Barbara KELLNER-HEINKELE (Berlin)

At this 59th annual meeting of the Permanent International Altaistic Conference, it is especially appropriate to remember Denis Sinor, one of the founding fathers and organizers of this series of scholarly meetings. On 17 April, 2016, he would have celebrated his 100th birthday, but alas, he passed away on 12 January, 2011, three months before his 95th birthday. At this point, I would like to share a few thoughts about his life and scholarly achievements.

It was thirty years ago, in 1986 that the 29th Meeting of the PIAC took place in Tashkent, Uzbekistan, USSR. Yet, this was only the second time, after Ankara (1973), in which the meeting was being held in a country where one of the Altaic languages was the national language. In his report on the meeting, a Chinese participant mentioned Denis Sinor, longtime secretary general of the PIAC, as a Ural-Altaist by specialization.[1] This was quite correct in two senses: first, Denis Sinor published extensively on Altaic and, less so on Uralic topics and, second, from 1962 to 1981, he was the chairman of the Department of Uralic and Altaic Studies at Indiana University in Bloomington, Indiana, USA. However, his scholarly interests and activities were actually much wider. The annual PIAC Meeting was one of the more pleasant tasks he had set himself. At that Tashkent PIAC Meeting, Sinor was 70 and flourishing as a scholar, university professor, administrator, editor, publisher and international consultant in academic matters. He considered the Tashkent Meeting an achievement, and rightly so. It should be remembered that in the years preceeding it, the world was frozen in the Cold War.[2] It was probably

---

1 *http://www.altaist.org/annual-meetings/29th-meeting-tashkent-1986-report-chen-wei/*

2 See SINOR 2001: 3, 4-5, 12. For decades, scholars from the Cold War's "West" had rarely been able to personally meet scholars from the Cold War's "East", particularly within the Socialist territories. However, already two earlier PIAC Meetings had offered such opportunities, one in East Berlin (GDR) in 1969 and

due to the beginning of *perestroika*, that the Tashkent Meeting could be realized as first PIAC Meeting in the Soviet Union. Denis Sinor liked to tell the story of how he convinced one of the influential representatives of Oriental Studies in the Soviet Union, Prof. Dr. Vadim M. SOL'NCEV (1928–2000), then director of the prestigious Institute of Oriental Studies in Moscow, that a PIAC Meeting should take place in the Soviet Union considering the great tradition of Oriental Studies in the Russian Empire and the Soviet Union. Sol'ncev and Sinor had met at an earlier PIAC Meeting, and they had got on famously, enjoying the same sort of humour and curiosity of the world (Sinor 2001: 15–17).

Denis Sinor on a South Atlantic cruise, 1999

The PIAC website (*www.altaist.org*) – which Oliver CORFF has turned into a wonderful source of information on people and publications of Altaic research – shows that the Tashkent Meeting counted 280 participants from 23 countries, among them 200 Soviet scholars. This was probably the largest meeting the PIAC ever

one in Szeged (Hungary) in 1971. Soviet scholars participated for the first time at the 9th Meeting in Ravello, Italy (1966) (Sinor 2001: 6).

convened and, at the time, a rare opportunity for exchanges – encounters being one of the basic motivations of the PIAC Meetings. It
took many years before the PIAC would hold meetings in East Asia:
Taipei (1992), Kawasaki (1995) and Huhhot (2009).

There is an irony here because in the beginning the PIAC meetings
were small, informal get-togethers, not conferences in the con-
ventional sense, but rather workshops where everyone could present
research findings, raising questions and making proposals concerning
the direction Altaic Studies should take. It had been the great German
scholar of Mongol Studies Walther HEISSIG (1913–2005) who proposed the idea of creating such a working group at the 24th International Congress of Orientalists in Munich in 1957.[3] In fact, as Denis
Sinor reminisces in an article he contributed to the Proceedings of the
40th PIAC Meeting in Provo, Utah, USA (1997, publ. 2001), he
personally thought that such an organization would not work (Sinor
2001: 1) – but he was wrong. But he went along out of friendship
(Sinor 2001: 1). We have to remember here that both men were in
their early forties at that time and in the process of rebuilding their
careers which had been seriously disrupted by the Second World War
and its aftermath. Keeping this in mind, it is enlightening to go back
in time and notice the influences and people that accompanied Denis
Sinor's rise to being one of the foremost Altaists of his time.

---

3   The Proceedings announce this in the following way: "The ‚Zentralasien und
     Altaistik' Section of the 24th International Congress of Orientalists [ICO] has
     found that the time available at Orientalists Congresses is insufficient, and the
     alternative obligations of its members too great, to make it possible for various
     large problems, such as those of the relationship between the so-called Altaic
     languages to be adequately discussed. The 24th ICO proposes therefore that
     arrangements should be made for holding periodically small Seminars in Altaic
     Studies which would be assembled to discuss subjects of common interest chosen
     in advance, and would be attended only by specialists in those subjects. It hopes
     that the various international and national bodies which are interested in
     international cooperation and desire to foster knowledge of the lesser known
     civilizations, will be prepared to give material assistance to this project." (Sept. 4,
     1957, cf. FRANKE, ed. 1959: 40). Sinor describes the event with slightly different
     words (SINOR, ed. 1963: 1).

From Budapest to Berlin, Paris, Cambridge and finally, Bloomington, Indiana

Sinor had a study-year in Berlin in 1937/1938.[4] There he became acquainted with, among others, the specialists working in the internationally-famous Turfan collection and a number of foremost German Orientalists such as the Sinologists Erich HAENISCH (1880–1966) and Otto FRANKE (1863–1946). Sinor then moved to Paris where in early August 1939 he presented himself to the renowned Sinologist and Mongolist Paul PELLIOT (1878–1945).[5] The latter had already worked with the young Lájos LIGETI (1902–1987), Sinor's teacher of Mongol, when Ligeti was in Paris 1925–1928.[6] At this first encounter, Pelliot might not necessarily have remembered the name Sinor, though two years previous to their meeting he had published a paper (in German) by the then 21 year old Sinor in *T'oung-pao* 33 (1937).[7] Then, shortly after his arrival in Paris, another paper by Sinor

---

4   He stayed at the Collegium Hungaricum which exists to this day, see Sinor 1994: 37–39. In a guest lecture at the Freie Universität Berlin, Sinor also spoke on the political atmosphere that reigned among Berlin orientalists (cassette recording = Sinor 1997b).

5   On his life and works see LIEU 2002 with further references. Pelliot was *vice-président* of the Société Asiatique 1928–1935 (see *Journal Asiatique* 213.1928): 359 to 228.1936, 148–149), its *président* from 1935 (see *JA* 228.1936, 148–149, 685) until his death in Oct. 1945 and also a member of the editors' commission of *Journal Asiatique* (*JA*). Sinor reminisces on his academic experiences in Berlin, Paris and Cambridge in an article published in *JAOS* (SINOR 1999) which refers back, among others, to lectures given at the Royal Asiatic Society in London (10 Oct. 1996) entitled "60 Years of Oriental Studies: A Recollection" (*JRAS*, 3rd series, vol. 7/3 1997: 519) and Freie Universität Berlin (12 Feb. 1997). In both talks – each adapted to the particular audience – he mentioned private memories that do not appear in the *JAOS* article.

6   RÓNA-TAS 2012: 123–136, here 125–126. Ligeti became a member of the Société Asiatique in January 1926, but rarely attended the *séances* of 1926–1928, see the reports (*procès-verbal)* on the Société Asiatique's meetings in *JA* 208.1926 to 213.1928. Pelliot published two of Ligeti's articles in *TP* 27.1930.

7   Sinor himself writes that it was an atrocious paper (SINOR 1999: 467), and indeed, it is a somewhat strange essay in Buddhist studies. – Pelliot co-edited *T'oung-pao* since 1921, from 1925 until 1935 as its only editor, and from 1935 until his death (1945) as co-editor with J. J. L. Duyvendak.

appeared in *Journal Asiatique* 231 (1939): 543–590. It was a comprehensive discussion of *Briefe der uigurischen Hüen-Tsang-Biographie* (1938) by Annemarie von GABAIN (1901–1993) whose acquaintance Sinor had made in Berlin the year before. In the next few years, the war years, Sinor saw three more of his articles and reviews published in *Journal Asiatique* and *T'oung-pao* (*TP*).[8]

Though Pelliot was to become Sinor's chief mentor or "patron" he was able to profit from the teaching and presence of many other French luminaries of Oriental Studies of various academic institutions such as the historian René GROUSSET (1885–1952), author of *L'empire des steppes,* one of Sinor's favorite books as all his students remember. Then there were Paul DEMIÉVILLE (1894–1979) with whom he studied Chinese, and the Turkologist Jean DENY (1879–1963) who gave him a teaching post at the École Nationale des Langues Orientales Vivantes (1946). The list also includes the Iranist Henri MASSÉ (1886–1969), the Sinologist Marcel GRANET (1884–1940), the specialist of Central Asian history Louis HAMBIS (1906–1978), Jean SAUVAGET (1901–1950), historian of the Arab world, Éveline LOT-FALCK (1918–1974), specialist of the North Siberian peoples, and many others.[9] Personal encounters with prominent Orientalists of the time were also possible during the member sessions of the Societé Asiatique which took place every month (except during the summer months), a general session (*assemblée générale*) taking place in June of each year. In those years, not more than a dozen members would usually participate in these monthly meetings (*séance*) which regularly lasted for about an hour and a half and had one member or more give a talk on personal research. "Monsieur Dines Sinor" was presented to the members by "Messieurs Pelliot et

---

8   See MESERVE 1986: 5–6 (3.5, 3.8, 3.11). Two of the articles touch on Ural-Altaic topics. From 1939 he also had several book reviews published, see *JA* 231.1939 ff.

9   Cf. *JA* 232.1940–1941 ff.; see also SINOR 1999: 470. He also mentioned the names of admired teachers in the Paris years in his guest lecture at Freie Universität Berlin, 12 Feb. 1997. For Ruth I. MESERVE's spirited biographical sketch of Denis Sinor, see Meserve 1986: 39–43.

Grousset" and elected a member on 10 May 1940.[10] Less than a year later he presented there the first of altogether seven talks (*communication*) before his departure from France for England in 1948.

Sinor survived the war years precariously between his academic pursuits and gaining a livelihood for his family (Sinor 1999: 470). The guarded way he himself was to write and speak of the years 1940–1945 permits only approximate reconstruction of his whereabouts. In various autobiographical texts, he mentions that he escaped with his new wife from Paris to the *zone libre* (non-occupied France) in October 1942 after having been declared "politically unreliable" during interrogation by German Security. They found refuge in a convent near Toulouse (not far north of the Pyrenees).[11] On the other hand, from the reports of the monthly *séances* of the Société Asiatique one may deduce that he took his membership very seriously because he attended these *séances* in Paris regularly after becoming a member in May 1940. His name is absent from the attendees of the *séances* of only November and December 1940, May and November 1941, November and December 1942, January–April[12] and November 1943, June 1944, October–December 1944, January–June 1945. The dates for 1944 and 1945 concur with his autobiographical information that he joined the French Forces of the Interior in the summer of 1944. His unit was later incorporated into the Forces of Liberation of General Charles de GAULLE (1890–1970) which formed part of the Allied occupation forces in Germany.[13] Considering the war situation, Sinor's scholarly output in German, French and Hungarian was remarkable. It touched already on a wide variety of subjects to which he would return repeatedly in later years such as Uralic and Altaic

---

10 *JA* 232.1940–1941, 307; see also Sinor's anecdote related to this event, SINOR 1999: 470 (reprinted in Walravens 2001: XXXI).
11 SINOR 1999: 470; MANDELSTAM (interview) 2009: 94. His bibliography includes a long essay on *L'Eurasie Centrale*, based on a lecture series given at the Institut catholique de Toulouse in Dec. 1942–Jan. 1943, see MESERVE 1986: 6 (item 3.9).
12 Non-occupied (southern) France was eventually occupied by German troups from 11 November 1942. The Sinors returned to Paris in March 1943, see SINOR 1999: 470, SINOR 1997b, MANDELSTAM 2009: 95.
13 Sinor 1999: 472; Sinor 1997b. Cf. MESERVE 1986: 22 (item 10.6) and 41.

linguistics[14], Old Uighur texts, European perceptions of the Mongols, and general observations on Central Eurasia or *L'Eurasie centrale*[15] as he put it in those years.

By the end of the Second World War, the course of Sinor's scholarly life had already taken a decisive turn, largely due to PELLIOT about whom Sinor says: "It was my good fortune that late in his life, when I knew him, Pelliot was more and more attracted to Inner Asian history and to Altaic studies." (SINOR 1999: 470). Along with the lasting imprint of the Hungarian school of Oriental Studies, Pelliot and his approach probably exerted the deepest influence on young Sinor, although still another period of lasting influences was to come, namely, the Cambridge years. In autumn 1948, fate carried Sinor from the scene of French Oriental Studies in Paris – that paradise of libraries, institutions and people he had come to consider his future – to Cambridge University (UK). This was another such paradise, where he was offered a lecturership in Mongol studies and where he eventually also created a course in Manchu studies[16] – fields that had not previously been taught on a regular basis at Cambridge University. In their *Introduction into Altaic Philology* Igor de RACHE-WILTZ and Volker RYBATZKI comment briefly on this development:

---

14 His first contributions to Uralo-Altaic linguistics appeared in *T'oung-pao* 37.1944, see MESERVE 1986: 5–6, items no. 3.8, 3.11 and also 3.15.

15 MESERVE 1986: 5 (3.5, 3.9, 3.10, 3.12, 3.13, 3.14). There were also reviews (see item 5.5) and lectures on these topics (see chapter 10 in Meserve 1986: 22). The war and post-war constraints as well as the passing of a number of great representatives of Oriental Studies all affected the publishing of orientalist journals, such as the annual *Journal Asiatique* (which issued five volumes between 1940 and 1948) and the annual *T'oung Pao* (which appeared only in 1940, 1942, 1944 and 1948). *The Journal of the Royal Asiatic Society of Great Britain and Ireland* proceded without interruption throughout the war years.

16 He had first taught a course of Manchu at the École nationale des langues orientales in the academic year of 1947–1948 (MESERVE 1986: 22 (item 10.15). In 1949, he published with "La transcription du mandjou" and "Le verbe mandjou" his first articles on Manchu (see Meserve 1986: 6 (items 3.16, 3.17).

"In England, Mongolistics is largely a post-war development. The appointment at Cambridge in 1948 of Denis Sinor (b. 1916), a former student of Pelliot, created a favourable ground for Altaic studies in general."[17]

In his inimitable way, Denis SINOR gave his Cambridge teaching and research some more drama. As he wrote: "In 1949, at Cambridge University, when I proposed the introduction of a Mongol tripos (examination) so as to be able to examine the students I was paid to teach, a very pompous and asinine colleague raised the question: what, if any, was the educational value of Mongol studies? A stunned Faculty Council waited with bated breath for my reply and heard with relief the answer. In its *Divino afflante* encyclica (1943), said I, Pope PIUS XII declared that ‚All knowledge being part of God's infinite knowledge was *per se* valuable.' The argument carried the debate and, might be successful at a Higher Court where I will have to present my brief. Surely, if my work proved to be acceptable in Cambridge..."[18]

During the Cambridge years (1948–1962), Sinor published a large number of articles inspired by philological, historical and linguistic interests he had harbored for years. In many cases he would pursue these till the end of his life. For instance: The Türk and other early peoples in the steppes; medieval Europe's relations with Central Eurasian peoples; history, language and culture of the Mongols; Uralic and Altaic languages and cultures.[19] At the age of 85, he remarked: "Il y a des sujets d'étude qui vous accompagnent tout au long d'une longue vie, ou bien, je dirais, auxquels on ne se lasse pas de revenir. Le voyage de Julien est de ceux-là. Voilà très longtemps qu'il retient mon attention. J'ai abordé ce sujet pour la première fois le 24 avril 1944 dans une communication faite à la Société Asiatique." (SINOR 2002: 1153) Also while in Cambridge, he began publishing on

---

17 RACHEWILTZ, RYBATZKI (2010): 248. On the course of events, see Meserve 1986: 41–42.
18 SINOR 1997a: 11. He wrote these lines in Bloomington, Christmas 1996; 47 years had passed since the event.
19 Over the decades, three volumes of Sinor's favorite articles were published, together comprising 70 pieces, see SINOR 1977, SINOR 1990b, SINOR 1997a.

the yet much underrated importance of Manchu studies.[20] In a charming essay on Sinor's merits in Manchu studies – which he continued into the 1960s – Giovanni STARY pointed out that both his work on the Manchu language and its literature was pioneering and justifies granting Sinor a place of honor among western Manchurists.[21]

Uralic & Altaic – Inner Asia – Central Eurasia

Sinor's first major book – apart from his very well received *History of Hungary* (1957, 1976) – was *Introduction à l'étude de l'Eurasie Centrale*, a comprehensive *bibliographie raisonnée* of Uralic and Altaic Studies. He had started it in Paris in autumn 1945 and finished the manuscript in Cambridge in the beginning of 1962, practically on the eve of his transfer to Indiana University in the United States. (SINOR 1963: XI) The book is divided into three main parts: Les langues et les peuples, L'histoire, and Notes sur l'éthnographie. The first part containing a shorter section on the Uralic languages and peoples and a longer section on the Altaic languages and peoples as far as they were relevant to Central Eurasia. The second part is organized chronologically and is to a large extent devoted to "Altaic history". In the very short third part, Altaic references outweigh – as in the first part – the Uralic ones, thus reflecting, in a way, the state of research and the difference in the availability of historical sources and the geographical spread of the peoples in question. However, Sinors's objective as stated in his *Introduction* was not primarily to focus on "Uralic and Altaic", but on the concept of Central Eurasia, embodying, among others, Uralic and Altaic languages and cultures. Even nowadays when bibliographical searches are usually performed via the internet, Sinor's *Introduction* continues to be a ready mine of precious information.

---

20 MESERVE 1986: 6–7 (items 3.15–3.45).
21 Stary in MESERVE 1986: 53–55; cf. also SINOR 1968, where on p. 280 one can read: "Through no fault of his, Professor Sinor's contribution was left behind from 1958 until now."

Considering the *Introduction* and his other works[22] and the development of their author's ideas from Budapest via Paris and Cambridge to Bloomington, it comes as no surprise that Sinor's
subsequent development and activities went into studies which
spanned all of Central Eurasia. At Indiana University Denis Sinor
combined and represented the various aspects of his core concept: the
Uralic & Altaic Program (founded in 1956)[23] which became the
Department of Uralic & Altaic Studies (1965) and subsequently the
Department of Central Eurasian Studies (CEUS, 1993); further the
Inner Asian & Uralic National Resource Center (IAUNRC, founded
1963/1981) and the Research Institute for Inner Asian Studies
(RIFIAS, founded 1979), renamed in 2006 the Denis Sinor Institute
for Inner Asian Studies. These highly successful units of teaching and
research correspond to one part of what Jamsheed CHOKSY
considered Sinor's "prodigious contributions to Central Asian
Studies".[24] The Indiana University Publication "Uralic & Altaic
Series" should also be remembered here. It had been founded by
Thomas A. SEBEOK (1920–2001), the famous semiotician and linguist, in the late 1950s, but was directed by Sinor between 1979–1981
and 1985 to 2011. The last volume Sinor accepted for publication in
this series was number 173, the Festschrift for his friend Igor de
RACHEWILTZ (2009).[25]

---

22 Cf. e.g. Sinor's chapter "Central Eurasia" in SINOR 1954, 1970; *Inner Asia: A Syllabus* 1969, 1971; *The Cambridge History of Early Inner Asia* 1990.
23 In the sources there are some discrepancies in relation to the years the various institutions mentioned here were founded and/or directed by Sinor; no effort was successful in reducing this information to a common denominator.
24 CHOKSY 2011: 4.
25 RYBATZKI, Volker; Alessandra POZZI, Peter W. GEIER, and John R. KRUEGER (eds.) (2009). *The Early Mongols: Language, Culture and History. Studies in Honor of Igor de Rachewiltz on the Occasion of his 80th Birthday*. Bloomington (Uralic & Altaic Series, vol. 173.)

Here, another book series Denis Sinor directed and edited comes to mind: *Handbook of Oriental Studies* (Handbuch der Orientalistik), section 8 "Central Asia" (later "Uralic and Central Asian Studies") the founding volume of which was *The Uralic Languages* (1988).[26]

In a guest lecture at Freie Universität Berlin in 1997, Denis Sinor said that he invented the concept of "Eurasie centrale" as an historico-cultural entity in July 1940, i.e. in Paris.[27] But it needs to be said that he was indebted to the Budapest Orientalist School, represented, during his study years and later, mainly by Gyula NÉMETH (1890–1976) and Lájos LIGETI – "a splendid, ruthless Hungarian education", as he said in an interview titled "Scholar with a Dash of Derring-Do".[28] In the preface to his *Inner Asia, a Syllabus*, Sinor writes: "'Inner Asia' is a concept more readily understood [than Central Eurasia] and, in this book, it is virtually synonymous with ‚Central Eurasia'." (SINOR 1969: X) In this context he speaks of the "rather exhilarating intellectual experience" that a course on Inner Asia holds for a teacher and his students (Sinor 1969, IX). At the 12th PIAC Meeting held in Berlin (GDR) in 1969, Sinor discussed the various aspects of the concept and concluded: "'Inner Asia' has the merit that it includes Siberia whose importance for our studies becomes increasingly clear" thus opting for an indulgent attitude in using

---

26 Sinor contributed the preface, the introduction and an essay on "The Problem of the Ural-Altaic Relationship" (pp. 706–741). The idea of preparing a Handbook of Uralic Studies originated in a conversation between Professor Bertold SPULER (1911–1990), the founding editor of the Brill series *Handbook of Oriental Studies* (Handbuch der Orientalistik) and Sinor in October 1974 (p. IX). Sinor had first heard about Spuler from Pelliot during the war years (SINOR 1999, 469), and, incidentally, it was Spuler who recommended the present author when Sinor asked him to send one of his students as he had an IU Foreign Student Fellowship available (1966), and hence the author's first personal acquaintance with Denis Sinor. Sinor's student Nicola Di COSMO joined him as editor of the Handbook series in 2001. As of 2017 the series comprised twenty-four, usually hefty and influential volumes .

27 Cf. also SINOR 2003, 8, more accessibly quoted in KELLNER-HEINKELE 2006, 5–6.

28 MANDELSTAM 2009, 94; in a personal memoir devoted to his friend Tibor HALASI-KUN (1914–1991) Sinor sheds some very interesting light on the orientalist scene in Budapest and Paris in the 1930s and 1940s (SINOR 1993–1994, 31–42).

scholarly terms (Sinor 1974, 40–41). Two decades later, again both "Central Eurasia" and "Inner Asia" figure side by side in *The Cambridge History of Early Inner Asia* that covers the history of a large expanse of land inhabited mainly by peoples that are conveniently called Uralic and Altaic, but also by many that used or may have used other languages and practiced cultural traditions different from those we tend to ascribe to the so-called Uralic and Altaic peoples.[29]

Another line of his Central-Eurasian engagement was Sinor's involvement in the publication of handbooks and surveys, at a time when these were still sorely lacking. The most comprehensive of these projects was UNESCO's "History of Civilizations of Central Asia", first proposed in 1973 by the Tajik scholar B. G. GAFUROV and approved by the General Conference of UNESCO in 1976. Actual work started in 1981[30] and the first of six volumes appeared in 1992, the last in 2005. From the beginning and for all of the planned six volumes Sinor figured among the 15 members of the International Scientific Committee and contributed articles to volumes III, IV/1 and IV/2, while serving as one of the four members of the Reading Committee which comprised the inner circle where, as he used to say, the real work was done in cooperation with the fabulous Irène ISKENDER-MOCHIRI, the organizing soul of all six volumes. Denis Sinor loved this work on the *History* which took him back to Paris on a regular basis and offered him the opportunity to enjoy the collegiality of the Iranist Richard N. FRYE's (1920–2014) and that of the Islam historian Clifford Edmund BOSWORTH's (1928–2015).

Networking
In a way, the fourteen years Sinor spent teaching and researching in Cambridge (1948–1962) may have influenced his career even more than the years he spent in Paris. After the stormy and precarious war years, Cambridge war a real haven of security and quiet scholarly activities, even though the country was just starting to recover from

---

29 SINOR, ed. (1990): 1–18 (Introduction: The Concept of Inner Asia).
30 The story of the project's realization is addressed in the introduction of each volume (see "Preface" and "Description of the Project", History 1992–2005).

the hardships and scarcity of the post-war era. Compared to Paris, life at Cambridge University was necessarily modest, yet it offered all the glorious rituals and traditions of English academia – such as the college high table, the more generally practiced high tea and the Oxford and Cambridge Club in London.[31] At the same time, the inter-national network of scholars that had flourished in the inter-war period (and before) soon revived, and here was one of the fields where Sinor brought to bloom his uncommon organizational talent and his taste for unconventional solutions.

In 1938, the 20th International Congress of Orientalists (ICO, founded in Paris, 1873) met in Brussels and was scheduled to convene again in Paris in 1941. In those years this was still an event of great international academic importance. The Second World War pushed that date back to 1948. In spite of the material restrictions of the post-war years, the Congress, organized by the Société Asiatique and under the patronage of prominent state officials, was to be an eminent academic and diplomatic event with almost 300 communications (*Actes* 1949, 6–15, 401–408). The traditional sections of the ICO, "Iranian and Central Asian Studies" on the one hand and "Turkology" on the other, united the pre-war generation of famous orientalists (except the German ones) with a new generation, to which Denis Sinor, now from Cambridge, belonged.

The next, the 22nd International Congress of Orientalists was organized by Zeki Velidi TOGAN (1890–1970) in Istanbul in 1951. This offered the more than 600 participants the extraordinary adventure of encountering a modernizing, though economically-struggling Turkey, and the thrill of the region's charms during ex-cursions to inner Anatolia.[32] Sinor took the opportunity to travel to

31 When in London, then and in later years, Denis used to stay at his favorite club, the Oxford and Cambridge Club (founded 1830), housed in two adjacent venerable old palaces on Pall Mall (opened 1838).

32 TOGAN, ed. 1953: 222–228. One of the lasting results of this congress was the steps taken to advance the project for a "Grundriss of Turkish Philology and Cultural History", which was realized and published under the title *Philologiae Turcicae Fundamenta* (*PTF*) I (1959) and II (1965); for details see *PTF* I: IX–XII. The volumes became indispensible tools for Turkologists. Sinor contributed an

Istanbul overland on what turned out to be an exciting trip not many were ready to take in those days. With his Iranist colleague and friend Harold W. BAILEY (1899–1996), he drove in a Land Rover from Cambridge across western Europe, Yugoslavia and Bulgaria and into Turkey (Sinor, Berlin lecture 1997b).

If people, culture and academic traditions were completely familiar in Paris for one coming from Cambridge, the ICO in Istanbul turned out to be an almost exotic adventure. Possibly even more than the Paris Congress it brought together the cream of international orient scholars (except the Soviet scholars) and triggered new cooperations. For Sinor, participation in the International Congress of Orientalists in Paris (1948) and Istanbul (1951) created lasting impressions and experiences. He learned what large congresses could and could not achieve. In any event, after the bitter war years, the ICOs permitted the international networking to resume and open up new horizons of scholarship.

Already as a young scholar in his first semester at the University of Budapest (1934), Sinor had met and become familiar with scholars who set the tone internationally. We have seen that he continued subsequently to acquaint himself personally with scholars in, and related to, his area of studies. Now, after the Istanbul Congress he was ready to try his own hand at organizing the next International Congress of Orientalists. Supported by the president of The Royal Asiatic Society of Great Britain and Ireland,[33] Sir Ralph TURNER, and, among others, also H. W. Bailey, Sinor overcame much resistence in Cambridge itself for his ambitious plan. He succeeded in organizing and convening the Congress at Cambridge University in the summer of 1954.

It is in the context of the post-war recovery of international Oriental Studies and the high prestige of the International Congress of

---

article on "The Uighur Empire of Mongolia" to what amounts to vol. III: History of the Turkic Peoples in the Pre-Islamic Period, ed. by Hans Robert ROEMER, Berlin: Klaus Schwarz 2000, 187–204 (Philologiae et Historiae Turcicae Fundamenta I).

33 Sinor had been elected a member on 14 May 1953, see *JRAS* 1953, 183.

Orientalists that we have to see the convening of the Twenty-Third International Congress of Orientalists in Cambridge. Sinor, at 38 years of age, was the Secretary-General, and in this capacity, the main organizer of the Congress, and afterwards, the editor of the bulky volume of its proceedings.[34] In his preface to the Proceedings, Sinor mentions that his colleagues in the organizing committee gave him complete freedom of action (p. 7), but he also does not fail to mention that without the "unobtrusive persistence" of H[arold] W[alter] BAILEY, the chairman of the organizing committee, "the Congress would never have met in Cambridge." (ibid.)

With 908 participants from 40 countries the 1954 congress was a great achievement and acclaimed as a big success. Even a delegation of 18 Soviet scholars had made it to Cambridge (SINOR, ed. [s. a.], 18). The speeches held on various occasions and the list of events (SINOR, ed. [s. a.], 11–53) perfectly reflect the high esteem participants and public institutions expressed for the Congress. It was a time of "remarkable growth of interest in Oriental studies at our universities", as the President of the Cambridge Congress, Sir Ralph Turner said (SINOR, ed. [s. a.], 28).

Interestingly, it was the first time that the venerable old International Congress of Orientalists had an official section for "Altaic Studies" besides the section "Iranian, Armenian and Central Asian Studies", and it might not be far-fetched to believe that Denis Sinor, as the organizer, stood behind this new feature.[35] The section's program lists among others the names of Sir Gerard CLAUSON, Alessio BOMBACI, Omeljan PRITSAK, Pertev Naili BORATAV, Louis BAZIN, Zeki Velidi TOGAN, Kaare GRØNBECH, Helmuth SCHEEL, Pentti AALTO, Walther HEISSIG, Erich HAENISCH, Rahmeti ARAT, Mecdut MANSUROĞLU, Karl Heinrich MENGES, A. N. KONONOV,

---

34 SINOR, ed. [s. a.]. Issued in connexion with the Congress and distributed among the participants was, among other volumes, the collection of *Orientalism and History*, edited by Denis Sinor, which contained, one may assume, his "credo", the article on Central Eurasia (Cambridge: Heffer 1954: 82–103, 2nd ed. Bloomington – London: Indiana University Press 1970, 93–123).

35 SINOR, ed. [s. a.], 181–202 (abstracts and program of sessions).

Denis Sinor at the 44th Annual Meeting of the PIAC in
Walberberg, 2001

Annemarie von GABAIN, Charles R. BAWDEN –most of whom would
in later years follow the call to the meetings of the Permanent
International Altaistic Conference.[36]

During the Cambridge years, Denis Sinor became ever more
involved in international organizations of Oriental Studies, not only as
a member or organizer of conferences, but also as a "mover" and pre-
senter of ideas. The international network of colleagues, acquaintances and friends in Oriental Studies into which he had been drawn
during the Paris years expanded quickly. We have to see his involvement in the emerging PIAC in this context. In his short history of

---

36 Another section was "Turkology (history)" where today we would speak of
   Ottoman studies. It was represented by Osman TURAN, Akdes Nimet KURAT, Halil
   İNALCIK, Franz TAESCHNER, F. R. UNAT, Jean DENY, Bernard LEWIS, Abdülkadir
   KARAHAN, Gotthard JÄSCHKE, Zeki Velidi TOGAN, Tayyib GÖKBILGIN, Paul
   WITTEK, Claude CAHEN, Irène MÉLIKOFF, Richard F. KREUTEL a. o. (SINOR, ed.
   [s. a.], 203–214).

the PIAC Sinor mentions (Provo 1997: 1) that in 1957 there were in the small informal gathering – as far as he recalls – Annemarie von GABAIN (1901–1993) whom he had met in 1937 during his student year in Berlin, and Omeljan PRITSAK (1919–2006) apart from Walther HEISSIG and himself. The next year, 1958, the first PIAC meeting on record assembled in Mainz just a dozen people from six countries: Pentti AALTO (1917–1998), Charles R. BAWDEN (1924–2016), Gerhard DOERFER (1920–2003), Wolfram EBERHARD (1909–1989), Walther HEISSIG (1913–2005), Karl JAHN (1906–1985), Karl H. MENGES (1908–1999), Udo POSCH, Omeljan PRITSAK (1919–2006), Klaus SAGASTER (b. 1933), Kaare THOMSEN HANSEN (1924–1997) and Denis SINOR. During the second and third meeting in 1959 and 1960, they were joined by Mecdut MANSUROĞLU (1910–1960), Reşit Rahmeti ARAT (1900–1964), Ahmed TEMIR (1912–2003), Alessio BOMBACI (1914–1979), Tourhan GANDJEI, Ananiasz ZAJĄCZKOWSKI (1903–1970), Nicholas POPPE (1897–1991), Walther FUCHS (1902–1979) and Erich HAENISCH (1880–1966). If one looks at the ages of the scholars in this list, it becomes clear that most of them are of about the same age, i.e. they attained their full intellectual and academic development after the Second World War. Only a few, such as R. R. Arat, Nicholas Poppe, Annemarie von Gabain and Ananiasz Zającz-kowski were half a generation older.

Within a year of his arrival in Bloomington to direct Indiana University's Uralic and Altaic Studies Program, Denis Sinor organized the fifth Annual Meeting of the Permanent International Altaistic Conference (PIAC), June 4–9, 1962, to be held in Bloomington. Of the earlier four meetings three had been held in Germany and the fourth in Cambridge (1961), the latter under Sinor's aegis. The Bloomington Meeting was the first that led to a collective volume of the papers offered, and it was the first at which a larger number of American scholars was able to participate (Sinor, ed. 1963: 5–7, Conference report). It was at this meeting that the "Indiana University Prize for Altaic Studies" was announced and a first medal committee elected. Father Antoine MOSTAERT (1881–1971), the outstanding Mongolist, was the first recipient. It is not impossible to think that the Triennial Gold Medal of the Royal Asiatic Society[37] was the model for the IU Prize for Altaic Studies, or, perhaps, the Lidzbarski Medal that had played a prominent role at the International Congress of Orientalists which Sinor had organized in Cambridge eight years earlier (1954).[38] It seems appropriate to mention here that it had been at the Cambridge event that the Semitist and Arabist Franz ROSENTHAL (1914–2003) of the University of Pennsylvania finally received the Lidzbarski Gold Medal. This corrected the fact that Rosenthal, who had been awarded the Lidzbarski Prize in monetary form at the ICO in Brussels in 1938, never received it. The award had been withheld from the German Jewish citizen Rosenthal owing to the pressure of the Deutsche Morgenländische Gesellschaft which had overall charge of the Lidzbarski awards.[39] Perhaps, Sinor was instrumental in this rectification as he played the leading role in the organization of the Cambridge ICO. That would have been fully characteristic.

It is perhaps not widely known that there also exists a **Denis Sinor Medal.** It was inaugurated in 1993 by Denis Sinor, specifically to honour scholars in the field of Inner Asian Studies. It is awarded by The Royal Asiatic Society. In 2001 it was awarded to Academician Shagdaryn BIRA (b. 1927) for his outstanding work on Mongolia and Inner Asian historiography. Previous recipients were Sir Harold W. BAILEY (1899–1996) in 1993 and Karl JETTMAR (1918–2002) in

---

37 This medal was awarded between 1897 and 1990 and then replaced by the Royal Asiatic Society Award. *http://royalasiaticsociety.org/the-triennial-gold-medal/* (Accessed 2 Feb., 2018).

38 See BUCKLEY 2012, chapter 5 and BOSWORTH 2001: passim.

39 ROSENTHAL 1998, 361–366; see also SINOR, ed. [s. a.], 44-46. In 1928, the Semitist Mark LIDZBARSKI (1868–1928) of Göttingen University founded an endowment with the aim of honoring the scholarly work of Semitists at the International Congresses of Orientalists. The recipient was to be chosen by representatives of the Deutsche Morgenländische Gesellschaft, Société Asiatique, The Royal Asiatic Society and the American Oriental Society. The award was conferred for the last time in 2007 and then discontinued, because the Deutsche Morgenländische Gesellschaft was no longer able to provide the funds for the Medal, s. minutes of the annual meeting of Deutsche Morgenländische Gesellschaft in *ZDMG* 159.2009, 518.

1998. It was awarded in 2007 to the Mongolist Igor de RACHEWILTZ (1929–2016) and the Iranist Nicholas SIMS WILLIAMS (b. 1949) in 2015.[40]

Epilogue

In his later years, friends and colleagues were especially impressed by Denis Sinor's continuing energy and discipline. His bibliography of published works for the years after his retirement is indeed impressive and full of zest.[41] In spite of his very frail health and of being in constant pain since the late 1990s, he continued to edit to his death the "Journal of Asian History" which he had founded in 1967, proof-reading articles to be published, making notes with his fine, very characteristic handwriting, and, assisted by his esteemed colleague Ruth I. MESERVE as book-review editor and his secretary[42], conducting business with the publishing house.[43] In the context of his contributions to Comparative Altaic Linguistics, he wrote: "I consider myself a historian and not a linguist (a statement with which, I suppose, most linguists would gladly agree), and the aim of any research I have undertaken was always meant to serve – at least in my own mind – the clarification of a historical process." (SINOR 1990b, IX).

Looking back on his life, Denis Sinor remarked: "Let me assure those who may question the ‚utility' and the ‚relevance' of my scholarly work that they will find in me no determined foe of their views. I have no doubt that my friends, such as a policeman on the beat, a mechanic in the garage, a nurse in a hospital ward, do more

---

40 See Homepage of The Royal Asiatic Society, Awards, Prizes & Visiting Fellow-ships.
41 See CHOKSY, ZAI 2011, 6–15. Their bibliography continues the bibliography presented in Meserve 1986 for the years 1986–2010.
42 Ruth I. MESERVE was book-review editor from 1983–2011. Secretaries who assisted with the *JAH* were in particular Karin L. FORD (1968–1997) and Jill ZAI (2002–2011).
43 The *Journal of Asian History* was one of his very personal matters of concern. In the first number he wrote: "This new periodical is intended to fill a gap which both general historians and orientalists have long felt to exist in the coverage of Asian Studies." (*JAH* 1.1967, 1).

good than I could ever achieve with my writing." (SINOR 1997a: 11).
He is not exaggerating when he speaks here of policemen, nurses or
mechanics as his friends. As eye-witnesses confirm, they *were* his
friends, because he had a natural friendliness with everyone, be he or
she a scholar, administrator, employee, craftsman or worker. It was
coupled with genuine interest, an extraordinary sense of humour and a
much-admired quick-wittedness.[44] He could be scathing, sarcastic or
even frightening, as well, but what most people experienced was his
unusual charm, I would even say, his charisma.

References

Actes du XXe Congrès International des Orientalistes, Bruxelles, 5–
    10 Septembre 1938. Louvain 1940.
Actes du XXIe congrès international des orientalistes, Paris, 23–31
    juillet 1948. Paris: Société Asiatique de Paris 1949.
ALPATOV, V. M. (2001). Denis Sinor. Yubilej uchenogo. In: *Altaica*
    V: 9–13.
BAZIN, Louis; Alessio BOMBACI; Jean DENY; Tayyib GÖKBILGIN;
    Fahir IZ; Helmuth SCHEEL; Pertev Naili BORATAV (1965).
    Philologiae Turcicae Fundamenta II. Mainz: Steiner.
BUCKLEY, Jorunn J. (2012). *Lady E. S. [Ethel Stefana] Drower's
    scholarly correspondence. An intrepid English autodidact in Iraq.*
    Leiden: Brill.
BOSWORTH, C. Edmund (ed.) (2001). *A century of British
    Orientalists, 1902–2001.* Oxford: Oxford University Press for The
    British Academy.
BOYKOVA, Elena V.; Giovanni STARY, with the assistance of
    Elizabeth and Charles CARLSON. *Florilegia Altaistica. Studies in
    honour of Denis Sinor on the occasion of his 90th birthday.*
    Wiesbaden: Harrassowitz. (Asiatische Forschungen, 149.)
CHEN Wei (1987). A short introduction to the 29th meeting of the

---

44 "[...] mit seiner viel bewunderten Schlagfertigkeit" [...], see DÉCSY in HEISSIG et
    al. (eds.) 1976, 122.

PIAC. (Translation: O. Corff) *http://www.altaist.org/annual-meetings/29th-meeting-tashkent-1986-report-chen-wei/* (accessed 16 July 2017).

CHOKSY, Jamsheed K. (2011). Denis Sinor, Doyen of Central Eurasian Studies. In: *Journal of Asian History* 45: 3–6.

CHOKSY, Jamsheed K.; Jill ZAI (2011). Bibliographical addendum. In: *Journal of Asian History* 45: 6–15.

DENY, Jean; Kaare GRØNBECH; Helmuth SCHEEL; Zeki Velidi TOGAN (eds.) (1959). *Philologiae Turcicae Fundamenta* I. Mainz: Steiner.

DUYVENDAK, J. J. L. (1947/48): Paul Pelliot. In: *T'oung Pao* 38: 161–164. [Reprinted in WALRAVENS (2001): XIII–XXIV.]

FRANKE, Herbert, ed. (1959). *Akten des Vierundzwanzigsten Internationalen Orientalisten-Kongresses München, 28. August bis 4. September 1957.* Wiesbaden: Steiner, in Kommission für die Deutsche Morgenländische Gesellschaft.

FUTAKY, István; Wolfgang VEENKER, Hrsg. (1994*): Julius von Farkas zum 100. Geburtstag.* Wiesbaden: Harrassowitz. (Veröffentlichungen der Societas Uralo-Altaica, 41.)

GOSH, A. et al., ed. (1969*). Proceedings of the Twenty-sixth International Congress of Orientalists, New Delhi 4–10th January, 1964.* Vols. I–II. New Delhi 1966, 1968.

HAZAI, Georg; Peter ZIEME (eds.): *Sprache, Geschichte und Kultur der altaischen Völker. Protokollband der XII. Tagung der Permanent International Altaistic Conference 1969 in Berlin.* Berlin: Akademie. (Schriften zur Geschichte und Kultur des Alten Orients, 5.)

HEISSIG, Walther; John R. KRUEGER; Felix C. OINAS; Edmond SCHÜTZ, eds. (1976). *Tractata Altaica. Denis Sinor sexagenario optime de rebus altaicis merito dedicata.* Wiesbaden: Otto Harrassowitz.

HEYWOOD, Colin (1991). Review of Denis SINOR: Essays in comparative Altaic linguistics. Bloomington, IN 1990. In: *Journal of the Royal Asiatic Society* XX: 445–447.

History of Civilizations of Central Asia. Vols. I (1992), II (1994), III

(1996), IV/1 (1998), IV/2 (2000), V (2003), VI (2005). Paris: UNESCO.

LIEU, Samuel (2002): Paul Pelliot. *Encyclopaedia Iranica*, online edition, available at http://www.iranicaonline.org/articles/pelliot-paul (accessed on 25 Sept. 2017).

KELLNER-HEINKELE, Barbara (2006). Hommage à Denis Sinor. In: *Florilegia Altaistica. Studies in honour of Denis Sinor on the occasion of his 90th birthday*. Edited by Elena V. BOYKOVA and Giovanni STARY with the assist. of Elizabeth and Charles CARLSON. Wiesbaden: Harrassowitz, 1–10. (Asiatische Forschungen, 149.)

KELLNER-HEINKELE, Barbara (2013). Prologue. In: Tatiana PANG, Simone-Christiane RASCHMANN, Gerd WINKELHANE (eds.): *Unknown treasures of the Altaic World in libraries, archives and museums. 53rd Annual Meeting of the Permanent International Altaistic Conference, Institute of Oriental Manuscripts, RAS, St. Petersburg, July 25–30, 2010*. Berlin: Klaus Schwarz, 8–10. (Studien zur Sprache, Geschichte und Kultur der Türkvölker, 13.)

MANDELSTAM, Janet (2009). Denis Sinor, Scholar with a Dash of Derring-Do! In: *Bloom Magazine*, June/July: 92–96.

Mémoires du Congrès International des Orientalistes, Paris 1873. 1–3. Paris: Maisonneuve, 1874.

MESERVE, Ruth I. (1986). *Denis Sinor bibliography*. Bloomington, In. (Arcadia Bibliographica Virorum Eruditorum, 9.)

PANG, Tatiana; Simone-Christiane RASCHMANN; Gerd WINKELHANE (eds.): *Unknown treasures of the Altaic World in libraries, archives and museums. 53rd Annual Meeting of the Permanent International Altaistic Conference, Institute of Oriental Manuscripts, RAS, St. Petersburg, July 25–30, 2010*. Berlin: Klaus Schwarz. (Studien zur Sprache, Geschichte und Kultur der Türkvölker, 13.)

RACHEWILTZ, Igor de; Volker RYBATZKI (2010). *Introduction into Altaic philology*. Leiden: Brill. (Handbook of Oriental Studies, section 8, vol. 20.)

RÓNA-TAS, András (2012). In Memoriam Lajos Ligeti (1902–1987). *Acta Orientalia Academiae Scientiarum Hungaricae* 65: 123–136.

ROSENTHAL, Franz (1998). Die Lidzbarski-Goldmedaille. In: *Zeitschrift der Deutschen Morgenländischen Gesellschaft* 148: 361–366.

SINOR, Denis, ed. (1954). *Orientalism and history.* Cambridge. [A second enlarged edition was published in 1970 by Indiana University Press, Bloomington, IN.]

SINOR, Denis, ed. (s. a.). *Proceedings of the Twenty-Third International Congress of Orientalists.* Cambridge 21st–28th August 1954. London: The Royal Asiatic Society.

SINOR, Denis (1959, 1976). *History of Hungary.* London: George Allen & Unwin.

SINOR, Denis (1963). *Introduction à l'étude de l'Asie centrale.* Wiesbaden: Otto Harrassowitz.

SINOR, Denis, ed. and assisted by David FRANCIS (1963/1981). *Aspects of Altaic civilization. Proceedings of the Fifth Meeting of the Permanent International Altaistic Conference held at Indiana University, June 4–9, 1962.* Westport, Conn.: Greenwood. (Indiana University Publications. Uralic and Altaic Series, 23.)

SINOR, Denis (1968). La langue mandjoue. In: *Tungusologie.* Mit Beiträgen von W. Fuchs, Ivan A. Lopatin, Karl H. Menges, Denis Sinor. Leiden, Köln: Brill: 257–280. (Handbuch der Orientalistik, 1. Abteilung, 5. Band, 3. Abschnitt.)

SINOR, Denis, ed. with the Assistance of Tanja JACQUES, Ralph LARSON, Mary-Elizabeth MEEK 1971). *Proceedings of the Twenty-Seventh International Congress of Orientalists, Ann Arbor, Michigan, 13th–19th August 1967.* Wiesbaden: Otto Harrassowitz.

SINOR, Denis (1974). Stand und Aufgaben der internationalen altaistischen Forschung. In: Georg Hazai, Peter Zieme (eds.): *Sprache, Geschichte und Kultur der altaischen Völker. Protokollband der XII. Tagung der Permanent International Altaistic Conference 1969 in Berlin.* Berlin: Akademie, pp. 35–43. (Schriften zur Geschichte und Kultur des Alten Orients, 5.)

SINOR, Denis (1977). *Inner Asia and its contacts with medieval Europe.* London: Variorum Reprints.

SINOR, Denis, ed. (1988). *The Uralic languages. Description, history and foreign influences.* Leiden etc.: E. J. Brill. (Handbuch der Orientalistik, 8. Abteilung: Handbook of Uralic Studies, vol. 1.)

SINOR, Denis (1990a). *The Cambridge history of early Inner Asia.* Cambridge: Cambridge University Press.

SINOR, Denis (1990b). *Essays in comparative Altaic linguistics.* Bloomington, IN. (Indiana University Uralic and Altaic Studies, 143.)

Sinor, Denis (1993–1994). Tibor Halasi-Kun. A personal memoir. In: *Archivum Ottomanicum* XIII: 31–42.

SINOR, Denis (1994). [Julius von Farkas] 1937–1938. In: István Futaky, Wolfgang Veenker (Hrsg.): *Julius von Farkas zum 100. Geburtstag.* Wiesbaden: Harrassowitz, pp. 37–39. (Veröffentlichungen der Societas Uralo-Altaica, 41.)

SINOR, Denis (1997a). *Studies in medieval Inner Asia.* Aldershot: Ashgate. (Variorum Collected Studies Series.)

SINOR, Denis (1997b). *Reminiscences.* Guest lecture at Freie Universität Berlin, Faculty of Philosophy and Social Sciences II, 12 February 1997 (unpublished casette).

SINOR, Denis (1999). Remembering Paul Pelliot, 1878–1945. In: *Journal of the American Oriental Society* 119/3: 467–472. [Reprinted in WALRAVENS (2001): XXV–XXXV.]

SINOR, Denis (2001). Forty Years of the Permanent International Altaistic Conference (PIAC): History and Reminiscences. In: David B. Honey & David C. Wright (eds.): *Altaic affinities. Proceedings of the 40th Meeting of the Permanent International Altaistic Conference (PIAC), Provo, Utah (1997).* Bloomington, IN: Research Institute for Inner Asian Studies, pp. 1–21. (Indiana University Uralic and Altaic Series, 168.)

SINOR, Denis (2002). Le rapport du dominicain Julien écrit en 1238 sur le péril mongol. In: *Académie des Inscriptions & Belles-Lettres. Comptes rendus des seances* de l'année 2002 novembre – décembre: 1153–1168.

SINOR, Denis (2003). [Reminiscences]. In: *Inner Asian & Uralic National Resource Center Newsletter.* Winter: 1, 8–9.

SINOR, Denis (2004). Rediscovering Central Asia. In: *Diogenes* 204: 7–19. [French version pp. 19–24.]

TOGAN, Zeki Velidi (ed.) (1954, 1957). *Proceedings of the Twenty Second Congress of Orientalists held in Istanbul, September 15th to 22nd, 1951.* Vol. I, Istanbul 1953; vol. II, Leiden: Brill 1957.

WALRAVENS, Hartmut (2001*): Paul Pelliot (1878–1945). His life and works. A bibliography.* Bloomington, IN. (Indiana University Oriental Series IX.)

http://royalasiaticsociety.org/awards-prizes-visiting-fellowships/ (accessed 2 Feb. 2018).

On the Theory of Regular Script in Uighur Calligraphy

LIU Ge (Professor, College of History and Culture, Shaanxi Normal University)

Translated by LI Zhaojun (Xijing Institute, Xi'an)
and John MCGOVERN (New College, University of Oxford)

The term Uighur corresponds with the *pinyin* transliteration of today's Chinese word 维吾尔 (*weiwu'er*). Uighurs were Turkic speakers. The so-called Uighur script refers to a kind of Turkic writing, using the writings of Sogdians who spoke Eastern Iranian. According to Geng Shimin, among ethnic groups who spoke Turkic in China, it is the Toxsis who were the first to use Sogdian to write their own language, with the evidence that "there exist 8th century coins with Toxsi letters on them."[1] Uighur people later also used this kind of writing, and because of their long existence and great influence, it became later known as Uighur script.

In the late 9th century Islam began to spread throughout the Xinjiang region. Ethnic groups speaking Turkic began to use Arabic script to spell Turkic. At present, the author has collected many Uighur documents, which were written after the main body of Uighur people had migrated westwards, with most contracts written in the Yuan dynasty, that is, the 13th–14th centuries.

The direct consequence of Uighurs using Arabic instead of their old writing system is that Uighur script gradually became a dead script, and their history and culture of pre-Islamic times written in Uighur has been sealed up along with it. Now, if we want to understand this period of history, we will have to know of this kind of writing, and that is why Uighur texts are very precious.

---

1 GENG Shimin: *An Introduction to the Ancient Culture and Literature of the Uygur Nationality*. Urumqi: Xinjiang People's Publishing House, 1983, 103.

Uighur calligraphy includes the writing tools, Uighur text structure, artistic effect and so on. The writing tools and text structure have the features of the age, therefore research into Uighur calligraphy is an important part in the study of its history and culture.

MORIYASU Takao's 森安孝夫 research is the most famous among many on Uighur calligraphy. He divides the calligraphy in Uighur literature into four styles: regular script, semi-regular script, semi-cursive, and cursive, and has made special descriptions of the characteristics of each style. However, I do not agree with his classification and discussions. This article mainly focuses on his theory of regular script.

Moriyasu Takao's theory of regular script in Uighur calligraphy
MORIYASU Takao's standards of Uighur regular script are mainly as follows. First, narrow spaces between words: "writing intensively." Second, clear strokes. As the initial letter A or N is easy to identify, A, N, X, Y, etc. are "easily distinguished". The strokes are clear, just like being printed. Third, "neat handwriting". There seem to exist interval lines of equal distance between them, so the words cannot be confused. Fourth, he thought "this kind of handwriting was mostly written by specialists from Manichean or Buddhist organizations, and mostly seen in religious texts," and "it is rarely seen in the secular documents, and also has nothing to do with the time period."[2]

---

2 森安孝夫：《ウイグル文書劄記》、（その四）、《内陸アジア言語の研究》IX、1994、第 66 頁:"字間は密につまっているが、アレフ（または N）と R、ダブルアレフ（またはアレフと N）と X、Y と β、語頭のアレフと N とが容易に区別できるほど字画がはっきりした、一見印刷かと思われるような整然とした書体。多くは予め等間隔に罫線を引き、文字の中心線がぶれないようにしてある。恐らくはマニ教教団や仏教教団内の専門の書記や寫字生によって筆寫されたもの。マニ教典や仏典に多くの例が見られる。実例: Pelliot: Ouïgour 1=Hamilton, MOTH, No.1, pp. 267–270; Or. 8212–104= Hamilton, MOTH, pp. 331–350. 俗文書に使用されることはまずないと言ってよく、従って『集成』にも実例はない。この書体だけは時代に無關係である。"

My own comprehension and cognition about the theory of regular script in Uighur calligraphy

There is regular script (楷書) in Uighur texts, just as Moriyasu Takao holds. I infer that he equates certain writing styles of Uighur texts with Chinese regular script. I believe this is debatable.

The basic characteristics of Chinese regular script

There are many rules in Chinese regular script. Compared with the Uighur writing styles, the main characteristics of Chinese regular script are as follows. First, the Chinese regular script is made up of square characters, using horizontal, vertical, left-falling, right-falling, dot and hook strokes. Second, of each Chinese regular script character the number of strokes is fixed and the strokes cannot be omitted. If a stroke is omitted, the character or phrase cannot be found anywhere in etymology dictionaries compiled according to the stroke order. Due to strokes omitted or lost, or those linked together which shouldn't be, from the structures of Chinese characters this writing style cannot be called regular script.

Third, the stroke configuration of regular script Chinese characters is relatively fixed. Because of the way of placing, moving, and finishing the brush, and of the location of the stroke in the Character, the formation of horizontal and vertical strokes have various styles such as *cangfeng* 藏鋒 (hiding the tip of the brush), *zhongfeng* 中鋒 (centralizing the tip), *cefeng* 側鋒 (side-cutting the tip), *huifeng* 回峰 (returning the tip), *dunbi* 頓筆 (pressing the brush), *tibi* 提筆 (lifting the brush) and *zhebi* 折筆 (folding the tip). The forms of the stroke also have rules, for example, the horizontal is like an array of clouds, different in height. The vertical is like a dry vine, abundant in knobs but full of vigor. The left-falling is like a swallow sweeping down across the eaves, and the right-falling is like a golden blade. Although calligraphers have different styles, Chinese characters have basic principles of stroke order and placement. If a character is written out with the principles, or horizontal is not horizontal and vertical not vertical, relatively speaking, or straight characters are written into a round, oval, or irregular shape, that does not make regular script.

Comparing Chinese regular script characters with Uighur ones, according to the author's experience in copying, the difference of the above points is significant.

The basic characteristics of Uighur script

From the respect of the word structure, Uighur and Chinese are totally different. First, Uighur is an alphabetic script, with a single word made up of two or more letters (discussed in another essay). Most letters have three forms: initial, medial, and final, and a few letters only have two forms. The style of each letter varies due to the location in the word. The initial letter "d", for example, is not identical to the form when it is in the middle or at the end of a word.

Second, most Uighur letters assume round forms, such as b, p, d, t, o, u, ö, ü. Some letters are semicircle, such as g, k, h, γ. Some are similar to a lying triangle, such as s, and so on. If in a written document, the part of the angle is not written pointed, they are often in the form of a lying semicircle. Third, there is the phenomenon of homographs (different pronunciation, but same spelling), b, p, d, t, o, u, ö, ü as mentioned above, are in the similar form. Fourth, according to GENG Shimin, Uighur word lines are arranged in two kinds: "Early Uighur is written horizontally from right to left, and later on, which is commonly seen as documents of Uighur literature, is written vertically with the lines progressing from left to right. This is likely to be affected by Chinese."[3] Most Uighur documents I have seen are written vertically with a new line starting from left to right, and a few from right to left.

When writing Uighur words, the writing order is according to their position in a word, Uighur letters are written continuously in se-quence. Their basic appearance changes with the different position in the word, except connecting to "z". Even in the middle of a word, it is naturally disconnected, because it is a requirement for "z".

---

3   GENG Shimin: Researches on Uighur Social and Economic Documents. 《回鹘文 社会经济文书研究 *The Study of Ancient Uighur Socio-Economic Documents*》, 中央民族大学出版社 Central University for Nationalities Book Press，2006, p 39.

There is space between words in the sentence, even if the space is very little in some documents, and a literate person can still notice it according to the length of the specific word suffix.

When copying Uighur contract documents, the author usually finds that most of Uighur words are long, or even joined up, connecting to each other. In some documents which are written very fluently, the trace of the joint can't be seen between characters. From the above points, the author agrees that written Uighur script is just like Chinese cursive.

Fifth, Uighur has no horizontal or vertical strokes similar to Chinese regular script characters. In the conjoining position, the "horizontal" of Uighur looks like a bud. While copying, the author feels that it was even more like a rose thorn, some like a broken wood (Uighur calligraphy art is discussed in another essay). The vertical strokes of Uighur in the conjoining position are formed naturally from top to bottom between different letters. Some have a joint, as said earlier, and some are joints without trace. There is also a hook in the Uighur words, but they are not the same as in square Chinese characters regular script. The Uighur hook takes on the form of an arc. The initial and medial L, as the author copies, feels either like dogstail grass swaying in the breeze, or a woman's curved eyebrow which is up side down. Some final L have plenty of angles, but all the hook-tips move upwards.

Sixth, some Uighur vowels and consonants can be omitted in the spelling of the word. Von GABAIN, for example, once said: "Incomplete writing and omitting a vowel between words may make us come to the conclusion of vowel reduction." Her example is that *yiti* (sharp) is written as *yti*, and she said: "This shows the vowel reduction in the first syllable." R, she said, is "an example of consonant loss, as *bar* (have) stands for *bar-ïr*."[4] ZHANG Jieshan discusses the problem of vowel and consonant loss, which mainly includes the vowels a, ï, ä, I, u, ü and the consonants t, l, and r, and in one chapter of his book, he gives enough examples of this.[5] If there is vowel or consonant loss in the pronunciation of a word, it will inevitably be reflected in its

---

4   Annemarie von GABAIN: *Alttürkische Grammatik*, trans. GENG Shimin, pp 36-48.
5   ZHANG Tieshan: *The structure and features of Uighur literature language*. Beijing: China Minzu University Press, 2005, 84–86.

written form, resulting in the connection of letters which are not to be connected. Here is a random example found in a Uighur contract: *barz* (tiger), as shown below. Two letters, a and r, are omitted in the word. It is the first word in the first line in Mi02. In Chinese calligraphy however, it is not regular script if a stroke is omitted.

Here we are just making some comparisons from the aspect of character structure and stroke features. Chinese and Uighur are entirely different languages. In a word, it is inappropriate to equate Chinese regular script with the Uighur one. No regular script in written Uighur documents exists. Of course, if the document is not hand-written but engraved or printed by movable type, it will have some characteristics of its own. For example, the length and the size of each character are relatively the same. The affix can be made respectively, so as to make up a word or a sentence. The author thinks that its general writing rules are the same.

In his article Moriyasu Takao mentioned interval lines in "regular script" documents. As Mr. Moriyasu sees plenty of Uighur documents, it may exist. But the author didn't find the phenomenon he has mentioned in a few hundred Uighur contract pictures in Mr. Nobuo YAMADA's works.

On "book style" in Uighur calligraphy
Moriyasu Takao said that Uighur regular script is often seen in Buddhist and Manichean texts, but rarely in secular documents. Some related works published in China mentioned "book style" in Uighur calligraphy.[6] I estimate that this "book style" is probably the regular

---

6 NIU Ruji: *An introduction to Uygur ancient writing and ancient literature*. Urumqi: Xinjiang People's Publishing House, 1997, page 88: "Uighur chirography is divided into three kinds: carving style (prominent edges), book style (round stroke) and cursive." Page 270: "Uighur chirography can be roughly divided into five kinds: carving script, regular script, running script, cursive, and hard-pen calligraphy."
YANG Fuxue: *Uighur Literature and Uighur Culture*. Ethnic Publishing House, 2003, pp. 120–121: "There are many forms of Uighur chirography: the carving style which is in the form of prominent edges, the book style which has round strokes, the cursive in which the strokes are more connected and flamboyant, the running style which is written more fluently and smoothly, the hard-pen

script, which Moriyasu Takao has claimed, often found in Buddhist and Manichean texts.

The author believes that, no matter the "book style" or Uighur "regular script" often seen in religious texts, as long as it is hand-written Turkic, Uighur which is spelled in the Sogdian language, its writing style is basically the same because of the restriction of the Turkic language and the regulations of text structure. Only religious texts, which are copied by organized religious groups, are more beautifully written. They may invite some professionals, or even calligraphers, to copy the texts, and the paper, pen, ink and the decoration are exquisite. Civil contracts have nothing comparable. Differences maybe exist in the writing style and skills, but there is no difference between the religious texts and the written civil contracts in terms of the language structure. So, it is not appropriate to determine certain Uighur writing style in the name of religious content. In the Tang dynasty there were writing styles such as *yan*, *liu* and *ou* in calligraphy circles. If we use these styles to copy religious canons, can we call it "book style" but not the style of *yan*, *liu* or *ou*?

Making a summary of the above discussion, the author's basic view is that Chinese characters are square and the framework for every character is a square. Every character has its fixed number of strokes which should not be omitted, and Chinese character stroke configuration is fixed. If the horizontal isn't horizontal and vertical not vertical, it can't be called the regular script. Uighur is an alphabetic written language, and the styles of a lot of letters are similar. Some letters have the round or semicircle parts. Each word is composed of several letters. Handwritten documents are often written from the top to bottom with the lines from left to right. Therefore, specific Uighur words present a long form. If a word has too many round, semicircle or similar letters, it will look like a long string of intertwined circles. In addition, affected by Uighur language rules, the number of the compositions of a word, the letters, is changing. Due to these important factors, Uighur regular script does not exist, and it cannot be equated with the regular script in Chinese.

---

calligraphy which is hard and straight style, and the movable-type style which is more compact."

MORIYASU Takao's theory of Uighur semi-regular script and semi-cursive is also established on the basis of comparison with Chinese "running script", so it has the similar problems of regular script. Even if the feature of Uighur cursive is similar to the Chinese one, his description of the features of Uighur cursive still remains to be discussed. The author will discuss it in another essay.

A Comparison of (Jap) *kuni* "land, country, state", (Mo) *ulus* and (Ma) *gurun*

Kyoko MAEZONO (Jena)

1 Introduction

The Japanese word *kuni* has the meaning "land, country, state". If a Japanese asks a non-Japanese: "*Okuni wa dochira desu ka.* Where is your *kuni?* / Where do you come from?" *kuni* means "home country". If a Japanese asks the same question from a fellow Japanese, *kuni* means "home region". Since the very beginnings of the written Japanese language this word has been documented and it is still used very often in the daily life.

The modern Khalkha-Mongolian word улс (< *ulus*) has the meaning "state, government, people, dynasty".[1] This Mongolian word corresponds often to the Manchu word *gurun*. In this paper the Japanese word *kuni* as it appears in Japan's oldest chronicle *Kojiki* 古事記 (712 A.D.) will be compared semantically with the Mongolian word *ulus* and the Manchu word *gurun* in their earliest attested usages. In this paper, it will be also discussed which meanings these words had originally and how they were used especially at the time of foundation of their nations or states.

The following texts are consulted for our comparison:

- Japanese: *Kojiki* 古事記 "Records of Ancient Matters" (712 A.D.)
- Mongolian: *Manghol-un Niuca Tobca'an* 元朝秘史 "Secret History of the Mongols" (13c.)
- Manchu and Mongolian: *Manju-i yargiyan kooli* 満洲實録 "Veritable Records of the Manchus" (1781)

As a multilingual-dictionary for Manchu, Tibetan, Mongolian, Turki and Chinese will be used for the comparison especially between Manchu and Mongolian in this paper:

---

1   Cf. TÖMÖRTOGOO, D. (1979): *A Modern Mongolian-English-Japanese Dictionary*. Tokyo: 開明書院 Kaimei Shoin.

• Manchu and Mongolian: *han-i araha sunja hacin-i hergen kamciha manju gisun-i buleku bithe* 御製五体清文鑑 "Pentaglot Dictionary" (1794?)

2.1 Japanese *kuni* "land, country, state" in *Kojiki* 古事記 "Records of Ancient Matters" (712 A.D.) and (Jap) *Izanaki* and *Izanami*

The Japanese *Kojiki* 古事記 "Records of Ancient Matters" is the oldest surviving book dealing with the ancient history of Japan dating from 712 A.D.[2] It was written in Chinese characters which are partially used phonetically and partially used semantically.[3] The grammar of the *Kojiki* text features both Japanese and sometimes Chinese elements. The text in Chinese characters was read traditionally all in Japanese pronunciation and grammar.

In this oldest chronicle, we find the word (Jap) *kuni* from the very beginning and it is possible to observe a major shift in meaning. In the following sentences, the word (Jap) *kuni* and its translation into English is emphasized, while its feature or explanation is underlined. In the following sentence (Jap) *kuni* has features like "floating oil", "drifting matter" or "medusa-like or jellyfish-like":

(Jap) 國稚如浮脂而　久羅下那洲多陀用幣流之時 (上 18:4)[4] く に わかくうけるあぶらのごとくして、くらげな すただよへる[の]とき、 (上 19:4) **Kuni** *wakaku ukeru abura no gotoku shite, kurage nasu tadayoheru [no] toki,*

---

2 *Kojiki* 古事記 starts with myths and legends (Vol. 1), from the enthronisation of the first Emperor of Japan JINMU 神武天皇 (660 B.C.?) to the 15. Emperor ÔJIN 応神天皇 (Vol. 2), and from the 16. Emperor NINTOKU 仁徳天皇 to the 33. Emperor SUIKO 推古天皇 (592–628 A.D.) (Vol. 3).

3 In most cases, the word (Jap) *kuni* is written with the Chinese character 國 (国) for its meaning, but it is also written as 久邇 (70:6) for its Japanese pronunciation *kuni*.

4 The page and line numbers between brackets are from: AOKI, Kazuo 青木和夫 et al. (ed.) (1982): 『古事記』 *Kojiki*, 日本思想大系〈1〉 Nihon Shisô Taikei <1>. Tokyo: 岩波書店 Iwanami Shoten.

(Eng) when the **earth**, <u>young and like unto floating oil, drifted about medusa-like</u>,[5]

In the next sentence (Jap) *kuni* is the "drifting land" which should be consolidated. *Izanaki* 伊耶那岐 and *Izanami* 伊耶那美 were the Two Deities, male and female, who became the ancestors of all things. The place where everything began is to be called Onogorojima 淤能碁呂嶋（自凝島）"self-condensed island", located possibly near Awaji-shima 淡路島 between Honshû 本州 and Shikoku 四国 as the place names which follow in the text seem to indicate.

(Jap) 於是天神諸命以　詔伊耶那岐命　伊耶那美命　二柱神　修理固成是多陀用弊流之國 (上 20:4–5) ここに、あまつかみもろもろのみこともちて、いざなきのみこと・いざなみのみことのふたはしらのかみにのらさく、「この<u>ただよへる</u>**くに**ををさめかためなせ。」とのらして、(上 21:5-6) *Kokoni, amatsu kami moromoro no mikoto mochite, Izanaki no mikoto, Izanami no mikoto no futahashira no kami ni norasaku, "Kono <u>tadayoheru</u> **kuni** wo wosame katame nase" to norashite,*

(Eng) Hereupon all the Heavenly Deities commanded the two Deities His Augustness the Male-Who-Invites and Her Augustness the Female-Who-Invites, ordering them to "make, consolidate, and give birth to this <u>drifting **land**</u>".

The Two Deities *Izanaki* 伊耶那岐 and *Izanami* 伊耶那美 were ordered by all the Heavenly Deities to give birth to islands after the conception of (Jap) *kuni* "the earth". (Jap) *kuni* developed from a fluid to a solid in this stage. The Two Deities *Izanaki* 伊耶那岐 and *Iza-nami* 伊耶那美 gave birth to islands:

(Jap) 識孕土産嶋之時 (序 10:6) **くに**をはらみしまをうみしときをしり (序 11:6) ***Kuni** wo harami shima wo umishi toki wo shiri,*

(Eng) …, we, …, learn the time of the conception of the **earth** and of the birth of islands;

---

5   The English translation is from: CHAMBERLAIN, Basil Hall (1919): *The Kojiki.* *http://www.sacred-texts.com/shi/kj/index.htm*

2.2 Japanese *kuni* "land, country, world, realm" in *Kojiki* 古事記 "Records of Ancient Matters" (712 A.D.)

From the Chaos Heaven and Earth first parted and up in the Heaven there was *Takama no Hara* 高天原 "the Plain of High Heaven", not a (Jap) *kuni*. Under "the Plain of High Heaven" there were (Jap) *kuni* as follows. In these cases, (Jap) *kuni* means "land, country, world, realm", or the place where one originally belongs.

> (Jap) 葦原中国 (上 34:15-16) あしはらのなかつ**くに**(上 35:16) *Ashihara no nakatsu* **kuni**
> (Eng) the-Living-**Land**, the Middle **Country**

> (Jap) 黄泉国 (上 32:11) よもつ**くに** (上 33:11) *Yomotsu* **kuni**
> (Eng) the **Land** of Hades, **World** of Darkness, **Realm** of the Dead, Under**world**

> (Jap) 根之堅州国 (上 42:9) ねのかたす**くに** (上 43:9) *Ne no Katasu* **kuni**
> (Eng) the Nether-Distant-**Land** (far away over the seas)

2.3 Japanese *kuni* "land, country, region, province" in *Kojiki* 古事記 "Records of Ancient Matters" (712 A.D.)

The word (Jap) *kuni* is combined with many words in *Kojiki*. There are concrete place names of regions or provinces:

> (Jap) 伊豫國 (上 24:1) いよの**くに** [6] (上 25:1) *Iyo no* **kuni**
> (Eng) the **Land** of Iyo

> (Jap) 讚岐國 (上 24:2) さぬきの**くに** (上 25:2) *Sanuki no* **kuni**
> (Eng) the **Land** of Sanuki

---

6   Readings in Hiragana according to: AOKI Kazuo 青木和夫 et al. (ed.) (1982): *Nihon Shisô Taikei* <1> 日本思想大系 〈 1 〉 *Kojiki* 『 古事記 』 . Tokyo: Iwanami Shoten 岩波書店.

(Jap) 筑紫國 (上 24:5) つくしの**くに** (上 25:5) *Tsukushi no* **kuni**
(Eng) the **Land** of Tsukushi

(Jap) 熊曾國 (上 24:6) くまその**くに** (上 24:7) *Kumaso no* **kuni**
(Eng) the **Land** of Kumaso

(Jap) 出雲國 (上 30:6) いづもの**くに** (上 31:7) *Izumo no* **kuni**
(Eng) the **Land** of Idzumo

(Jap) 无耶志國 (上 48:7) むざしの**くに** (上 49:7) *Muzashi no* **kuni**
(Eng) the **Land** of Muzashi

(Jap) 茨木國 (上 48:8) うばらきの**くに** (上 49:8) *Ubaraki no* **kuni**
(Eng) the **Land** of Ubaraki

(Jap) 倭國 (上 72:7) やまとの**くに** (上 73:6) *Yamato no* **kuni**
(Eng) the **Land** of Yamato

Such regions or provinces in Japan were named as *kuni* already in the section "倭人 Woren" at the end of fascicle 30, "烏丸鮮卑東夷傳 Biographies of the Wuhuan, Xianbei, and Dongyi" of the Chinese historical book "Sān guó zhì 三國志 *Records of the Three Kingdoms*" at the end of the 3rd century. Rulers of these *kuni* sent tributary delegations to China. At the time of the Taihô-Code 大宝律令 enactment (701 A.D.), there were 66 *kuni*-provinces which were divided further in smaller political units.

2.4 Japanese *kuni* "land, the whole country, state" in *Kojiki* 古事記 "Records of Ancient Matters" (712 A.D.)

In the next sentences *kuni* means "land, the whole country, state". The subject is the 10. Emperor SUJIN 崇神天皇 （148–29 B.C.）：

> (Jap) 爾天皇愁歎而　坐神牀之夜　大物主大神　顯於御夢日　是者我之御心　故　以意富多多泥古而　令祭我御前者　神氣不起　國安平 (中 148:9-12) しかして、すめらみことうれへなげきて、かむどこにいますよ、おほものぬしのおほかみ、みいめにあらはれてのらさく、「こはわがみこころそ。かれ、おおほたたねこをもちて、わがまへをまつらしめば、かみのけおこらず、**く**にもたひらけくあらむ。」 (中 149:9–11) *Shikashite, sumera mikoto urehe nagekite, kamu doko ni imasu yo, ohomono nushi no oho kami, miime ni araharete norasaku, "Ko ha waga mikokoro so. Kare, oohotataneko wo mochite, waga mahe wo matsurashimeba, kami no ke okorazu, **kuni** mo tahirakeku aramu".*

> (Eng) Then the Heavenly Sovereign grieved and lamented, and at night, while on his divine couch, there appeared [to him] in an august dream the Great Deity the Great-Master-of-Things, and said: "This is my august doing. So if thou wilt cause me to be worshipped by Oho-tata-ne-ko, the divine spirit shall not arise, and **the land** will be tranquillized."

In the next sentence the subject is the 40. Emperor Tenmu 天武天皇 (631–686 A.D.).

> (Jap) 設神理以獎俗　敷英風以弘國 (序 12:13-14) あやしきことわりをまけてならはしをすすめ、すぐれたるおしへをしきて**く**にひろめたまひき。 (序 13:15) *Ayashiki kotowari wo makete narahashi wo susume, suguretaru oshihe wo shikite **kuni** ni hirome tamahiki.*

> (Eng) He established divine reason herewith to advance good customs; he disseminated brilliant usages wherewith to make **the land** great.

As we have seen, the meaning and the usage of the (Jap) *kuni* developed from "fluid" via "earth" further to "island" and then to "land, province" and at last to "nation, state" at the time of the foundation of the state of Yamato or Japan which started in the southwest of Japan.[7] The whole state was called *kuni* and each province was also called *kuni*.

(Jap) *kuni* means a place to live together with common social agreements. In modern Japanese, it still means "land, country, state".

3.1 Mongolian *ulus* in *Manghol-un Niuca Tobca'an* 元朝秘史 "Secret History of the Mongols" (13c.) (Mo) *börte činu* "a blue-grey wolf" and *γoγai maral* "a fallow doe"

The Mongolian history begins with a blue-grey-wolf and a fallow doe in the *Manghol-un Niuca Tobca'an* 元朝秘史 "Secret History of the Mongols" which was written in the 13th century. The oldest version that we can find is written in Chinese characters in a manner similar to *Kojiki* 古事記 of Japan.

At the very beginning of the "Secret History" it is told that the ancestors of the Mongols were a blue-grey wolf and a fallow doe which came crossing the Tenggis(-River) ordained by Heaven.

3.2 Mongolian *ulus* "state, empire" in *Manghol-un Niuca Tobca'an* 元朝秘史 "Secret History of the Mongols" (13c.)

In the "Secret History of the Mongols" we find many times the word (Mo) *ulus*[8] which, in modern Khalkha-Mongolian, has the meaning "state, government, people, dynasty"[9].

> (Mo) *Монгол Улс* (Mongol **Ulus**) 1911-
>
> (Eng) Mongolia (1911: declared independence from the Qing Dynasty)

---

7   Archeologically the oldest remains of human beings in Japan, stone tools of 110,000–120,000 years ago, were found in 2009 in Izumo 出雲, more to the southwest. Cf. MATSUFUJI, Kazuto 松藤和人 (2014): *Nihon-rettô Jinruishi no Kigen – "Kyûsekki no karyûdo"-tachi no chôsen to kattô*『日本列島人類史の起源　—「旧石器の狩人」たちの挑戦と葛藤—』. Tokyo: Yûzankaku 雄山閣, pp. 165–173.

8   Cf. STAROSTIN, Sergei; Anna DYBO; Oleg MUDRAK (2003): *Etymological Dictionary of the Altaic Languages*, p.14: PT *uluí 'country, city' (OT *uluš*) > WMong. *ulus*.

9   Cf. TÖMÖRTOGOO, D. (1979): *A Modern Mongolian-English-Japanese Dictionary*. Tokyo: 開明書院.

(Mo) *Их Монгол Улс* (**Yeke** Mongol **Ulus**) 1206-1634/38[10]
(Eng) Mongol **Empire**

3.3 Mongolian *ulus* "common people" in *Manghol-un Niuca Tobca'an* 元朝秘史 "Secret History of the Mongols" (13c.)

Looking at the sentences in the *Manghol-un Niuca Tobca'an* 元朝秘史 "Secret History" (abbr. SH) that was written in the 13th century there are many examples of *ulus* for the meaning "people", e.g. in paragraph §96.

> (Mo) *qara buluɣan daqu-yin qariɣu qaɣačaɣsan* **ulus**-*i čin-u qamtudqaǰu ögsü;*
>
> *buluɣan daqu-yin qariɣu butaraɣsan* **ulus**-*i čin-u bügüdkeldüǰu ögsü.* (SH §96)
>
> (Eng) "In return for the black sable coat, I shall bring together for you Your divided **people**;
>
> In return for the sable coat, I shall unite for you Your scattered **people** ...."[11] (Ong Qan said to Temüjin)

Even nearly at the end of the "Secret History" in the paragraph §254 we find the Mongolian word *ulus* for the meaning "people". YESÜI Qatun, wife of Cinggis Qagan, asks for his successor among his four sons in case he would not come back alive after a battle.

> (Mo) *Negüle metü beye čin-u negüs oduɣasu nedkel metü* **ulus**(*i*)*-yan ken-e gemü.*
>
> *Tulu metü beye čin-u tulbas oduɣasu tuɣal metü* **ulus**(*i*)*-yan ken-e gemü.* (SH §254)
>
> (Eng) "When your body, like a great old tree, Will fall down, To whom will you bequeath your **people** Which is like tangled hemp?

---

10 Их Монгол Улс (Yeke Mongol Ulus) was from Genghis Khan's time till the beginning of the Ming 明 Dynasty in China.

11 English translation for *Manghol-un Niuca Tobca'an* "Secret History of the Mongols" is from: RACHEWILTZ, Igor de (2015): *The Secret History of the Mongols: A Mongolian Epic Chronicle of the Thirteenth Century* (*http://cedar.wwu.edu/cedarbooks/4/*, last access)

When your body, like the stone base of a pillar, Will collapse,
To whom will you bequeath your **people** Which is like a flock
of birds?" (YISÜI Qatun said to ČINGGIS Qa'an)

3.4 Mongolian *ulus* "people" in *Manju-i yargiyan kooli* 満洲實録 "Veritable Records of the Manchus" (1781)

In the following sentences in *Manju-i yargiyan kooli* 満洲實録
"Veritable Records of the Manchus" (abbr. MY) (1781), the original
in Manchu with its Mongolian translation, we see the Mongolian word
ulus means "people". The verbs combined with the subject (Mo) *ulus,*
"wondered and asked" can only be used for human beings.

> (Ma) **geren** gemu <u>ferguweme fonjime,</u> (MY I:23)
> (Jap) 諸人共、奇しとし問ひける、[12]
> (Eng) The **people** <u>wondered</u> all and <u>asked,</u> ...

> (Mo) *tere **ulus** bügüdeger <u>ɣaiqaɣad asaɣur-un,</u>* (MY I:23)
> (Jap) その人々 共々奇しとし，問いけるは，
> (Eng) The **people** <u>wondered</u> all and <u>asked,</u> ...

3.5 Mongolian *ulus* "dominion, state" in *Manghol-un Niuca Tobca'an* 元朝秘史 "Secret History of the Mongols" (13c.)

At the beginning of the *Manghol-un Niuca Tobca'an* 元朝秘史
"Secret History of the Mongols" (13c.) we find (Mo) *ulus* for the
meaning "dominion, territory".

> (Mo) ***ulus** ülü temeĉed ...* ***ulus** irgen ülü temeĉed ba.* (SH §64)
> (Eng) We do not strive for **dominion**. ... We do not strive for **dominion**, nor for people.

The same Mongolian word *ulus* was also used for the meaning "state"
for example:

---

12 The Japanese translation is from: TAMURA Jitsuzô 田村實造 et al. (ed.) (1966): *Gotai Shinbunkai Yakkai* 『五體清文鑑譯解』. Kyoto.

(Mo) ***ulus*** *baiɣululčaɣsad ǰoboldulɣsad-i mingɣad-un noyad bolɣaǰu* (SH §224)

(Eng) *"Činggis Qa'an made commanders of a thousand those who had established the* **state** *with him and who had suffered with him."*

Comparing the various usages of the Mongolian word *ulus* in the "Secret History" one can say that in many cases the word *ulus* had the meaning "people" and in fewer cases the meaning "state". In the 13th century, the Mongolian word *ulus* generally meant "the people who live, cooperate and unite together", a concept which developed later to "state".

4. Manchu *gurun* "country, empire, people" in *Manju-i yargiyan kooli* 滿洲實錄 "Veritable Records of the Manchus" (1781) (Ma) *abkai ilan sargan jui* and (Mo) *tngri-yin ɣurban ökid* "three celestial maidens"

Manju-i yargiyan kooli 滿洲實錄 "Veritable Records of the Manchus" (abbr. MY) starts with three celestial or heavenly maidens who are bathing in a lake. The youngest one of the three sisters cannot go back to the heaven because she ate a red fruit, a transformation of a God, which leads her to conception. Giving birth to a boy she goes back alone to heaven. This boy is told to be the ancestor of the Manchu.

4.1 Manchu *gurun* and Mongolian *ulus* "state, empire; country, land" in *Manju-i yargiyan kooli* 滿洲實錄 "Veritable Records of the Manchus" (1781)

At the beginning of *Manju-i yargiyan kooli* 滿洲實錄 we have the Manchu word *gurun*[13] for the meaning "state, Empire" which is

---

13 Thanks to a comment of Alexander Vovin it was examined which word corresponds to the (Mo) *ulus* and (Ma) *gurun* in the Kitan language. It corresponds to the Kitan word <g.úr> "country"; <g.úr:n> (genitive), <g.úr:se> (plural). Cf. Kane, Daniel (2009): *The Kitan Language and Script*. Leiden: Brill, p. 89, 3.031. It is also transcribed as <gur> like in: Aisin Gioro Ulhicun and Yoshimoto Michimasa 愛新覚羅 烏拉熙春・

translated into the Mongolian word *ulus*:

> (Ma) *Manju **Gurun**[14]* (MY I:13)
> (Mo) *Manǰu **Ulus*** (MY I:13)
> (Ch) 満洲
> (Jap) 満洲國
> (Eng) the Manchu-**Empire**

> (Ma) *Daiming **Gurun*** (MY V:94)
> (Mo) *Daiming **Ulus*** (MY V:94)
> (Ch) 明國
> (Jap) 大明國
> (Eng) the Ming-**Empire**

Smaller countries or lands are also named:

> (Ma) *hadai **gurun*** (MY I:83)
> (Mo) *Hada **Ulus*** (MY I:82)
> (Eng) the **Land** of Hada

> (Ma) *ulai **gurun*** (MY I:83)
> (Mo) *Ula **Ulus*** (MY I:82)
> (Eng) the **Land** of Ula

吉本道雅 (2011): 韓半島から眺めた契丹・女真　*The Khitais and Jurchens as seen from the Korean Peninsula*, p. 96:24 etc.

Cf. also LESSING, Ferdinand D. (1960): *Mongolian-English dictionary.* Berkeley and Los Angeles: University of California Press, p. 392b: gürün [Ma. gurun] n. Country, state, people, nation.

ROZYCKI, William (1994): *Mongol elements in Manchu.* Bloomington: Indiana University Research Institute for Inner Asian Studies, p. 93: MA gurun 'country, tribe, people; ruling house, dynasty' J gurun 'country' SL guru ULC, OK guru(n) N guru Mo gürün 'country, state, nation' (MA → MO on phonological basis; the fronting of the vowels in MO indicates this is not a recent loan.) S 681

14 Cf. (Ma) *Daicing **Gurun*** （大清国）1616–1912

(Mo) *Чин улс, манж Чин улс, Дайчин гурэн*

(Eng) the Manchu **Dynasty**, Qing **Dynasty** （清朝）1616–1912

(Ma) *hoifa i* **gurun** (MY I:96)
(Mo) *Hoifa* **Ulus** (MY I:98)
(Eng) the **Land** of Hoifa

4.2 Manchu *gurun* "state, people" and Mongolian *ulus* "people" in *Manju-i yargiyan kooli* 滿洲實錄 "Veritable Records of the Manchus" (1781)

In the 18th century the Manchu word *gurun* corresponded to the Mongolian word *ulus* yet the Mongolian word *ulus* had not only the meaning "land, country, empire" but also the meaning "people". The Mongolian *ulus* thus had a wider meaning than the Manchu word.

Looking at the modifiers in the sentences we find that the words (Ma) *gurun* and (Mo) *ulus* do not always mean the same. In the next sentence the Manchu word *gurun* "state" was translated into Mongolian with the word (Mo) *ulus*. But because of the modifiers we see that the Mongolian word *ulus* means "people":

(Ma) *amba* **gurun** "big **state**"   ⇔   *ajige* **gurun** "small **state**"
(Mo) *olan* **ulus** "many **people**" ⇔ *čögen* **ulus** "few **people**"
(Ma) *amba* **gurun** *be ajigen obuci ajige* **gurun** *be amban obuci gemu abkai ciha kai.* (MY IV:44-45)
(Ch) 然大國成小。小國成大。皆出於天。
(Eng) It's all Heaven's wish to make a big **state** small or a small **state** big!
(Mo) *olan* **ulus**-*i čögen bolɣabasu, čögen* **ulus**-*i olan bolgabasu ber deger-e tngri-ner medem ǰ-a,* (MY IV:44-45)
(Eng) High Deities know to make many **people** few or few **people** many!

In the next sentence (Ma) *Monggo gurun i niyalma* "people of the Mongolian state" corresponds to (Mo) *Mongɣul Ulus* "Mongolian people, Mongolians". The Mongolian word *ulus* means therefore "people".

(Ma) *yehei aiman i da mafa monggo gurun i* **niyalma**, … (MY I:89)
(Ch) 葉赫國始祖蒙古人。

(Eng) The origin of the Yehe-tribe were the **people** of the Mongolian state, …

(Mo) *Yehege-yin iǰaγur inu Mongγul **Ulus** bülüge,* (MY I:90)
(Eng) The origin of the Yehege were the Mongolian **people**, …

In some sentences, we see that the Mongolian word *ulus* means – "people" because of the meaning of the verb. The acts of the next sentences of the subject (Mo) *ulus* are "believe, kill and follow" which were done by human beings. The Mongolian word *ulus* means in this sentence also "people". The original Manchu word from which the Mongolian word *ulus* was translated is (Ma) *niyalma* "people": (Ma) *niyalma* "people" – (Mo) *ulus* "people".

(Ma) *... hoton i dorgi **niyalma** akdafi ini ejen atai janggin be wafi lii ceng liyang de dahaha.* (MY I:110-111)
(Ch) 城中人信其言。遂殺阿太而降。
(Eng) ... the **people** in the city-wall <u>believed</u> it, <u>killed</u> their own lord Atai Janggin and <u>followed</u> Ceng Liyang.

(Mo) *... qota dotur-a ki **ulus** inu tere üge-yi itegeǰü öber-ün eǰen-iyen Atai-yi alaγad, Lii Ceng-Liyang-dur oruǰu ögbei,* (MY I:112)
(Eng) … the **people** in the city-wall <u>believed</u> his words, <u>killed</u> their own lord Atai and <u>followed</u> Lii Ceng-Liyang …

In the next sentence (Ma) *gurun* and (Mo) *ulus* mean both "people":
(Ma) ***gurun** gemu*
(Mo) ***ulus** bügüdeger*
(Eng) all the **people**

(Ma) *ere be waha de, **gurun** gemu muse be neneme dain deribuhe sembikai* (MY I:179)
(Jap) こを殺したるときは、國皆我等をさきに戦始めたりと云ふにぞ。
(Eng) If we will kill him all the **people** would say that we would have started the war first.

(Mo) *egün-i alabasu* **ulus** *bügüdeger man-i-yi urida daisun egüskebe kemekü buyu,* (MY I:179)

(Jap) こを殺さば国人諸人我等[を指して] 先に戦さを起こしたりと言うあり。

(Eng) If we will kill him all the **people** would say that we would have started the war first.

4.3 Manchu and Mongolian: in *Han-i araha sunja hacin-i hergen kamciha manju gisun-i buleku bithe* 御製五體清文鑑 "Pentaglot Dictionary" (1794?)

In the *Han-i araha sunja hacin-i hergen kamciha manju gisun-i buleku bithe* 御製五体清文鑑 "Pentaglot Dictionary" (abbr. SG) from the 18th century Manchu word *gurun* corresponds as a rule to the Mongolian word *ulus*.

(Ma) *gurun* (SG 2713.3)

(Mo) *ulus*

(Ch) 國

(Jap) 國[15]

(Ger) Reich, Staat, Land[16]

(Eng) country, tribe, people; ruling house, dynasty; country-side[17]

(Ma) *gurun* and (Mo) *ulus* are combined with other words in the same way:

(Ma) *tulergi* **gurun** (SG 2713.4)

(Mo) *γadaγadu* **ulus**

(Ch) 外國

(Ger) auswärtiger **Staat**, Aus**land**

(Eng) foreign **country**

---

15 Cf. for the Japanese translation: TAMURA Jitsuzô 田村實造 et al. (ed.) (1966): *Gotai Shinbunkai Yakkai* 『五體清文鑑譯解』. Kyoto.

16 Cf. for the German translation: CORFF, Oliver; Kyoko MAEZONO, et al. (ed.) (2013): *Auf kaiserlichen Befehl erstelltes Wörterbuch des Manjurischen in fünf Sprachen – "Fünfsprachenspiegel"*. Wiesbaden: Harrassowitz Verlag.

17 Cf. for the English translation: NORMAN, Jerry (2013): *A comprehensive Manchu-English dictionary*. Cambridge (Massachusetts) and London: Harvard University Asia Center.

(Ma) *tulergi **gurun**-i bithe* (SG 0730.4)
(Mo) *γadaγadu **ulus**-un bičig*
(Ch) 外國書
(Ger) ausländisches Schriftstück
(Eng) foreign document

As in the next examples from "Pentaglot Dictionary" (Ma) *gurun* and
(Mo) *ulus* were used for the country or state names, contemporary or
in history:

(Ma) *solho **gurun**-i kuren* (SG 2831.3)
(Mo) *solungγus **ulus**-un küriyɤä*
(Ch) 高麗館
(Ger) Absteigequartier der koreanischen Gesandtschaften in
Peking
(Eng) Residence of the Goryeo (918–1392) legation in Peking

(Ma) *lio kio **gurun**-i kuren* (SG 2831.4)
(Mo) *liu kiu **ulus**-un küriyɤä*
(Ch) 琉球館
(Ger) Absteigequartier der Ryûkyû-Nation in Peking
(Eng) Residence of the Ryûkyûan (1429–1879) legation in
Peking

(Ma) *jeo **gurun**-i jijungge nomun* (SG 4603.2)
(Mo) *zeü **ulus**-un ziruxayitu nom*
(Ch) 周易
(Ger) das heilige Buch der Wandlungen, auch 易經 Yìjīng
(Eng) the book of changes of the Jeo (1046–256 BC) State

(Ma) *ho lan **gurun**-i loho* (SG 4639.1)
(Mo) *xo' lan **ulus**-un ildü*
(Ch) 賀蘭刀
(Ger) holländisches Schwert
(Eng) a Dutch sword

5. Conclusion

(Jap) *kuni* "land, country, state", (Mo) *ulus* and (Ma) *gurun*

It can be shown that (Jap) *kuni*, (Mo) *ulus* and (Ma) *gurun* which correspond to each other in the modern language for the meaning "land, country, state" used to have different meanings and usages in earlier stages of their respective languages.

The corpora which were used for this paper were written in the 8th century (Japanese sources stating *kuni*), in the 13th century in the case of Mongolia (*ulus*) and in the 18th century in the case of (Ma) *gurun* respectively. At the time of their writing these states or empires had already established the political and social systems for their whole nations.

According to *Kojiki* 古事記 "Records of Ancient Matters" (Jap) *kuni* developed from "fluid" to "solid", to "earth" where all things could live on. *Kuni* was then the place to live together as a community with social agreements which developed later to "state". In *Manghol-un Niuca Tobca'an* 元朝秘史 "Secret History of the Mongols" (Mo) *ulus* was used first for the meaning "people"[18] which developed later to "state, empire". In *Manju-i yargiyan kooli* 滿洲實錄 "Veritable Records of the Manchus" (Ma) *gurun* was often used for the meaning "teritorry" which developed later to "state, empire".

In the comparison between Manchu and Mongolian in *Manju-i yargiyan kooli* 滿洲實錄 "Veritable Records of the Manchus" it becomes clear that the Mongolian word *ulus* was much more often used than the Manchu word *gurun* due to the fact that (Mo) *ulus* covers a wider semantic scope than (Ma) *gurun*.

At the times of these corpora we can say, semantically as well as quantitatively, that (Jap) *kuni* and (Ma) *gurun* had more in common than with (Mo) *ulus*. For (Jap) *kuni* and (Ma) *gurun* "place to belong" and for (Mo) *ulus* "people belonging to each other" were the semantic cores. In other words in the Japanese and the Manchu worlds the

---

18 Cf. HAENISCH, Erich (1962): *Wörterbuch zu Manghol un Niuca Tobca'an (Yüan-ch'ao pi-shi) Geheime Geschichte der Mongolen.* In this dictionary for *Manghol-un Niuca Tobca'an* 元朝秘史 "Secret History of the Mongols", p. 163, (Mo) *ulus* means "百姓 zugehöriges Volk, 部落 Stamm; 國 Staat, Reich; 人烟 Bevölkerung, Bewohnerschaft".

states were established by developing and widening "land" while in the Mongolian the state was established by uniting and organizing "people".

Bibliography

- AISIN GIORO Ulhicun and YOSHIMOTO Michimasa 愛新覚羅 烏拉熙春 吉本道雅 (2011): 『韓半島から眺めた契丹・女真』*The Khitais and Jurchens as seen from the Korean peninsula*. Kyoto: 京都大学学術出版会 Kyôto-daigaku Gakujutsu Shuppankai.
- AN Shuangcheng 安双成 (ed.) (1993): 满汉大辞典 *Man-Han da cidian*. 沈阳 Shenyang: 辽宁民族出版社 Liaoning minzu chubanshe.
- AOKI Kazuo 青木和夫 et al. (ed.) (1982): 『古事記』*Kojiki*, 日本思想大系〈1〉Nihon Shisô Taikei <1>. Tokyo: 岩波書店 Iwanami Shoten.
- CHAMBERLAIN, Basil Hall (1882 translated): *Kojiki http://www.sacred-texts.com/shi/kj/index.htm*
- CORFF, Oliver; Kyoko MAEZONO, et al. (ed.) (2013): *Auf kaiserlichen Befehl erstelltes Wörterbuch des Manjurischen in fünf Sprachen – "Fünfsprachenspiegel"*. Wiesbaden: Harrassowitz Verlag.
- DORJ, Dorjpalam; Oliver CORFF (ed.) (2014): *Auf kaiserlichen Befehl erstelltes Wörterbuch des Manjurischen in fünf Sprachen – "Fünfsprachenspiegel"*. Index 3: Mongolisch. Wiesbaden Harrassowitz Verlag.
- HAENISCH, Erich (1962): *Wörterbuch zu Manghol un Niuca Tobca'an (Yüan-ch'ao pi-shi) Geheime Geschichte der Mongolen*. Wiesbaden: Franz Steiner Verlag.
- HAUER, Erich (1952, 2007): *Handwörterbuch der Mandschusprache*, 2., durchgesehene und erweiterte Auflage herausgegeben von Oliver Corff. Wiesbaden: Harrassowitz Verlag.
- HANEDA Tôru 羽田亨 (1937): 『満和辞典』*Man-Wa Jiten*. Kyoto.
- HU Zengyi 胡增益 (ed.) (1994): 新满汉大词典 *Xin Man-Han da cidian. A comprehensive Manchu-Chinese dictionary*. Urumchi, P.R.C.: 新疆人民出版社 Xinjiang renmin chubanshe, Xinjiang People's Publishing House.
- IMANISHI Shunjû 今西春秋訳 (1938, 1992): 『満和蒙和対訳満洲實録』*Manwa-Môwa Taiyaku Manshû-Jitsuroku*. Tokyo: 刀水書房 Tôsui Shobô.

- KANE, Daniel (2009): *The Kitan language and script*. Leiden: Brill.
- LESSING, Ferdinand D. (ed.) (1960): *Mongolian-English dictionary*. Berkeley and Los Angeles: University of California Press.
- KIYOSE, Gisaburo N. (1977): *A study of the Jurchen language and script – Reconstruction and decipherment*. Kyoto: Hôritsubunkasha.
- MAEZONO, Kyoko; Oliver CORFF (ed.) (2014): *Auf kaiserlichen Befehl erstelltes Wörterbuch des Manjurischen in fünf Sprachen – "Fünfsprachenspiegel"*. Index 1: Manjurisch. Wiesbaden: Harrassowitz Verlag.
- MATSUFUJI Kazuto 松藤和人 (2014): 『日本列島人類史の起源 ― 「旧石器の狩人」たちの挑戦と葛藤―』 *Nihon-rettô Jinruishi no Kigen – "Kyûsekki no karyûdo"-tachi no chôsen to kattô*. Tokyo: 雄山閣 Yûzankaku.
- MURAKAMI Masatsugu 村上正二 (1970, 1972, 1976): 『モンゴル秘史 1・2・3』 *Mongoru Hishi 1,2,3*. Tokyo: 平凡社 Heibonsha.
- NORMAN, Jerry (2013): *A comprehensive Manchu-English dictionary*. Cambridge (Massachusetts) and London: Harvard University Asia Center.
- RACHEWILTZ, Igor de (2015): *The Secret History of the Mongols: A Mongolian epic chronicle of the thirteenth century*. *http://cedar.wwu.edu/cedarbooks/4/*
- ROZYCKI, William (1994): *Mongol elements in Manchu*. Bloomington: Indiana University Research Institute for Inner Asian Studies.
- SHIRATORI Kurakichi 白鳥庫吉 （1943）:『音譯蒙文元朝秘史』 *On'yaku Môbun Genchô-hishi*, 東洋文庫 Tokyo: Tôyô Bunko.
- STAROSTIN, Sergei; Anna DYBO; Oleg MUDRAK (2003): *Etymological dictionary of the Altaic languages*. Leiden: Brill.
- TAMURA Jitsuzô 田村實造 et al. (ed.) (1966):『五體清文鑑譯解』 *Gotai Shinbunkan Yakkai*. Kyoto.
- TÖMÖRTOGOO, D. (1979): *A modern Mongolian-English-Japanese dictionary*. Tokyo: Kaimei Shoin 開明書院.

Crimean Toponyms in the Court Registers of the 17th–18th Centuries and the Issue of the Crimean Tatars' Tribal Composition

Oleg RUSTEMOV (Ardahan, Turkey)

Abstract
This paper is concerned with the analysis of the Crimean toponyms from the point of view of identifying the Turkic tribes that participated in the ethnogenesis of the Crimean Turks. A similar task has already been posed in Crimean linguistics. Currently, it becomes possible to significantly expand the range of sources on the Crimean toponymic nomenclature. It is known that the renaming of geographical names in the peninsula began immediately after the conquest of the Crimean Khanate (1783). This process assumed a total character after the deportation of the Crimean Tatars in 1944 and the abolition of the Crimean ASSR. In its present form the Crimean toponymy, with some minor exceptions, represents no historical or philological value. But the historical names of the settlements and geographical features (*yer adları*) preserved in the written monuments, such as the *sicil*s (registers) of the Sharia courts, provide rich material for a wide variety of philological research. One of the urgent tasks of the linguistic analysis of the Crimean toponymy is the identification and definition of the tribal composition of the Crimean Turks who arrived to the peninsula at different times. Contrary to the prevailing point of view in Crimean history, the role of the Oghuz Turks is much bigger than it has hitherto been believed.

Keywords: Crimean *sicil*s, Crimean toponymy, philological analysis, geography in Crimean texts, Crimean Khanate.

Introduction
Along with the written sources and archaeological data, toponymy makes the reconstruction of nation formation possible with high

accuracy. The importance of toponymy as a historical and simultaneously linguistic witness can hardly be overestimated. This is
equally true for the Crimean toponymic nomenclature. The Turkic
names of numerous villages, mountains, valleys, rivers, districts, etc.
can give a detailed description of the role peoples and tribes played in
the formation of the Crimean Tatars, inhabitants of the Crimean
Khanate which included both the Crimea and the vast steppe space
stretching from the banks of the Dnieper to the banks of the Volga
river and known by ancient chroniclers under the name of Desht-i
Qipchaq.

The purpose of this paper is to demonstrate the necessity of
introducing the notion of the whole array of insufficiently studied
documents called "*sicil*s (registers) of the Crimean Khanate", which
are an important source of information on the etymology of the
Crimean toponyms. The paper's tasks also include the correction and
clarification of some etymological interpretations of the geographical
names given by previous researchers. Another more global task of this
paper is to present the ancient "pre-Tatar" Turkic layer of the toponyms extracted from the Crimean court registers. An analysis of the
information contained in the Kazasker's (*kadıasker*) court records
combined with data from other sources referred to below makes it
possible to define many names in the "pre-Tatar" toponymic nomenclature as names of Oghuz or ancient Oghuz-Qipchaq origin. This fact
largely explains the features of the written language of the Crimean
Turks of the Crimean Khanate period, in particular, the language of the
court registries of the Bakhchisarai *kadılık* (judicial district), which
has a pronounced Oghuz type of language with some admixture of the
Qipchaq language.

The history of the study of the Crimean geographical names
probably started with the essay "The cameral description of the
Crimea" (Камеральное описание Крыма) by Fedor Lashkov containing large-scale fact-based material and published in 1888 in the
Bulletin of the Tauric Scientific Archival Commission.[1] This essay
presents an almost complete list of all *kaymakam*ships (districts),
judicial districts (*kaza/kadılık*) and names of the villages related to

---

1   Лашков 1888–1892.

them. The information given by the author dates to 1783, i.e. the last year of the independent Crimean Khanate's existence as it was found by the Russian occupation command.

By this time, according to the peace treaty of Küçük Kaynarca of 1774, the Crimean Khanate was an independent state which comprised *kadılık*s of the former Ottoman sancak (sub-province) of Kefe, with the exception of Kerch (Kershin) and the fortress of Yeni Kale which passed to the Russians based on the same treaty. According to the information provided by F. LASHKOV, there were seven *kayma-kam*ships on the territory of the Crimean peninsula: Bakhchisarai (6 *kadılık*s), Akmescit (9 *kadılık*s), Karasuvbazar (9 *kadılık*s), Kezlev (5 *kadılık*s), Kefe (7 *kadılık*s) and Or-Kapu (6 *kadılık*s). According to LASHKOV, the *kadılık*s numbered in all 42.[2] In turn, the Turkish historian Ömer BIYIK suggests that there were 46 *kadılık*s at the beginning of the XVIIIth century in the Crimean Khanate, and 8 *kadılık*s located within the boundaries of the Kefe *vilayet* (province) subordinated directly to Istanbul.[3]

Thus, despite Lashkov's statement that part of the former Turkish *kadılık*s in the Crimea passed to the Khanate, the number of judicial districts in "The cameral description of the Crimea" is less than the quantity given by Ömer BIYIK referring to other sources. This can be explained by the fact that Lashkov's list misses the *kadılık*s located outside the Crimea, namely in the North Caucasus and the steppes between the Don and the Dnieper rivers. In any case, this information should be carefully checked by historians according to the different periods of the existence of Crimean Tatar rule. As for the villages, they amounted to about 1411 of at least partially populated villages in the list of *kadılık*s, while 1470 completely ruined villages are also listed.

However, Lashkov's list cannot be called exhaustive, because it lacks a number of villages and towns known from other sources. Furthermore, Lashkov himself reports that some *kaymakam*s provided incomplete information.[4] In addition, Lashkov's list has not any choronyms and hydronyms. We can also make the assumption that in 1783, a part of the villages disappeared or were renamed, and that the

---

2   Лашков 1888: 36–38.

3   BIYIK 2014: 41–69.

4   Лашков 1888.

urban settlements also under the Crimean Khanate's rule, but located outside of the Crimea, are not represented at all except for a small number of nomad camps.

The names of a number of settlements from "The Cameral Description" have obvious errors in writing, such as "Bolta Çekrak" instead of "Balta Çoqraq"; "Byesala" instead of "Büyük/Biye sala", "Kokos" instead of "Kökköz", etc. The distorted phonation of the names of Crimean settlements, including the prevailing phonation in the Crimean Tatar environment (cf. originally "Fettakh sala/Fetkh sala" and later "Foti Sala") prevents their etymological analysis, which can create some difficulties in addressing some issues, especially in the creation of an Crimean linguistic atlas.

Previous Research

The well-known Russian historian, ethnographer, and archaeologist, academician Arseniy Ivanovich MARKEVICH (1855–1942), also considered scientific and linguistic problems in his writings concerning the Crimean toponymic system. His detailed article "The geographical nomenclature of the Crimea" presents a large number of names of all geographical objects, including choronyms and oronyms, which currently are completely lost and forgotten, but can be reproduced either based on archival materials, or scientific works such as Markevich.[5]

Markevich tried to address multiple problems of an etymological nature systematizing the toponyms under the principle of linguistic components. He names five such language layers in total: 1) Greek, 2) an Iranian-language component introduced to the Crimea by the Alans (the same language tradition also includes Scythian and Taurian which, in our opinion, is doubtful, since today the appurtenance of the Tauri and Scythians to the Iranian-language tribes is the subject of scientific debates), 3) Italian, associated in our understanding with the Genoese of Kaffa (Kefe) and other colonies,[6] 4) German or Gothic (Goths of Mangup), 5) Tatar as such, which today is understood as a variety of the Turkic dialects which existed in the Crimea from the

---

5   Маркевич 1928: 17–32.
6   YAŞA 2017a: 417–429.

moment of its conquest by the Khazars and Bulgars, Pechenegs, Seljuk Turks and Kipchaks, and finally by the Tatars and Nogais.

In addition to the "official" languages, which are certainly accepted by all scholars of the Crimea as toponym-forming, Markevich also refers to the Hungarian language, probably alluding to the fact that some Pecheneg families, after their defeat by the Kipchaks, settled on the territory of the Magyar state. Perhaps this is due to the connection with the Huns or even much later the Kuns associated with the Cumans (Polovtsy) which also have found shelter on the banks of the Danube, this time seeking safety from the Mongol invasion. Anyway, the phonological parallels between the Crimean toponyms and certain Hungarian lexemes, to their possible correlation or relationship Markevich draws attention, look artificial[7]. Some errors in Markevich's etymological and linguistic analysis of entire groups of toponyms are probably due to the lack of sources. The original, correct formants or prototypes of various geographic names will be discussed in a separate paragraph of this paper in connection with the analysis of toponyms from the kazasker *defter*s (registers).

The Crimean historian Z. Sh. NAVSHIRVANOV made an attempt to study the issue of the tribal composition of the Crimean Turks largely relying on toponymic data. In our opinion, his article "Preliminary notes on the tribal composition of the Turkic tribes residing in the south of Russia and the Crimea"[8] is extremely informative and scientifically sound in most of its assumptions and hypotheses. Navshirvanov used the then existing Crimean toponymic nomenclature and involved into his scientific work quite a large range of historical and philological sources, which made it possible to draw analogies and parallels between the Turkic tribes settled in the Crimea and those located in Central Asia, Iran (Turan) or the Caucasus according to the description of medieval Arab and other chroniclers. This concerns to a larger exent the Türkmen and Kipchak tribes because their settlement in the Crimea occurred in a more distant past than the arrival of the tribes brought in by the Mongol invasion.

Regarding the Crimean toponymic system in the past, the Crimean Tatar monuments and written sources can provide a more correct

---

7   Маркевич 1928: 22, note 1.
8   Навширванов 1929.

picture. As a rule, all these sources date back to a much earlier time than "The cameral description of the Crimea" drawn up by order of Baron O. A. IGEL'STROM (1737–1818).[9] The Crimean *sicil*s of the Shariah courts, also called, as stated above, "Kazasker records", are one of such important monuments in terms of their significance.

After the conquest of the Crimea by the Russian Empire, these records lay idle in the archives for almost a hundred years before they were presented to the world at first by Vladimir SMIRNOV, professor at Kazan University,[10] then by the historian Fedor Lashkov and finally the first translator of these texts, Murat BIYARSLANOV[11].

To date, the historical aspect of the Crimean *sicil*s is thoroughly studied thanks to the efforts of the Turkish scholars Halil İNALCIK[12], Ahmet Nezihi TURAN[13], as well as Zeynep ÖZDEM[14], Ömer BIYIK[15], Nuri KAVAK[16], and some others. Based on material from the Crimean court registers Fırat YAŞA wrote his historical work on the districts of Bakhchisaray.[17] From the philological point of view, the texts are being studied in detail by the author of this paper[18].

The geography of the Crimean *sicil*s is quite extensive and it is not confined only to villages and geographical features of certain *kadılık*s (*kaza*). The Shariah courts conducted the hearing of lawsuits which concerned both the whole Crimea and the settlements of the Ottoman Empire and even beyond its borders. In this regard, such suits (*da'va*) can be divided into 1) commercial suits which refer to a variety of ports, where the cargo was delivered to, and the towns or regions where certain commodities were produced or purchased, for example,

---

9   JANKOWSKI 2006.
10 Смирнов 1887.
11 Биярсланов 1889–1891.
12 İNALCIK 1996.
13 TURAN 2003.
14 ÖZDEM 2010.
15 BIYIK 2014.
16 KAVAK 2014; KAVAK 2009.
17 YAŞA 2017b.
18 Рустемов 2013 a; Рустемов 2014; Рустемов 2013 b; Рустемов 2015 a; Рустемов 2015 b; Рустемов 2015 c.

salt, fabrics, etc., 2) cases related to campaigns, which refer to the various military events, including the capture of prisoners. Foreign geographical names are also found in the texts which refer to the acquisition of real estate (land) beyond the Crimea, and, in texts involving slaves, their origin is also reported: *Boğdaniyet ül-asl* (originating from Moldova), *Eflakiyet ül-asl* (from Walachia), *Moskoviyet ül-asl* (from Moscovy), etc.[19]

Names of settlements are also mentioned in the disputes related to land located in a particular area or settlement. Finally, toponymic nomenclature is present in the proper names of the parties involved in legal proceedings and witnesses of a given case listed below each entry.

Studies of court texts and Crimean toponymy

In the records of a commercial nature in the 1st volume of the *sicil*s the most frequently used toponyms are Istanbul in the form of *İslambolu*, *İstanbul*, *Kostaniye*, and also *Ak Kerman*, *Varna*, *Trabzon*, *Selânik* (Thessaloniki), and others. Personal names include *el-Cendi*, *Cezairlü*, *el-Sivasi*, *Bursalı*, *Bursevi*, *el-Kayseri*, *el-Tebrizi*, etc., which indicate close links between the Crimea and Central Asia, Iran, and almost all corners of the Ottoman Empire.

The military events of the period to which the first volume of the *sicil*s refers are reflected in names such as: Magyar (*Macar seferi* – Hungarian campaign) and Korel (*Körel seferi* – campaign on Korel/ Eastern Poland). Special mention should be made of the name of river Özü (Dnieper), the etymology of which presumably refers to the name of an Oghuz tribe wandering in the Black Sea steppes in the Xth to XIIIth centuries[20].

The system of identification or fixation of the land (*arazi*) which appears in cases on the sale of land or buildings is of a certain philological interest as shown in the text below:

Line 1: Oldur ki, Mehmed bin Mevlüd Ağadan sabitü'l-vekâlet olan Mehmed bin Abdullah mahfil-i qaza-yı celili'l-qadride Allah-ahmar bin İbrahim beyi ihzar

Line 2: idüb müşarün-ileyh Allahahmardan nehr-i Salğırda bir pay

---

19 For detailed information, see YAŞA 2014: 657–669; YAŞA 2017c: 38.
20 Навширванов 1929.

arz-ı mezraa ki, hududı beyan olunur qıblası Üç obaya

Line 3: ve şimali Qañglıya ve ġarbı Bek Cemaatına ve şarqı asiyata muttasılı. İşbu hudud-i erbaa ile mahdud ve beyne'l-ciran

Line 4: malûm arzı on dört hasene ile bir ġuruş iştira' idüb teslim-i semen ve qabz-i mebi' vaki olmuştur, sicil olunsun

Line 5: dicek, bi'l-müvacehe Allahahmardan sual olunduqta mezbûr Muhammedin kelâmını tasdiqi ile cevap verecek sıhhat-ı bey'e ve şiraya hükm olunub qayd olundı. Cera zelik fi evasit-i Muharrem sene 1018 (1609).

Line 6: Şühûdü'l-hâl: Nur Muhammed bin Mahmud, Çomay bin Külek, Teke bin Taymas, Temir Sufi bin Esen Keldi, Arslan bin Emrullah ve ġayruhum.

Translation: *Mehmed b. Abdullah, an authorized representative (house-keeper) of Mehmed b. Mevlud Aga, having summoned Allahahmar bin İbrahim bey to the highranking Court Session (declared): The land on Salgir river was purchased from said Allahahmar for cultivation. The boundaries thereof: in the south (Qibla) it borders on Üç Oba – "Tree Hills" (possibly the name of the village), from the north on "Qanglı", from the west on Bek Cemaatı (to the Bek community), from the east on the mill on the river. This land, within the established boundaries on four sides, located between the known neighbors, being purchased, was transferred to (the buyer) and fourteen khasenes (florin) and one gurush were paid for it. Let it be recorded (in the sicil). And immediately after him, Allahahmar was directly questioned. Once he confirmed the words of the said Mehmed, the purchase and sale deal was recognized as legitimate and registered. Present day: the middle of the month of Muharram, year 1018 (1609).*
Present witnesses: Nur Muhammed b. Mahmud, Comay b. Külek, Teke b. Taymas, Temir Sufî b. Esen Keldi, Arslan b. Emrullah, and others.

[Crimean *sicil*s, vol. 1, page 5 B, text no. 3, translated by the author]

This method of geographical description is similar to the one that was used in the Ottoman *sicil*s, i.e. the area of the land location and its neighbors or the objects to which it is adjacent according to the four points of the compass are reported. But in the Crimean *sicil*s we face other toponymic, tribally based realities. In the above text, there are toponyms such as Salğır – the name of a river – and Qanglı (probably the name of the village, but it may be an oronym, or even a choronym). Both toponyms relate to the names of Oghuz clans. In other words, toponyms of old Oghuz origin are found in the heart of the Crimea. Salğır – in the form of "Salğur" is found in the dictionary of MAHMUD AL-KASHGARI *Diwan Luġat al-Turk*[21]. Mahmud al-Kashgari designates it as a branch of the Oghuz tribe. At the same time, he notes the type of brand (*tamġa*) used by that branch.

Another toponym – Qangly/Qanglı – is also recognized by most turkologists as an Oghuz tribe, which came into contact with the Finno-Ugric tribes, while for Mahmud al-Kashġari Qangly is the name of a famous man of the Kipchak. In turn, we tend to relate the toponym "Qangly" to the days when the Pechenegs stayed in the Crimea (according to MAHMUD AL-KASHGARI: «ال بجنك» *el-becenek*)[22] which does not contradict the statement that Qangly is an Oghuz tribe, as well as the fact that it comes from the Kipchaks. It should be noted that the Kipchaks and Oghuz can be traced to a single branch of the Turkic tribes originating from the legendary Oghuz Khan[23]. *Diwan Luġat al-Turk* repeatedly emphasizes the linguistic identity of these two branches[24], although it can be assumed that the linguistic differences between the Oghuz and Kipchaks started before the XIth century. Most likely, this process started from about the VIIIth century, when a part of the Türkmen and Kipchak tribes started to move in the direction of the Caucasus and Eastern Europe. The Crimea was not left aside. The work by ABULGHAZI BAHADIR khan in particular, the "Genealogy (or tree) of the Türkmens" (*Şecere-i terakime*), also known as the Muslim version of the epic "Oghuz-name"[25], reports the arrival of a part of the Salğır (Salur/Salor) *il/el* (sub-tribe) (900 hooded carts) and of the Karkyn (Karykyn) clan (100 hooded carts) to the Crimea, led by a certain Ogurcuk, seeking refuge from the persecution of another Oghuz *il*, the Bayundur.

Abulghazi also describes how Oghuz khan went to war with a great

---

21 KAŞGARLI MAHMUD 1991, vol. 1: 56.
22 KAŞGARLI MAHMUD 1991, vol. 1: 56–57.
23 Навширванов 1929: 86–87.
24 KAŞGARLI MAHMUD 1991, vol. 1.
25 Кононов 1958: 43.

tribe of Tatars, who lived in the neighbourhood of the Cürcet country, suddenly attacked, defeated them and captured a large booty. In order to carry this booty, a certain man invented the *arba* (cart) which emitted sounds like "qanq-qanq" while moving. This *arba*, allegedly, was named "qanq", and the person who invented it was nicknamed *Qanqly*. Later, his whole family was called *Qangly*[26].

In turn, Constantine Porphyrogenitus, writing about the origin of the Pechenegs, mentions that in the old days the Pechenegs were called Kangar, and now only the three most powerful families of them are called Kangar.[27] The phonological identity of the radicals in the words of qanq+lı and qanq+ar is obvious. However, currently we have to abstain from semantic parallels because of the lack of linguistic material. In addition, according to Abulghazi, the Pechenegs (*becene*) are often the military competitors and outspoken enemies of the Qanqly, and, indeed, the Salors (Salğır), who even called them *it-becene* (dog Pechenegs).[28]

When leaving inhabited places, in the course of movements and migrations, the migrating Turkic tribes were faced with another language environment, which, naturally, was reflected in the phonetic and lexical aspects of language changing over time. For a long time, there was the hypothesis that the language of the Bulgars, Khazars and Saburs, compared by a number of researchers with that of the modern Chuvash, was transformed under the influence of the Finnish and Slavic languages.[29] In the XIth century, Mahmud al-Kashgari puts the Pechenegs on a par with the Bulgars and Suvars (Saburs?), noting their common language features: "The language of the Bulgars, Suvars and Pechenegs up to the boundaries of Rome (Rum/Byzantium) is a Turkic dialect with truncated word endings".[30] Consequently, by this time the Pechenegs had moved to the Bulgar branch of the Turkic languages, although it is known that before their appearance between the rivers Don and Dnieper, as well as in the Crimea, they were certainly perceived as one of the sub-tribes (*il*) of the Oghuz Turks.

---

26 Кононов 1958: 43; Ebulgazi Bahadır Han 1996: 131–132.
27 CONSTANTINE PORPHYROGENITUS 1967: 171.
28 Кононов 1958: 56.
29 Худяков 1923.
30 KAŞGARLı MAHMUD 1991, vol. 1: 30.

Abulghazi mentions the *becene* clan among other clans dating back to Oghuz khan, i.e. the Oghuz *il*. He also notes the meaning of the name of this clan: "he who is doing" (probably from the verb *becermek* – "to cope, to be able to perform, to execute"), their *tamga*, and their *ongon* ("bird" totem) – the variegated falcon.[31]

Constantine Porphyrogenitus also mentions the dwelling of the Pechenegs in the Crimea at the end of the IXth century noting "This nation of Pechenegs is neighbour to the district of Cherson [...]."[32]

At the same time the Crimea was part of the Khazar Khanate, which suggests that the Pechenegs and the Khazars for quite a long time coexisted in the same territory. In addition to the Khazars and Pechenegs, as well as other Turks, which were discussed above, the Bulgarians, coming from Danubian Bulgaria, settled in the Crimea at the same time, whom the Khazars willingly hired as soldiers[33]. Thus, most likely, in spite of the existing military confrontation, there was close proximity to the Khazars and Bulgars who assumed a higher degree of cultural development which influenced the language of Pechenegs as recorded in the XIth century by Mahmud al-Kashgari.

Coming back to the toponymic nomenclature of the peninsula, in addition to the above mentioned Qangly and Salgyr (in Crimean Tatar: *Qaṅġlı* and *Salġır*), other toponymic facts should also be noted which attest to the presence of Oghuz Turks, including the Pechenegs, in the Crimea. In his essay on the Pecheneg language, A. M. Shcherbak mentions, among other geographical names, which he correlates directly with the tribe, two names which fit well into the toponymic picture of the Crimea: *Almatay* and *Bürlük*.[34] According to Shcherbak, both names are hydronyms, i.e. the names of rivers (potamonyms).

In his work "De Administrando Imperio", CONSTANTINE PORPHY-ROGENITUS also indicates the hydronym "Almatay" placing it in the territory between the Danube and the Khazar city Sarkel. He writes that the distance between them is a 60 days' journey. Among other rivers located in the same area, he emphasizes two large rivers, Dnieper and Dniester, and a number of smaller rivers: Syngul /

---

31 Кононов 1958: 53.
32 CONSTANTINE PORPHYROGENITUS 1967: 55.
33 Живков 2010: 14.
34 Щербак 1997: 108.

Syngoul (Singöl?), Hybyl, Kophis and Bogou[35], the latter clearly corresponding to the Bug.

Due to the ancient nature of the Pecheneg hydronyms, as well as due to the fact that Constantine Porphyrogenitus gives quite a large number of potamonyms ending in "-tai"such as Toungatai, Salmaktai, Sakaktai, Kraknakatai,[36] we tend to see here the frequently used Turkish appellative *çay* (*say, şay, tsay, etc.*) – river. Thus, according to our assumption Almatai corresponds to Alma + çai – Apple River. By analogy with the collocation Almachai (*Almaçay*) other word combinations appeared in the Crimea: *Alma Tarhan* – Tarhan possession on the Alma[37], *Alma Saray* (Palace on the Alma), *Alma Tamaq* (Mouth of the Alma). The location of the village Burlyuk/*Bürlük* in the lower reaches of the Crimean river Alma also indicates toponymic parallels (even if we exclude that Constantine Porphyrogenitus' "Almatai" was located in the Crimea, since he gives no specific reference to its location). According to a so-called folk etymology the origin of this name is associated with the word *bür* – ovary (bot.), inflorescence. İt is not unreasonable to assume the location of "Flower" or "Bud" village on the "Apple river".

A. M. SHCHERBAK gives the option for writing this name in the form of *Burlik*, and, at the same time, offers the version of its origin from *bur* (more precisely: *bor* [O.R.]), which means "chalk, limestone".[38] In this case, *Burlyuk (Burlik/Bürlük)* would have to appear in the form of: Borlıq (Borlyk or Borluk), as required by the laws of vowel harmony. Violation of these laws caused by the influence of the Iranian substrates is inherent in the Uzbek language, in which, for example, the polysemous suffix "-lik" forming abstract substantive meanings with quality semantics regardless of sound composition in the stem has only one single form.[39] However, we cannot say anything like this about the Kipchak or Oghuz languages, to which we refer the Pecheneg language of the Xth century. Vowel harmony in these languages is an immutable rule. Thus, it would be

---

35 CONSTANTINE PORPHYROGENITUS 1967: 185.
36 CONSTANTINE PORPHYROGENITUS 1967: 169.
37 About Tarhans see: Усманов 1979; Kurat 1940.
38 Щербак 1997: 108.
39 On Uzbek grammar see: Боровков 1959: 679-727.

possible to conclude that Shcherbak's version is erroneous, but at the same time, we find surprising confirmations of it from other sources.

In the Crimea there is a river *Byuryulcha/Bürülça*, which flows into the Salgır and is located far away from the Alma. The meaning of the verb *bürül-* is "to revolve", "inturn", "wrap", etc. The suffix *-l* provides the verb with a passive meaning. The particle *-cha/-ça* in this name is the word we already know: "chay"– "river", in other words, "rapid" or "revolving" river. However, at the same time on the map of the Crimea dating from the end of the XVIIth century (republished in 1854 by the Ottoman Imperial Land Engineering School/ Mühendishane-i Berri-i Hümayun), there is a settlement Borluca «بورولجا» (most likely originally Borluchay [O. R.]), which is located on the banks of the same river. Here, there is no doubt that the village name is derived from the hydronym and means "Lime river". In this case, we can acknowledge the process of sporadic change in the sound structure of the word expressed primarily in the appearance of an epenthetic vowel at the junction of the sonorants: *Borluchay* > *Burulcha*, under the influence of which the assimilation of "o" in "u" occurred and further palatalization of the consonants resulted in labialization and narrowing of the vowels, probably due to the correlation with the similar word *burul-*. As for the river Alma (*Almaçai*), there are still limestone quarries located in the area which are used in construction, known as "Alma stone". Thus, the name of the Alma village *Bürlük* (Burlyuk / Byurlyuk) can also be formed according to the same model. In any case, we have to acknowledge A.M. Shcherbak's assumption as correct.

When studying another Crimean hydronym of uncertain origin, *Kacha* (in Crimean Tatar *Къачы / Qaçı*), this leads us to Oghuz roots. In the form of *Gachy* this word is registered in the dictionary of the Türkmen language and means "pond", "dam"[40]. In the form *qaçı/ къачы* with the same semantics it can be found in the dictionary of Lazar Budagov with the note "Khiv." (Khivan dialect)[41]. As is known, Khiva and the Khivan oasis (present-day Uzbekistan) were situated in the past on the territory of the empire of the Khorezmshahs, where the

---

40 *Туркменско-русский словарь* 1968: 166.
41 Будагов 1871, vol. 2: 7.

language of the Oghuz Turks was the literary language before the arrival of the Mongols, which still retains its dialectal features of light-vowel pronunciation, bringing it close to the Türkmen and Azerbaijanian languages.

The next wave of Turkish tribes that found their second home in the Crimea were the Kipchaks, also known in the Crimean written sources as Comans or Cumans. Abulghazi has a legendary story about the tribe's eponymos, Kipchak: During the battle with a certain It Barak Khan, Oghuz Khan was defeated and fled. Some honourable Bey (Bek) of Oghuz Khan's committed bodyguard fell in battle, and his pregnant wife, who was among the troops, was left completely alone. At night it was cold, and she had no shelter. Therefore, she hid in the hollow of a large tree and gave birth to a son. Oghuz Khan took care of the boy and gave him the name Kipchak, i.e. hollow tree (according to Abulghazi). In view of the fact that in those days the common people were not accustomed to a literary pronunciation, they pronounced the word "Chypchak". Subsequently his descendants multiplied and wandered in the area between the three rivers Yaik (Ural), Itil (Volga) and Tin (Don). (For some reason the Dnieper is not mentioned – O. R.) The tribe was so numerous that these lands were named Dasht-i Kipchak. They ruled there for three hundred years, until the appearance of Chenghis Khan.[42]

In this passage, even if it is in the genre of folk tales, we see another confirmation of the fact that Oghuzes and Kipchaks have common ancestors, and their language also goes back to a common root. In future works, this fact will be used by us as the starting point for identifying the language of the *sicil*s of the Crimean Khanate and for the solution of etymological problems, especially in the toponymy of the Crimea.

Currently, no toponymic data are known in the Crimea from the Turkic tribes known as Comans, whose name appears in the title of the dictionary *Codex Cumanicus*. Perhaps, most likely, they were not separated from the general register as such. The name Coman (Cuman) remains enigmatic. They are associated by some researchers with one of the Kipchak tribes, while others relate them to some

---

42 EBULGAZI BAHADIR HAN 1996: 133–135.

Kipchak tribe, largely mixed with the Bulgars, at least in terms of language. These "Bulgar" elements found in the language of the *Codex Cumanicus* prevented some researchers from adding this dictionary to the monuments of the Oghuz language[43]. Despite the steady trend in Turkic studies to derive the genealogy of the Comans from a branch of the Türkmen tribe "Kon", as well as a number of other hypotheses, this issue needs to be clarified. In any case, Mahmud al-Kashgari lists no separate tribe of Comans. When listing the Turkic tribes from the west to the east, there are Pechenegs, Kipchaks (in the Arabic form "Kifčak") and only then Oghuzes.[44] Given the fact that the *Diwan Lughat al-Turk* was written at the end of XIth century (1072–1073), the situation with the resettlement of the Turks in Eurasia is different from the situation described by Constantine Porphyrogenitus 140 years earlier. In addition, it is necessary to take into account the fact that Mahmud al-Kashgari represents in the dictionary the largest tribal associations and only occasionally gives information of the smaller divisions or tribal units, mostly of Oghuz origin.

There are quite a large number of toponyms in the Crimea formed from the ethnonym *Kipchak*. Thus, it is necessary to recognize the earlier settlement of the Oghuzes and Kipchaks of the Crimea, as well as of the descendants of the Khazars, Bulgars, Suvars and Pechenegs who mixed with them, in relation with the Mongol tribes and confederations, that came to the Crimea in the next era of turkization of the peninsula – at the beginning of the XIIIth century. However, the tribal structure of Turks who settled there during the annexation of the Crimea by the Golden Horde was not uniform. There was a complicated mixing process of a variety of tribes and clans, which in varying degrees was reflected in the languages of the Turkic peoples, that currently can be characterized as non-homogeneous language forms in terms of dialect composition. The Crimean Tatar language is a vivid reflection of this linguistic phenomenon.

Another popular ethnonym in Crimean toponymy, "Kongrat/ Kungrad", can serve as an example for the migrations of the Turkic tribes. The Kongrat tribe was widespread in Central Asia. Today, as

---

43 Навширванов 1929: 94.
44 KAŞGARLı MAHMUD 1: 26.

before in the Crimea, there are many geographical denotations with that name. The descendants of the Kongrat tribe are present among the modern Kyrgyzes, Kazakhs and Uzbeks. In other words, this is basically the traditional Kipchak area, even with an admixture of the Karluk branch that can be related to the Uzbeks. However, there is a hypothesis that this tribe is of Türkmen, i.e. again Oghuz origin. Navshirvanov writes that the Kongrats were powerful in the Khiva Khanate, and later the Khan's dynasty belonged to that same tribal group,[45] but he associates the name of the Kongrat tribe with the name of a Kipchak khan named Kongur oglu.

Conclusion

In addition to the geographical maps, important material on the Crimean toponymic nomenclature is preserved in books and manuscripts of the Crimean Khanate, primarily of a historical nature (including the decrees/*yarlık* of the Crimean khans). As we have already noted, the most detailed such source is the *sicil*s or *kazasker* records of the Crimean Khanate. According to our preliminary linguistic analysis, these documents are written in the southern Turkic Oghuz dialect comparable to the eastern dialect of Old Ottoman (Pre-Ottoman/Seljuk).[46] Thus, it is logical to assert that in these documents the spoken language of the Crimean Turks appears, in this case that of the inhabitants of Bakhchisarai, mixed with a large number of Arabic terminology which was the norm in the written language both of Ottoman and Seljuk Turks. Toponymic data, in turn, confirms our assumption that a large percentage of the inhabitants of the Crimea belonged to a particular Oghuz tribal group. Anyway, following Choban-zade, we can say that the language of the Crimean Tatars, not only in the southern coastal part of the peninsula, but also of the urban population was largely similar to the Ottoman Turkish language belonging to the South Oghuz branch of the Turkic languages.[47] Using this language signalled education and refinement. The Oghuz-Kipchak nature of the spoken language is also evidenced by samples of speech

---

45 Навширванов 1929: 83.
46 On the Old-Ottoman dialects, see: Гузев 1979.
47 Чобан-заде 1925/2003: 25.

of the inhabitants of Bakhchisarai, recorded by V. V. RADLOV at the end of the XIXth century.[48]

The importance of the Crimean *kazasker* books in solving toponymic problems can be made clear, for example, by the spelling of the name of the village Urkusta which Markevich connects to old-Greek names of unknown etymology[49]. In the court papers, this name is presented as Oğrı Kosta[50], which means Thief Kosta. We do not know the history of this toponym's origin, but its spelling shows its Turkish-Greek origin.

Markevich also offers an interpretation for another well-known toponym – the name of the village of Suren – via the Hungarian word (?) *sairen* (white, whitish)[51], whereas in the *sicil*s this name is spelled *Sürentaş (Syuren Tash)*, which means "pointed rock".

A number of such errors and wild guesses accumulated in studies devoted to Crimean toponymy. Comparative work should be done with the available texts, the number of which is very large, e.g. the toponyms contained in the *sicil*s should be compared with toponyms extracted from other sources, and an atlas of the Crimea should be compiled, which would reflect all the historical names of the peninsula and beyond. Such a time-consuming and extensive work can only be performed by a group of scholars of a research institute or laboratory. But it should be performed and we hope that it will be done in the near future.

References

In Russian

БАСКАКОВ, Н. А. (1981). *Алтайская семья языков и ее изучение.* Москва: Наука.

БИЯРСЛАНОВ, М. (1889–1891). Выписи изъ кадіаскерского сакка

---

48 Радлов 1896, vol. VII.
49 Маркевич 1928: 24.
50 *Sicil*s of Crimean kadis, I. Gasprinskiy Library, Simferopol, archival fund 67 A90.
51 Маркевич 1928: 31.

(книги) 1017–1022 хиджры (1608/9 – 1613 г. хр. лет.), хранящагося в архіве Таврического Губернского Правления. *Известия Таврической ученой архивной комиссии (ИТУАК).* №№ 8; 9; 10. Симферополь: Типография Таврического губернского правления.

БИЯРОВ, Б. Н. (2012). Особенности монголоязычных топонимов казахского Алтая. *Инновации в науке: сб. статей по материалам XI международной научно-практич. Конференции.* Часть I. Новосибирск: СибАК.

БОРОВКОВ, А. К. (1959). Краткий очерк грамматики узбекского языка. *Узбекско-русский словарь.* Москва: Государственное Издательство Иностранных и Национальных Словарей, С. 679–727.

БУДАГОВ, Лазарь (1871). *Сравнительный словарь турецко-татарскихъ нарѣчій со включеніемъ употребительнѣйшихъ слов арабскихъ и персидскихъ и съ переводомъ на русскій языкъ.* Санктпетербургъ: Типографія Императорской Академіи Наукъ, Т. 1, Т. 2.

ГУЗЕВ, В. Г. (1979). *Староосманский язык.* Москва: Наука.

ЖИВКОВ, Борис (2010). *Хазария през IX и X век.* София: Гутенберг.

Кононов, А. Н. (1958). *Родословная туркмен. Сочинение Абу-л-гази, хана хивинского.* Москва, Ленинград: Изд. АН СССР.

Копии сиджилей крымских кадиев, хранящиеся в библиотеке имени И. Гаспринского в Симферополе. Архивный фонд: 67 А90.

ЛАШКОВ, Ф. Ф. (1888). Камеральное описание Крыма. *ИТУАК.* Симферополь, № 6, с. 36–65.

МАРКЕВИЧ, А. И. (1928). Географическая номенклатура Крыма, как исторический материал. Топонимические данные крымских архивов. *Известия Таврического Общества истории, археологии и этнографии.* Т. 2. (59). Симферополь: Крымлит, с. 17–32.

НАВШИРВАНОВ, З. Ш. (1929). Предварительные заметки о племенном составе тюркских племен, пребывавших на юге Руси и в Крыму. *Известия Таврического Общества истории, археологии и этнографии.* Т. 3 (60). Симферополь: Крымлит, с. 78–99.

РАДЛОВ (1896). *Образцы народной литературы сѣверныхъ тюркскихъ племенъ.* Собраны В. В. Радловым. Часть VII. Нарѣчія Крымскаго полуострова. Санкт-Петербургъ: Типографія Императорской Академіи Наукъ.

РУСТЕМОВ, О. Д. (2013a). Внутренняя стилистика бахчисарайских сиджилей. *Сходознавство* № 64. Інститут Сходознавства им. А. Ю. Кримського, НАН України. Київ, с. 108–116.

РУСТЕМОВ, О. Д. (2014). Вопросы стилистических соответствий при переводе текстов судебных решений бахчисарайского сакка на русский язык. *Ученые записки Таврического национального университета им. В.И. Вернадского.* Том 27 (66), №. 3 Филология. Симферополь, с. 181–187.

РУСТЕМОВ, О. Д. (2013b). Источники по изучению становления официально-делового стиля крымскотатарского языка эпохи Крымского Ханства. *Ученые записки Таврического национального университета им. В. И. Вернадского.* Том 26 (65), №2. Филология. Симферопол, с. 232–238.

РУСТЕМОВ, О. Д. (2015a). Крымские сиджили XVII-XVIII вв. жанровая структура юридического документа «хукм». *Вестник СПб Университета. Востоковедение. Африканистика.* Серия 13. Выпуск 1. Санкт-Петербург, Март, с. 55–63.

РУСТЕМОВ, О. Д. (2015b). Словесные портреты и описания людей в крымских судебных книгах XVII–XVIII вв. *Золотоордынское обозрение. Научный журнал.* № 2. Казань, с. 37–42.

РУСТЕМОВ, О. Д. (2015c). Языковые параллели русского и крымскотатарского делового письма в юридических документах XVI–XVII вв. *Восток/Oriens.* № 4. Институт Востоковедения РАН. Санкт-Петербург, с. 168–175.

СМИРНОВ, В. Д. (1887). *Крымское Ханство под верховенством Оттоманской Порты до начала XVIII века.* Казань: Издательство Казанского университета.

Туркменско-русский словарь (1968). Под общей редакцией Н. А. Баскакова, Б. А. Каррыева, М. Я. Хамзаева. Москва: Советская энциклопедия.

УСМАНОВ, М. А. (1979). *Жалованные акты Джучиева Улуса XIV–XVI вв.* Казань: Изд-во КазГУ.

ХУДЯКОВ, М. Г. (1923). *Очерки по истории Казанского Ханства.* Казань: Государственное издательство.

ЧОБАН-ЗАДЕ, Б. ([1925] 2003). *Къырымтатар ильмий сарфы.* Научная грамматика крымскотатарского языка. Транслитерация с арабской графики издания 1925 г. Симферополь: Доля.

ЩЕРБАК, А. М. (1997). Печенежский язык. *Языки народов мира: Тюркские языки.* Под редакцией Тенишева Э. Р. Бишкек: Кыргызстан, С. 107–110.

In Turkish and English

BIYIK, Ömer (2014). *Kırım'ın idarî ve sosyo-ekonomik tarihi.* İstanbul: Ötüken.

CIHAN, Ahmet; YILMAZ, Fehmi (2004). Kırım kadı sicilleri. In: *İslâm Araştırmaları Dergisi* 11: 131–176.

CONSTANTINE PORPHYROGENITUS (1967). *De Administrando Imperio.* Greek text edited by Gy. Moravcsik. English translation by R. J. H. Jenkins. Washington DC: Center of Byzantine Studies.

EBULGAZI BAHADIR HAN (1996). *Şecere-i Terākime (Türkmenlerin soykütüğü).* Hazırlayan: Zuhal Kargı Ölmez. Ankara: Simurg.

İNALCIK, Halil (1996). Kırım Hanlığı kadı sicilleri bulundu. In: *Belleten* LX/227: 165–189.

JANKOWSKI, Henryk (2006). *A historical-etymological dictionary of pre-Russian habitation names of the Crimea.* Leiden, Boston: Brill.

KAŞGARLI MAHMUD (1991–1992). *Divanü Lûgat-it-Türk.* Çeviren: Besim Atalay. Ankara: Türk Tarih Kurumu.

KAVAK, Nuri (2014). *Karasu Kazası (1683–1744). Kırım Hanlığı'nda bir yerleşme örneği.* Bursa: OnMat Öner.

KAVAK, Nuri (2009). Kırım Hanlığı Şer'iyye Sicillerinde yer alan avariz ve para vakıfları üzerine. In: *Eskişehir Osmangazi Üniversitesi Sosyal Bilimler Dergisi* 10: 273–287.

KURAT, Akdes Nimet (1940). *Topkapı Sarayı Müzesi Arşivindeki Altın Ordu, Kırım ve Türkistan Hanlarına ait yarlık ve bitikler.* İstanbul: Burhaneddin.

ÖZDEM, Zeynep (2010). *Kırım Karasubazar'da sosyo-ekonomik hayat (17. yüzyıl sonlardan 18. yüzyıl ortalarına kadar).* Ankara: Türk Tarih Kurumu.

RUSTEMOV, O. D. (2015). History of discovering and problems in studying Crimean court books of the 17th–18th centuries. In: *Manuscripta Orientalia. International Journal for Oriental Manuscript Research* 21/2: 58–68.

TURAN, Ahmet Nezihi (2003). Kırım Hanlığı kadı sicilleri hakkında notlar. In: *Türk Kültürü İncelemeleri Dergisi 9*: 1–16.

YAŞA, Fırat (2014). Kırım Hanlığı'nda köleliğin sosyal ve mali boyutları. In: *Gaziantep University Journal of Social Sciences* Vol. 13/3: 657–669.

YAŞA, Fırat (2017a). The importance of the archives of Venice, Bologna and Modena for the Crimean Studies. In: *Acta Orientalia Academiae Scientiarum Hungaricae* 70/4: 417–429.

YAŞA, Fırat (2017b). *Bahçesaray (1650–1675).* Sakarya: Sakarya Üniversitesi Sosyal Bilimler Enstitüsü. (Doktora Tezi).

YAŞA, Fırat (2017c). Han'ın mutfağından Bahçesaray'daki kölelere: Toplumsal ilişkilerin odağında Kilercibaşı Mehmed Ağa. In: *Bilig Türk Dünyası Araştırmaları Dergisi*, Vol 81: 27–49.

ZEKIYEV, Mirfatih Z. (2002). Bolgar-Tatarların etnogenezi ve genel gelişme aşamaları. *Türkler*, vol. 2, Ankara: 425–442.

XVII. ve XVIII. yüzyıl Kırım Kadı Sicillerinde geçen yer isimleri ve Kırım Tatarlarında aşiret sorunu

Öz

Bu makalede Kırım Hanlığı'na ait ve daha önceki Türk kökenli yer isimlerine odaklanılmaktadır. Kırım Hanlığı kurulmadan önce bölgeye yerleşen Türk boy ve kabilelerinin kullandıkları yer adları çok büyük bir öneme sahiptir. Bilindiği gibi Rusların Kırım'ı işgalinden sonra Kırım ve etrafındaki step topraklarında var olan Türk isimleri değiştirilerek yerine Rus veya Rum kökenli adları kullanılmıştır. Kırım Tatarları sürgün edildikten sonra ise bir iki isim hariç neredeyse bütün Türk kökenli yer adlarının kullanımı yasak edilerek mevcut köy ve şehirlere yeniden isimlendirilmiştir. Sovyet zamanında Kırım toponimisi üzerine çalışan bazı araştırmacılar elinde sağlam kaynakları olmadığından yer adları konusunda büyük yanılgıya düşmüş ve etimolojik hatalar yapmışlardır. Bu çalışmada bölgenin en önemli kaynaklarından biri olan Kırım kadı sicilleri kullanılarak yer adları yeniden ele alınmıştır. Kadı sicillerinin yanı sıra çeşitli sözlükler de kullanılarak yer adlarının filolojik tahlili yapılmıştır.

Anahtar kelimeler: Kırım sicilleri, Yer adları, filolojik analiz, Kırım Hanlığı.

Аннотация

В статье представлен анализ отдельных крымских топонимов с точки зрения идентификации тюркских племен, которые приняли участие в этногенезе крымских татар. Подобная задача уже ставилась в крымском языкознании. В настоящее время появилась возможность значительно расширить круг источников по крымской топонимической номен-клатуре. Как известно, переименование географических названий на полуострове началось сразу после завоевания Крымского ханства. Массовый характер этот процесс принял после высылки крымских татар в 1944 году и упразднения Крымской АССР. В своем настоящем виде топонимия Крыма за редким исключением не представляет никакой исторической или филологической ценности. Но сохранившиеся в письменных памятниках, таких как сиджили судов шариата, истори-ческие названия населенных пунктов и географических объектов дают богатый материал для разнообразных филологических исследований. Одной из актуальных задач языкового анализа крымской топонимики является выявление и определение племенного состава крымских тюрок, в разное время приходивших на полуостров. Вопреки сложив-шейся в истории Крыма точки зрения, роль тюрок-огузов в ней гораздо масштабнее, чем это считалось до сих пор.

Ключевые слова: Крымские сиджили, географические названия, филологический анализ, Крымское Ханство.

Shall We Read the Verb About "God of Time" (*öd teñri*) Which Is in Köl Tigin (N 10) as *yaşamak* Living "to live", *yasamak* Legislate "to arrange, to organize" or *aymak* Telling "to say, to tell"?[1]

Osman Fikri SERTKAYA

(Istanbul University)

Abstract

In this paper, a discussion is offered about proposed readings by different authors concerning a verb interpreted first as *yaşamak* "living", "to live" and later as *yasamak* "legislating", "to legislate, to arrange, to organize" as well as the verb *ay-* "to say, to tell". Furthermore, the sentences where this verb occurs should be accepted as a conditional compound sentence. Finally, there are some comments about the statements *öd teñri / üd teñri*, "God of time".

Introduction

Göktürk (Runic) Alphabet Inscriptions have been read and published about 120 years ago, namely in 1895 and 1896 by RADLOFF[2] and THOMSEN.[3] In those 120 years, the inevitable mistakes made by the

---

1   The Turkish version of this article was published under the title "Köl Tigin (K-10)'da Geçen Öd Teŋri 'Zaman Tanrısı' ile İlgili Fiili Yaşamak 'Yaşamak' mı, Yasamak 'Tanzim Etmek, Düzenlemek' mi, Yoksa Aymak 'Demek, Söylemek' mi Okumalıyız?" *Journal of Old Turkic Studies* 2017, Cilt 1, Sayı 2, 55–63.
The editors express their profound gratitude to Dr. Simone RASCHMANN whose resourceful advice was instrumental for preparing the English version of this paper.

2   RADLOFF, W.: *Die alttürkischen Inschriften der Mongolei* (Erste Lieferung). St. Petersburg 1895.

3   THOMSEN, Vilhelm: *Inscriptions de l'Orkhon déchiffrées*. Helsingfors: La société de literature Finnoise, 1896. (Suomalais-ugrilainen seura, Helsinki Toimituksia, no. 5.)

first scholars and their followers were corrected by later researchers. As an example; instead of *öz(ü)t ogdı* we now accept *öz togdı,* and instead of *(a)ks(i)r(a)k ordu* we now read *k(a)s(a)r kord(a)n.* Unfortunately also some readings correct in the first place were turned wrong by later researchers. For example the word *pahra* meaning "Persian" was translated as *p(a)r* into Turkish and was read as *(a)p(a)r* meaning "Avar".

In this paper, I would like to share my opinion about a particular inscription fragment which was generally translated as "god lives the time".

The inscription and its early interpretations

1. The phrase, located in the 10th line of the inscription on the North Side of Köl Tigin, follows below:

: ⟩ⵣⴹⵂⵝ : ⵑ⟩ : ⵑ⟩ⵜⵝⵝⵂ : ⵝⵎⴹⵝ : ⵝⵜ⟩ : ⵝⵑⵅ⟩ ⵝⵝⵝ : ⵝⵝⵙ : ⵝⵝⵝⵂ ⵅⵝ : ⟩ⵣⴹⵂⵝ ⟩ⵂⵝ

This inscription has been read and interpreted in three different ways by prominent researchers.

1.1. The first group begins with Wilhelm RADLOFF who was the first scholar to publish his findings. He has read it as four sentences like "God lives human beings die" according to the opposite meaning of the verbs "live" and "die".
The reading and understanding of Wilhelm RADLOFF:
özmsknãm öḍtṅṛi jsr ḳiṣiogli qop ölgli ṭiṛimṣ. (11) nča sknãm
özŭm sakындım, öd mäӈpi jaшap кiшi oғлы кōn ölӯгli mipiмiш. (11)
Анча сакындım (1895:28–29).

"Ich selbst gräme mich, ewig nur lebt der Himmel, die Menschensöhne leben, aber sie müssen sterben. (11) Ich gräme mich" [I was sorry, only God lives forever. I was sorry because human beings were created in order die.]

1.1.1 Muharrem ERGIN[4] was the only representative follower of Wilhelm Radloff.
The reading and understanding of Muharrem ERGIN:

---

4   ERGIN, M.: *Orhun abideleri.* İstanbul: Milli Eğitim Basımevi 1970.

Özüm sakındım. Öd täŋri yaşar. Kişi oglı kop ölgeli törümis. Ança sakındım. (59) I thought deeply. God lives the time. Human beings have come into being in order to die. I thought. (1970:14)

1.2. The second group of readings began with Vilhelm THOMSEN. THOMSEN accepted the meaning of the inscriptions as the verbs "legislate" and "die" with the idea of "God arranges and organizes, human beings die". According to Thomsen and his followers the verb *yasa-* "legislate" of the inscription was "to organize, to arrange, to appreciate", *-r* being the present tense suffix.

The reading and understanding of Vilhelm THOMSEN:

öz^im s^ak^y nd^ym. öd t^aŋri y^as^ar, kisi oyty qop öl^ügli törüm^is. (I, 59) *anča s^ak^y nd^ym.* (1896: 113)

"Moi-même je me désolai. Le ciel dispose du temps, mais les nombreux fils des hommes sont nés mortels. Je me désolai en disant. Je me désolai tellement: [...]" [I am so sorry. God organizes the time but human beings are mortal. So sorry.]

1.2.1 Hüseyin Namık ORKUN[5] and Talat TEKIN[6] follow THOMSEN in their interpretations.

Interpretation by Hüseyin Namık ORKUN:

öz^üm s^ak^ind^m : öd t^enri : y^as^ar, kişi oglı kop öl^ügli : törümiş (I, 64) ^ança : s^ak^ind^m. (1936:50-52).

[I am sorry. God appreciates the time. Human being have come into being in order to die. I am so sorry.]

H. N. ORKUN has corrected his translation of the word in part IV of his dictionary (1941:135), *yaslan-* "being sorry" for *sakın-* as *yasa-* "to organize, to make".

1.2.2 The interpretation by Talat TEKIN:

özüm saqïntïm. öd täŋri yasar. kisī oyli qop ölgäli törümis. (N11) anča saqïntïm. (1968: 237)

5   ORKUN, H. N.: *Eski Türk yazıtları* 1. İstanbul: Devlet Basımevi 1936. ORKUN, H. N.: *Eski Türk yazıtları* 4. İstanbul: Devlet Basımevi 1941.
6   TEKIN, Talat: *A grammar of Orkhon Turkic*. Bloomington, The Hague: Mouton, 1968. (Indiana University Uralic and Altaic Series, vol. 69.)

"I mourned. Human beings have all been created in order to die, (N11)
I mourned in the following way: [...]" (1968:271)
yasa- "to determine, rule, order (1968:398)"

1.2.3 In his dissertation *Turkish Calendars in Middle Ages and Old
Ages* published 1972, Louis BAZIN[7] writes about the phrase *öd teñri
yasar*.

> *öd täŋri yasar*. (dans le passage où *Bilgä kagan* se livre, à propos
> de la mort de son frère, à des réflexions sur la précarité de la vie
> humaine: *kiši oglï kop ölügli törümiš* «les humains sont tous mortels
> par nature»).
>
> Les éditeurs ont compris: «Le Ciel (*täŋri*, Dieu-Ciel) règle le
> temps» (Thomsen, JB 113: «Le ciel dispose du temps»). C'est
> méconnaitrre la rigidité de l'ordre des mots dans tout ce texte, où le
> sujet précède nécessairement le complément d'objet, lui-même
> précédant le verbe. Une telle interprétation ne serait légitime que pour:
> «*täŋri öd yasar*».
>
> En réalité, *täŋri* n'a pas seulement le sens de «ciel» et de «Dieu-
> Ciel» (le Grand-Dieu des Turcs et des Mongols), mais encore celui de
> «dieu, divinité» en général, largement attesté dans toute la littérature
> turque ancienne (*uygur*), bouddhique, taoiste, manichéenne, ou
> chrétienne. Et le mot *täŋri*, en ce cas, suit immédiatement le nom
> spécifique de la divinité: *āy täŋri* «le Dieu-Lune» (HJ 176), *yōl täŋri*
> «le Dieu du Voyage» (HJ 73), *äzrua täŋri* «Brahma» (FA 259), *tïntura
> täŋri*, *yel täŋri*, *yaruk täŋri*, *suv täŋri*, *ōt täŋri* «le Dieu Zéphyr, le
> Dieu-Vent, le Dieu-Lumie, le Dieu-Eau, le Dieu-Feu» (FA 268); etc ...
>
> Ici, manifestement: *öd täŋri* «le Dieu-Temps», peut-être hérité du
> *Zervân* iranien. Donc: *öd täŋri yasar* «Le Dieu-Temps règle (tout)».
> C'est, par la voie détournée d'un concept religieux, un grand pas de
> fait vers l'idée abstraite de «temps». (1991: 194–195)

In my translation of the original text instead of *–gli*, I used *-geli* and
had translated it as follows: *kişi oglı köp ölgeli törümiş*. In the lines of
Louis BAZIN, the person who is concerned about the verb *öl-*, *kiši oglï
kop ölügli törümiš* "Human beings are created as mortal".

In the first paragraph of BAZIN's quote, the transcription "kişi oglı

7   BAZIN, Louis: *"Les calendriers turc anciens et medievaux"*. Lille, December 2,
     1972. Turkish translation: "Eski Türk dünyasında kronoloji yöntemleri", transl.
     by Vedat Köken. Turkish Language Association Ankara 2011.

köp ölügli. Törümiş", translated as "Les humains sont tous mortels par nature" should be transcribed as *kişi oglı köp ölgeli törümiş* and translated as "Human beings are created in order to die." Because the suffix of the the verb *öl-, -glı/-gli* which was translated as "*-an/-en*", more like *-galı/-geli* which can be translated as infinitives (*-mek/-mak*).[8]

1.3. The 3th reading group was introduced at the beginning of 1970s. At first Gerhard DOERFER, then Sir Gerard CLAUSON had interpreted the verb in the inscription as *ay-* "to tell" and the suffix *-sar* as a modal.

In his article "Gedanken zur Gestaltung eines idealen Türkischen Etymologischen Wörterbuchs."[9] of 1971, DOERFER says about that subject:

> *yasa-* 'ordnen' ist nicht ursprünglich türkisch, sondern mongolischer Herkunft: Es ist erst seit der Mongolenzeit belegt, s. TMEN Nr. 1794. Die ältesten türkischen Belege stammen aus dem 13. Jh., dagegen ist (gegen Räsänen 191, Drevnetjurkskij slovař 245) alttürk. "*yasa-*" anders zu erklären: es heißt nicht *öd täŋri yasar*, sondern *üd (so laut Brahmischrift u.a.) täŋri aysar* 'wenn der Himmel die Zeit bestimmt', von *ay-* 'sagen, bestimmen, festsetzen'. (Page 450)

In his article[10] about the word *ay-*, Sir Gerard CLAUSON also said:

> **ay-** (1) Intrans. 'to speak'; (2) 'to say, declare, prescibe (something *Acc.*)'; (3) 'to say' with the words said in *oratio recta*. There is little difference of meaning between **ay-**, **té-**, and **sözle-**, but at any rate in the earliest period **ay-** seems to be to same extent honorific, while the others are not. N.o.a.b.; apparently became obsolete when **ayıt-**, *q.v.*,

---

8   SERTKAYA, O. F.: "Louis Bazin: Les calendriers turcs anciens et medievaux (Eski ve orta çağlarda Türklerin takvimleri). Aralık 1972'de Savunulan Doktora Tezi, Lille 1974, 800 s.". *Türkiyat Mecmuası* 19.1980: 335–344. (Tanıtma)

9   DOERFER, Gerhard: "Gedanken zur Gestaltung eines idealen Türkischen Etymologischen Wörterbuchs." *Orientalische Literaturzeitung* 66.1971:9–10, 437–454.
     Translated by Dr. İlhan ÇENELİ: "Türkçenin ideal bir etimolojik sözlüğünün nasıl olması gerektiği hakkında düşünceler" başlığı ile Türkçeye çevirilerek Türk Dili. *Aylık Dil Dergisi*, Sayı: 392-393/Ağustos-Eylül, 1984, 366-374.

10   CLAUSON, Sir G.: *An etymological dictionary of pre-thirteenth century Turkish* [EDPT]. Oxford: Oxford University Press 1972.

came to mean 'to say', but in the transition period it is sometimes hard to say whether Perf. f.s represent **ay-** or **ayıt-**. Türkü VIII **öd teŋri: aysar** 'when heaven prescibes the time (all men are destined to die) I N 10. (EDPT 266a).

Because DOERFER and CLAUSON read it as *ay-*, Talat TEKIN changed his reading in 1968 *yasa-* to *ay-* in his book in 1988. When the verb is read as *(a)y-*, the rest *-sar* becomes conditional suffix.

1.3.1. The correction of reading and understanding of Talat TEKIN by himself:[11]

öz(ü)m s(a)k(ı)nt(ı)m : öd t(e)ñri : (a)ys(a)r : kişi oglı : koop : ölg(e)li : törüm(i)ş : (1988:38)

"Kendim düşünceye daldım. Zaman Tanrısı buyurunca insan oğlu help ölümlü yaratılmış.

(KT K11) Öyle düş ündüm." (1988:39)

[I thought deeply. When the God of Time commanded the human beings was created as mortals. I thought so.]

The verb *ay-* is not in the dictionary. Whereas the explanation on page 87 reads as follows:

118) KT K 10: *öd t(e)ñri (a)ys(a)r*. This text has been red by RADLOFF as "*yaşar*" and the whole sentence has been translated as "Ewig lebt (nur) der Himmel", that is "Only God lives forever". (1997:148). THOMSEN decided about the meaning of this word as the present tense of *yasa-* "to organize" and translated the sentences as "Le ciel dispose du temps" = "God organize the time (life)" (1896: 113). All those translations consist of the same meaning: ORKUN (I, 50), MALOV (1951: 33) and TEKIN (1968: 210).

CLAUSON was the first who suggested that the verb can not be *yasa-* because the Mongolian word couldn't be found in turkish documents before 13. and 14. Century. And he translated "öd teñri aysar" as "when heaven prescibes the time". (1972:974) DOERFER had also translated *öd* as *üd*. (TMEN IV: 72). This correction seems to be good. Because 1) the verb *yasa-* is Mongolian 2) Even it is Turkish, the verb which ends with present tense suffix with two syllable and

---

11   TEKIN, T.: *Orhon yazıtları*. Ankara: Türk Dil Kurumu Yayınları 1988.

with vowel sounds, it should have been -*yur* instead of -r (as *yaşa-yur*, *yorı-yur*).

No doubt that the verb clearly is *ay*-, but the meaning of *ay*- should be not "to tell" but "to command, to dominate, to appreciate". Conditional suffix -*sar* is also takes place for verb suffix indicates the time.

In his article "The relationship between compound sentences and head sentences in Orhon Inscriptions"[12] Mertol TULUM mentioned that it is a basic relationship to declare the cause of being or to connect to a cause of being in the sentence, and continued to say that was an example of a conditional helping sentence.

(auxiliary sentence) *öd tengri aysar* "Because God of Time commanded"

(head sentence), *kişi oğlu kop ölgeli törümiş* "The human being was created as mortal." (1994:197)

We should accept the way they expressed their thoughts because according to DOERFER, CLAUSON and TEKIN who accepted the sentences as conditional compound sentence have read Bilge Kağan's sentences (accepting the sentences as: *öz(ü)m s(a)k(ı)nt(ı)m: öd t(e)ñri: (a)ys(a)r: kişi oglı : kop: ölg(e)li: törüm(i)ş: a)nça: s(a)k(ı)nt(ı)m)*, as "I thought. That's why I tought God of time commended 'Human beings was created in order to die'."

The Readings of *öd* vs. *üd*

2. In Old Turkish the word was written as **Xⁱⁿⁱ** was read as *öd* which means "time". EDPT 35a-b *ö:ḍ* "time". The reason of reading it as *üd*, in Old Turkish text which was written in Brahmi letters, was that the wovels *ö* and *ü* were written differently in Brahmi alphabet.

In Old Turkish texts, *üç üd* "past, present and future" are called as *alku öd* "whole time". In other words it means "entire time". Saying *tört üd* indicates "four periods", four seasons "spring, summer, authum and winter". It also stands for "five times" prayer times in a day for Muslims.

---

12 Mertol TULUM: "Orhon yazıtlarında birleşik cümleler ve baş cümle ile yardımcı cümle ilişkileri" [The relationship between compound sentences and head sentences in Orhon Inscriptions]. *Belleten* [*Yearbook of Turkic Studies*] 1990. Ankara, 1994, p. 193–205)

Parallels in other languages – Conclusions

3. When we translate *öd teŋri* literally, it means "God of time".

The idea of *öd teŋri* In Old Turkish was matching up with *Zervan ~ Zurvan* in Persian. *Zervan ~ Zurvan* was accepted as "primordial, creator god". In Avesta *zurvan* comes from *zaman* "time". That why Louis BAZIN stated that the root of *öd teŋri* in Old Turkish might have been coming from *Zervan ~ Zurvan* in Persian. Zurvanism which has not many believers at all, is a branch of Mazdaism.

In Greek Mythology the synonym of *öd teŋri* in Old Turkish is the last Titan *Khronos > Kronos* who is the child of "God of Land" (Gaia) and Uranus. It is accepted that *Khronos* created the time and he is a time traveller. "Chronology" which means "putting in an order by time" was reproduced from *Khronos*. In Roman Mythology *Khronos* is known as Saturn. The name of the day Saturday also comes from Saturnus Ages.

It is known that in Islamic period of Turkish the name of who travels entire times was called Hıdır-Hızır (aleyhi's-selâm).

As a result we should accept the sentence *öd teñri aysar, kişi oglı kop ölgeli törümiş* as a conditional compound sentence "Because God of time commanded that human beings were created in order to die" in favour of understanding it as "God lives time" or "God organizes time."

Reevaluating the Role of the Native Language as Part of the Nation Building Process in Kazakstan

Orhan SÖYLEMEZ*

A theorist on nationalism has stated that "language is by no means the only binding force in modern societies."[1] However, even if it is not the only binding force, at least, language often plays an essential role in Kazak national or ethnic identity. Moreover, in an article published in 1996 a researcher emphasized the fact that "language is an integral part of society, its values, traditions, view of life; in short, its culture as a whole." Depending on this she also asserts that this is why nation-builders need a single official language pointing out the process of nation building in the case of the Turkish Republic where the language of the dominant ethnie is the base.[2] Some writers have touched upon another aspect of the language issue and have expressed their feelings about it. An article entitled "Of home and the world," for instance, describes the native language regarding Kazakstan:

The element of native language is the living air which we breathe. And if that air is short of the oxygen of fresh, real words, then the reader will suffer from "nitrous" word effacement.[3]

This statement clearly shows that language is deeply rooted, although not used all the time, in the Kazak society. It is a matter of life and death of grouphood, and is part of their everyday life and that of their identity.

This last assertion, moreover, can be supported by many examples, incidents, and reactions to them of Kazak intellectuals. Personal observations during the visits to different regions in Kazakstan over

---

* Prof. Dr., Ardahan University, Contemporary Turkic Languages and Literatures, Ardahan.

1 Anthony D. SMITH: *Theories of nationalism*. 2nd ed. London: The Gresham Press, 1983, p. 145.
2 Didem Mersin ALICI: The role of culture, history and language in Turkish national identity building: an overemphasis on Central Asian roots. *Central Asian Survey*, 15 (2).1996, p. 227.
3 V. LAKSHIN: Of home and the world. *The Soviet multinational state: Readings and documents*, ed. by Martha B. Olcott. New York: M. E. Sharpe, 1990, pp. 310–321.

the last five years indicate the fact that consciousness among the people on the street over Kazak language has been growing fast. The first visit during the academic year of 1998–1999 by the author proved that although awareness of own language began earlier than the declaration of independence, it is a very slow process to build a nation, depending on a local language. At that time it was difficult to come across people speaking to each other in Kazak even in cities like Shimkent, Kentau, and even in Turkestan, all located down in the South. Although populated overwhelmingly by Kazaks, people in these cities converse in Russian as a common language. However, even at that time, it was possible in bazaars, taxis or shops to find people answering back in Kazak unless Russian was used. This indicated the fact that common people know and use their mother tongue if either they want to or are requested to do so.

The incident reported in a Kazak language periodical that took place on a bus in 1989 and a Kazak intellectual's reaction to it shows the beginning of self-conciousness. In the bus from Ombi to Kökshetau an old woman begins to talk with appearently her grandchild in her broken Russian. Out of curiosity, the intellectual addresses the old woman with respect, calling her mother, and asks:

> Mother, during the travel you spoke in Kazak among yourselves and with the children, but with the grandchild you spoke in Russian. Why was it so? And with such Russian that it even upset the Russian travelers sitting next to my seat. Why do you not put the Kazak language into the soul and blood of this baby, along with its mother's milk on which it is dependent? Isn't it obligatory (*pariz*) for mothers to do so? The Russian language does not need your help to be taught to this baby! Your grandchild will soon grow up and schools and life will teach him Russian. So, isn't it your duty to help this baby move its tongue with its mother language?[4]

This is only one of many scenes that take place in Kazakstan everyday. However, they are not always handled and reacted against by an intellectual or another Kazak who is aware of the importance of the mother tongue. This incident describes how the Kazak people,

---

4   Qorghanbek AMANJOLOV: Ana tili degende. *Jûldïz*, 8 August 1989, p. 159.

literate or illiterate, began to show disrespect for their own language. It shows also that there are some Kazaks who care about it and have a great respect for it and its future. The result of the notion of the woman described above is tragic for a Kazak. The article that recorded it included another anecdote that projects the result with crystal clarity. In 1988, Kazak radio featured a program in which the radio anchors have a talk with the *komsomol* (youth organization) committees of the republic. As part of this program, the Kökshetau komsomol committee records their talk in Kazak and sends it to the radio. But there is no one working at the radio to read the text and make use of it.[5]

Nevertheless, the second visit to Kazakstan by the author two years later during the academic year of 2001–2002 to Astana, the capital of the country in the North, showed that Kazak is now being used even on the street, and also even by the Kazak youth. This wasn't entirely true a couple of years ago. This may be explained in two ways: 1. The city is the capital and people are living close to the center, 2. People are beginning to pay more respect to their mother tongue. Both are arguable.

This is a kind of reality that makes Kazak intellectuals feel sentimental about their language and makes them realize its real condition in the society. Thus, since their declaration of independence in 1991, the Kazaks have shown a great awareness of the language issue. Since then, most good jobs have required mastery of the Kazak language, which, according to the constitution (and as will be discussed later) is the only official state language, whereas Russian has been relegated to the level of the language of "inter-ethnic communication." This may seem a reactionary measure, given the harsh assimilation policy implemented by previous Soviet govern-ments which flooded Kazakstan with millions of Russian immigrants and essentially attempted to erase the Kazak language. At the same time, Kazak intellectuals have been writing about Kazak and trying to promote their modern Kazak language, which few Russians have bothered to learn, for Kazaks and Russians feel differently in regard to this matter. Kazaks want their language to dominate and permeate

5   Ibid., p. 161.

every level of society. While Russians feel discriminated against, Kazaks are proud of the promotion of Kazak.

Existence of a distinct Kazak language

Even before the 1917 Revolution, Kazak intellectuals remained preoccupied with creating and preserving the language legacy through which they could stay close to their roots. The efforts of intellectuals to promote the use of the Kazak language could only mean that language is a means to assert their national identity.

During the late 19th and at the turn of the 20th Centuries, Kazak reformers like Ibray ALTINSARIN were trying to set the base for the Kazak literary language on one hand, while intellectuals such as Dinmuhammed SULTANGAZI and Asilqozha QURMANBAYEV were expressing their conciousness about the loss of their language on the other hand. QURMANBAYEV in his article called "About the Kazak language" published in *Dala Velayeti Gazeti* in 1894 (no. 27) mentioning the fact that Kazak reformers already acknowledge the Arabic, Persian, and Turki languages, was warning against the loss of the native language. He asserted that knowing these languages does not mean that people are educated and that they are of no benefit for people. Eventually he suggests that they learn their own language beside Russian instead of all other unbeneficial ones. An answer for Qurmanbayev comes from the journal *Qazaq*. The article "Orinbor. 10 Fevral" signed by some "Turk-balasi" (Turkish son) aims at the important role of the language in the process of identity building. He says that "for a nation to live up or disappear depends on the language. If a nation loses its language it is also bound to disappear. If we are to become a Kazak nation we had better think about our own language rather than feed ourselves."[6]

The publication of such articles resulted in an increase in the number of articles in the press. In his book the Kazak scholar Amantai SHERIP sums up these efforts using what had been said in the journal *Aiqap*: "Literature and language are the life and soul of a nation." He also mentions the Kazak nationalist Mirjaqip DULATULI's article published in the journal *Qazaq* and shows the worries of some other

---

6   The articles by QURMANBAYEV and TURK-BALASI were cited in Amantai SHERIP: *Qazaq poeziyasi jane ulttik ideya.* Almatï: Bilim, 2000, p. 198.

reformers about the future of the Kazak language. Dulatuli warns that the Kazak language will not be able to protect itself and will loose its originality with the bulk of loan words from other languages without naming them. Journals like *Aiqap* and *Qazaq* opened their pages for those intellectuals who were concerned about the language. In general they came up with the idea that "Kazak as a national language should serve the Kazak people." Once setting Kazak as the language of their identity, they turn to search for ways to save and enhance it. Mirzahmet QOZHAKLANOV published his poem called "To my mother tongue" in *Aiqap* in 1914 (No. 13). It can roughly be translated as follows:

> Oh my mother tongue, don't go backward,
> Make efforts now and go forward.
> Before your sun and moon rose
> You for sometime mourned.
>
> ...
>
> To this world spread your light,
> Now enlighten your homeland.
> Let your homeland in light
> Rest as becoming sober from happiness.[7]

Other Kazak writers and poets also began to write in this respect. For instance, Sultanmurad TORAIGIROV in his poem says as follows:

> I love my mother tongue, mother's tongue
> Even in the cradle it taught me science
> Since the minute I came to earth crying
> Your known voice has settled in my ear.

Ilias JANSUGIROV went even further valuing the language as follows:

> Dear, values as gold my mother's tongue,
> With your present baby's value rose.
> Waking up four times at night to cool down
> With you sung lullabies my mother.

Magjan CUMABAYEV with his poem "Qazaq tili" joined these intellectuals. Moreover he pointed out that the mother tongue with its features like "purity, deepness, sharpness, power, and wideness" is to

---

7   *Aiqap*, ed. by U. SUBHANBERDINA and S. DAVITOV. Almatï: Qazaq entsiklo-pediyasi, 1995, pp. 215–216. Two couplets of the poem were also cited in Amantai SHERIP: *Qazaq poeziyasi jane ulttik ideya*. Almatï: Bilim, 2000, p. 198.

bring the people closer to each other. He described this as follows:
> Braveness, patriotism, unity, honesty, effort, faith, and pride
> Bad fate made dissappear all what existed
> From the Golden days as invaluable document
> Shining star, my father's tongue only you remained.
>
> ...
>
> Clouds spread all over you
> You, my tongue, could bring together with a white hand.[8]

All these pieces of poems are to indicate that Kazak intellectuals were set to create and disseminate their own language during the first quarter of the 20th Century. This concern made Kazak a literary language. This was also part of the program set by the Soviets and remained the case until the last decade of the century.

Kazak being part of ethnic identity

As a result of efforts by Kazak reformists, school books and anthologies in the Kazak language came into print. This paved the way to the opening of new-method schools. With the new method schools, Russian began to make itself felt throughout the Kazak steppes. For the Kazak intellectuals it was inevitable and necessary to learn Russian. The Kazak reformers most of whom had already known the Turki language, Arabic, and Persian, learned Russian. Abay KUNANBAYEV as an outstanding Kazak reformer supported this process. Even Islamic oriented poets wrote on the matter. For instance, Ebubekir KERDERI in his poem spoke out loudly praising the Russian language:

> Prophet, God, you should know together
> Russian and the Islamic language you should know
>
> ...
>
> Useless in this world
> Any day without reading Russian.

In another poem, religion-oriented KERDERI says:

> If he doesn't acknowledge in Russian
> He doesn't benefit you

---

8   Amantai SHERIP: *Qazaq poeziyasi jane ulttik ideya.* Almatï: Bilim, 2000, p. 199.

Your Muslim mentor.[9]

Another very pious man like Kerderi, Hadji Makish KALTAYEV says in his poem entitled "Russian needed":

We call Russian not good in our religion,
Even if we need it today.
Better than bending down to salute the translator,
Know it to finish your job yourself.
We salute the translator somehow
Is our word worse than his?![10]

Kaltayev in this poem points out the practical need of learning Russian in order to avoid those double-faced translators as he describes. Mirjaqip Dulatuli as a great Kazak nationalist also evaluated this side of the situation calling this as a national issue. "... In our world to gather our rights, to protect our land and property, and to avoid outside influence we need to learn Russian and educate ourselves... It is even worse not to know Russian than to know it. In Russia there live more than 140 million people and they speak in 109 different languages among which Russian is the highest. All official documents are done in Russian, and laws are in Russian, too." Muhammedjan SERALIN, editor of the journal *Aiqap*, gives even more and direct reason to learn Russian. He says: "What looks after us is the Russian government, so that we will not be guilty if we say it is necessary to learn Russian. In order to live happily in Russian lands we need science, art, and the Russian language."[11]

As will be seen in Shakerim QUDAIBERDIULI's poem, those Kazak reformers who were at the front in the Alash Orda movement expressed their pride of knowing Russian besides other eastern languages. Qudaiberdiuli describes this as follows:

Since my youth I have mastered the Turki language
Into this language all sciences have been translated.
With an effort I have studied and seen the result
Shining from darkness my sun rose.
Awakened me earlier an eastern poem,
Like a mirror opened the world's secret

---

9   Amantai SHERIP: *Qazaq poeziyasi jane ulttik ideya*. Almatï: Bilim, 2000, p. 193.
10   Ibid., p. 194.
11   *Aiqap*, 1912, no. 3, p. 53, cited in A. Sherip, p. 194.

With an effort having learned Russian
The dirt of illiteracy has gone off.

This shows that at the beginning of the 20th century, one of the difficulties for the Kazaks was to overcome illiteracy. A number of plays, short novels, and stories were aiming at solving this problem. Here, QUDAIBERDIULI sees and depicts Russian as a remedy for it. All these pieces of poems indicate the importance of the language, i.e. the Kazak language, in the formation of the nation in general. This was the case before the Soviet Union. Now it is over, and the same issue is at the top of the agenda in Kazakstan at the turn of the 21th century and after more than a decade of independence.

Central Asian intellectuals in general have made attempts to strengthen their respective groups' ethnic identity. They have consistently shown a great interest in illuminating their history for the people of their republics, and in encouraging them to use their own language, a practice that had been a taboo for quite a long time. Despite this tendency among the intellectuals, however, sections of Central Asian society, particularly high-ranking officials, seemed to have been caught unprepared by the sudden moves for independence in the former Soviet Union. What some feared was that the local governments of these new independent states might favor tight control over the people, media, and intellectual activities, as well as political life. Local journals and newspapers have complained and questioned scholars about the inconsistent attitudes of the officials. For instance, editors of one local Kazak-language newspaper accused officials of not taking any action to encourage the use of the Kazak language:

It has been more than a year since [people] founded the Society for the Kazak Language. We had trusted the words of officials who occupied the posts, but we were wrong. The Party Oblast Organization is not aware of our existence... Although it has been more than a month since officials promised to take action on the base of the national language for Kazak, they have yet to move.[12]

MUQAEV's complaint came just a year before the Soviet Union's breakdown. As will be seen and examined later in this paper, officials

---

12   Baqqozha MUQAEV: Ulttïng rukhï – tili. *Aqïqat*, no. 2, 15–31 August 1990, p. 1.

with their independence in hand took some very serious actions towards turning the Kazak language into the official one.

Restoring the Kazak language

Even in the late 1950s, Kazak intellectuals wanted to protect the Kazak language, and so demanded that all persons holding executive posts in the Communist Party and state administration know Kazak. A French scholar discussed the opposition of Kazak intellectuals to linguistic Russification, and opposition to this resistance by another Kazak intellectual. She calls the latter and his like "Russified Kazaks." According to her, Kazak intellectuals had long centered their attention on two main questions: "the preservation of their national language and the safeguarding of their cultural heritage."[13] Intellectuals still demand the same thing today and oppose general usage of the Russian language as equal with the Kazak language, which was designated by the language law as the State language. A sign of the importance of language for nationalists was shown in a recent caricature that depicted an anti-independence movement as a dark devil flying over Kazakstan and Kazakstan's flag. The devil's mouth and his single eye were open, and a text in the devil's mouth reads: 1) The Russian language should be the language of the State; 2) A so-called Kazakstanian nation should be established (regardless of people's ethnic origins); and 3) It is not necessary that the President should be a Kazak. The caption underneath the picture warns of the existence of an opposition to independence in Kazakstan, and reads as follows: "People who do not want us to have independence may still exist."[14] Nevertheless, since September 1989, the Republic of Kazakstan (it was an SSR at that time) has passed a law on the language of the State many times, with subtle changes from one time to another. The next few paragraphs discuss these subtleties.

Examining the language law

In his comparative study of the language issue in the former Soviet Union and India, a scholar of political science and South Asian studies

---

13 H. CARRÈRE D'ENCAUSSE: Linguistic Russification and nationalist opposition in Kazakhstan. *The East Turkic Review*, vol. 1, no. 1, April 1958, p. 97.

14 *Ana Tili*, no. 50 (162), December 17, 1992, p. 1.

argues that the Russian language dominated during the former Soviet Union due to the lack of any kind of requirement for Russians living in non-Russian republics to learn the language of the republic in which they live.[15]

Some Kazak intellectuals brought this matter to public attention again by discussing it on the pages of Kazak language literary journals. They argued that the previous advantages for knowing Russian should be reversed and that those who have a knowledge of the new state language, that is Kazak, should have the priority in competitions for jobs. However, political pressure from Moscow was exerted on policy makers in Alma-Ata/Almatï, the capital city of Kazakstan up to 1998, in order to protect the rights of Russian inhabitants in the republic, and this resulted in the acceptance of equal rights for both Kazak and Russian. Part of the reason for this might also have been the concern of the incumbant government over political stability in the state.

Should Kazak be the only official language of Kazakstan? Deputies of the Kazak parliament and scholars from various schools recently discussed this aspect of the language law, and brief comments by some deputies on the topic appeared in the journal *Ana Tili*. Some Russian deputies, concerned about their Kazak constituency, support making Kazak the official language. Some of these Russian members of parliament were being more cautious and willing to leave the solution of the language issue to the passage of time. The Russian representative of the City of Almatï, for example, taking into account the fact that the population of Kazakstan consists of different ethnic groups, said:

None of our nations has yet established itself to build a new country. We do not have such a nation. All we have is ethnic groups. There is no nation of so-called Kazakstanis and there is a need to make an effort to strengthen our new country.[16]

---

15 Paul R. BRASS: Language and national identity in the Soviet Union and India. *Thinking theoretically about Soviet nationalities*, ed. by Alexander J. Motyl. New York: Columbia University Press, 1992, p. 111.

16 Til üshin küres-qasiyetti küres (editorial), (during the Ninth Session of the Supreme Council of the Republic of Kazakstan). *Ana Tili*, no. 51 (163), December 24, 1992, p. 1.

In general, regardless of their ethnic background, most of the representatives agreed that there should be a clause in the Constitution designating Kazak as the official language. Kazak intellectuals also showed concern over the issue of the functions of the Kazak language, and this matter received much attention. A Kazak writer described the duty that the Kazak people have toward their language:

Our mother tongue was recognized by law to become the language of the nation. And now, a long stretch of time lies ahead of us before our language regains its true strength. In recent years, a number of schools and kindergartens has been opened for our children. This is the beginning of a long path and of an important task.[17]

It appears that Kazak intellectuals rolled up their sleeves to lift the Kazak language to a respected level. Another Kazak scholar described the new era for the Kazak language:

In 1989, the Kazak language was recognized as the language of the Republic of Kazakstan. Kazak became the language of science. The day for Kazak has arrived. We can accept the fact that this is a beginning for the Kazak people by turning to a saying which goes as follows: "Every language serves in forty different ways."

In education, two-thirds of three million Kazak children used to get their education in the Kazak language, and the rest of them used to be taught in Russian. In recent years, the Kazak language has also begun to take priority in the universities. It can be said that a new era has started that favors the Kazak language.[18]

Kazak officials and intellectuals have been eminently sensible over the language issue. While attempting to enhance the status of Kazak, which became the language of the republic and is becoming the language of instruction in schools, policy makers have prudently recognized the reality of Russian. As a result, articles on the status of the state language have seen major changes in regard to the status of Russian. When the first law on the State language was passed, the situation among Kazaks was pointed out in a joint article by Kazak scholars. It shows the level of linguistic assimilation on one hand and

---

17 Kamal SMAILOV: *Oianghan oilar*. Almatï: Zhalïn, 1991, p. 238.
18 Rahmanqul BERDIBAEV: "Kazakh literary language and its development" (July 24, 1991), Department of Near Eastern Languages and Civilization of the University of Washington, Seattle.

linguistic awareness on the other. The study depending on the 1989 Census, in other words the last Census in the Soviet era, gives the numbers. The level of knowledge of the ethnic language among Kazaks is the following: a) Those not assimilated and who know only Kazak 39,6 %; b) Those not assimilated and who know the Kazak language as dominant 60,95 %; c) Those assimilated and know Russian as dominant 0,25 %; and d) Those assimilated and know only Russian 0,12 %."[19]

The following articles present the subtle changes in the society. Nevertheless, these adjustments do not necessarily mean that the language issue is over. These unsettled policies received criticisms as well. Even some scholars worry about the future of the Kazak language against Russian. A close examination will show it clearly.

(Excerpt) from the law on language passed on September (Qïrqüyek) 22, 1989:

Article 1. The Kazak language is accepted as the language of the Kazak SSR.

Article 2. The Russian language is accepted as an international language in the Kazak SSR.

The Kazak SSR guarantees the free use of Russian as equal to the language of the State, Kazak.

(Excerpt) from the Constitution accepted after having been discussed by all groups during the Ninth Session of the Supreme Council of the Republic of Kazakstan held in December 1992.

Article 8. In the Republic of Kazakstan, the State language is Kazak.

The Republic of Kazakstan guarantees the Russian language free usage equal to the State language.

It guarantees the rights of citizens to use their own language. Right after this event, on November 26, 1992, President Nazarbayev spoke at a meeting in the Muhtar Avezov Theatre during the Second Kurultay of The Kazak Tili Foundation. He said: "What is possible today may not have been possible yesterday, what is not possible today may be possible tomorrow. However, the place of the mother

19 Elenora SULEIMENOVA, Dana K. AKANOVA: Kazak dili ve 1990'lardaki yeni dil politikası. *Türkler*, vol. 19. Ankara: Yeni Türkiye Yayınları, 2003, p. 414.

tongue and respect for it may not be filled, and the negligence of it may cause a danger for our nation. If a future generation in the steppes of Kazakstan sadly does not converse in the Kazak language which exalts the souls, dangers may present themselves. Thanks God, people have pulled themselves together and understood that there exists no bigger treasury and honour than the mother tongue before it is too late."[20]

> (Excerpt) from the copy that was announced after a heated discussions among the deputies during the second meeting of the Ninth Session of the Supreme Council of the Republic of Kazakstan held in January (*Qantar*) 1993.

> Article 8. In the Republic of Kazakstan, the State language is Kazak.

> The Russian language is recognized as an international language.

> The State guarantees the usage of the international language and other languages and their development.

The Supreme Council of the Republic of Kazakstan passed this draft as it stands, announcing it on January 25, 1993.[21] A draft for the official language in the Constitution of the Republic of Kazakstan has received a great deal of attention from parliamentary representatives of the regions, intellectuals, and the public. During the Ninth Session of the Supreme Council of the Republic of Kazakstan, more than one hundred delegates, including President Nursultan Ä. NAZARBAEV, commented on the language law. As a first speaker, he referred to the right of having the Kazak language as an official language in the Republic as planned in the Constitution.[22]

President Nazarbaev also expressed his concern about the Russian language being given equality with the state language, Kazak. The representative of Qostanay Oblast, JETIQARA, said that his con-stituency wanted the constitution to show that Kazak and Russian stand side by side as the official languages of the Republic. As has been shown, all these different language laws stress equality in the use

---

20 Savitbek ABDRAHMANOV: *Tavelsizdik shejiresi*. Astana: Elorda, 2001, p. 47.
21 Til turalï zangnan-ata zanggha deyin. (Editorial). *Ana Tili*, no. 5 (169), February (*Aqpan*) 4, 1993, p. 1.
22 Ibid., pp. 2–3.

of Russian. With this definite provision for the use of Russian and other languages, it seems that despite the tolerance in President Mikhail GORBACHEV's era, it would have been impossible to make Kazak the exclusive official language. However, there is a strong sentiment in favor of Kazak in the arguments of the law's proponents. The only difference between these different articles on the language situation was the emphasis on Russian. In each, Kazak is recognized as the language of the state whereas the change was on the Russian language being lingua franca or just one of the other languages in Kazakstan. This is to eliminate the reason for using Russian all the time. However, in contrast to the intellectuals' effort to avoid having Russian as a lingua franca, in the final draft of the Constitution Russian was granted international status.

In point of fact, as stated earlier, Kazak intellectuals still deem the language an essential component of national identity and worry about the danger in having a weak language for the future of Kazak. For example, a Kazak from Semey Oblast pointed to the possible danger or inevitable worsening of the situation of the Kazak language as a consequence of having two languages as official languages. Moreover, he offered a subtle change in the draft:

I would state that the Kazak language is the language of the Republic. But, we guarantee the free use of the languages of other ethnic groups and nations in the Republic.[23]

The representative of the Sozaq Region, Northern (*Ongtüstik*) Kazakstan Oblast, referred to the present language law of the Republic of Uzbekistan and suggested that Kazakstan should have a similar one. The pertinent article states that Uzbek is the language of the Republic and that the Republic of Uzbekistan respects and guarantees the free use of the languages of all those who live in the Republic.

There are some representatives in the parliament, mostly Kazak, who not only oppose the latest draft saying that Russian is to be used equally, but also the idea of having two languages together as the languages of the state. A Kazak from the Arïs Region of Northern Kazakstan states his case:

A nation without a language is a dead one. Long-time

---

23   Ibid., p. 2.

oppressive politics restricted and diminished our language. We worry about and speak eloquently in our own language. When the day comes, who is going to worry about the Kazak language? Of course, this nation itself is. It is right to respect and let other languages flourish freely.

Many people are speaking about language.

Some say that Russian should be granted the same national/official level as Kazak. Who will ensure that those who support this two-languages idea will not demand to have Kazakstan divided into two countries with two flags?[24]

A Kazak academician approaches the issue from a different perspective. He says that "Russian is widely accepted and a lingua franca. What else does it need? Nothing." He suspects that there must be another reason for Russian continuing to be a dominant language. According to him, those who favor this plan want to have these two languages compete. And, this would amount to diminishing the Kazak language because it just cannot contest Russian. Another Kazak, a renowned writer, states that none of the other fourteen non-Russian republics has claimed Russian as equal to their own language. He argues, therefore, that it is time to change the three-year-old draft concerning language.[25]

As said earlier, language is only one of many components of national identity. Therefore, in the process of nation-building, Kazaks have paid attention not only to their language, but also their past.

Kazaks and Russians, and of course some other ethnic groups, even today live and work side by side using only Russian. Among themselves, they could only communicate in Russian due to the lack of Kazak language knowledge within the groups other than Kazak. This slows down the process. Even if some Russian speaking minorities show their respect and willingness to learn the official language saying that, as they live in Kazakstan, they are supposed to learn and use the language. For instance, the Center for Kazak language headed by Jenibek NELIBAYEV organized a contest among non-Kazak people. As a result, the journal *Ana Tili* announced four

---

24 Ibid., pp. 2–3. Til üshin küres-qasiyetti küres (Editorial). *Ana Tili*, no. 50 [162], December 17, 1993.

25 Ibid., p. 3.

young people together in a picture as the winners with some captions and smiles. Pavel PETROV, a student in the Military Academy in the Turksib region, Irina KIM, a student of the Faculty of Economics in the Jetisu region, Nadejda REGULOVA, a student of the New Technology College, and Nataliya KUTSAYA, a student of the 160th Middle School. Apart from the photo, there are two others announced as winners: Natello LITKE, a college student from the Avezov region and Diana KLIMOVA, a student of the Almatï State Conservatory.[26]

Finally, the language law passed on July 11, 1997 approved the Kazak language as the official language and clarified the usage of Russian describing it as equal to it.[27] Kazak scholars praised the changes in the society after the Constitution had been passed. They analized it as "linguistic normalization:" "The announcement of the Kazak language as the official language in Kazakstan made an outstanding impact on the matter in favor of the Kazak language. This encouraged the process of linguistic normalisation, balanced the functional relation between the Kazak and Russian languages, and from a social point of view, the Kazak language began to be used in many and important places to the necessary extent. All this helped that the evaluation of the linguistic situation move in a positive way."[28]

The Kazak language has not come to this point without any efforts from concerned groups of Kazak society. One of them was and still is the Kazak Language Society. As an outcome of the freedom given by the openness (glasnost') policy in the late 1980s, intellectuals founded the Kazak Language Society, which worked in co-operation with the Party and Soviet organizations, and gave priority to bringing the problems regarding language into discussion. At its first congress, this society adopted the slogan: "The fate of your mother tongue is in your hand, the responsibility for it is around your neck," and one of the most fundamental objects of the Society was to try to pass the law on the new status of the Kazak language. As a result of this action, the Kazak language received formal recognition in 1989.

The fate of Kazaks living outside Kazakstan also receives a great

---

26 Olar Kazaksha soleidi. *Ana Tili*, no. 39 (566), September 27, 2001, p. 2
27 Elenora SULEIMENOVA, Dana K. AKANOVA: Kazak dili ve 1990'lardaki yeni dil politikası. *Türkler*, vol. 19. Ankara: Yeni Türkiye Yayınları, 2003, p. 410.
28 Ibid., p. 410.

amount of attention from intellectuals. A Kazak poet, for example, expresses his concern about the need for publications to reach Kazak writers and poets living in China, Mongolia, and other countries. In 2001 a competition was organized among Kazak writers devoted to the 10th Anniversary of independence in Kazakstan. Tursinbay ZAKENULI, a recent immigrant from East Turkestan and currently lecturing Chinese and Chinese history at the Gumilev Eurasian State University in Astana, won a price with his novel on the life of Chingiz Khan.[29] This evidence shows that, as an immediate response to the new sovereignty of their language and of their people, Kazak writers and intellectuals are trying to bring together their own people back under the name "Kazak", and to help them rally around the Kazak language. They are making an effort to rid people's minds of Sovietness and to fill them with "Kazakness" in the short run.

One Kazak literary historian mentions a number of names of Kazak literary figures who disappeared, suffered from political oppression, or were dismissed from their positions.[30] However, Kazak intellectuals are now in a position from which they can control the future of their society. In order to have command of the ongoing nation-building process, intellectuals try every possible way. One of many ways to serve an emerging Kazak identity is to change the names of streets, schools, squares, and so on. For example, a Kazak pointed out that converting names to Kazak should be equivalent to having independence for their country:

Our country has gained its independence. Our republic has become an individual nation (*memleket*). So now, is it not necessary for our names to correspond to our families, and to be pronounced and written according to the Kazak language's own rules?[31]

Kazaks see their independence far from complete without having their language free of outside influence. Therefore, they have begun to purify its terminology from influences of Russian and other foreign

---

29 A. JUMABEKULI: Bas baygeni Shingis Khan jaili roman jengip aldi. *Qazaq Ädebieti*, no. 1 (2735), January 1, 2002, p. 3.
30 Rahmanqul BERDIBAEV: "Tokpe Aqïndar", at a conference held on August 8, 1991, at the University of Washington, Seattle, Wa. (Unpublished paper).
31 Bayïnqol QALIÛLÏ: Atï-jönimizdi qalay Qazaqshalaymïz? *Qazaq Ädebieti*, October 9, 1992, p. 7.

languages. For example, the street right behind the Parlament in Astana bore the name Komsomolskaya. It is now called Jeltoqsan indicating the national awakening in 1986.

In this process, one should mention an article by a Kazak researcher. She did an outstanding job in pointing out all kinds of changes in this sense. For example, *Sotsiyalistik Qazaqstan* which had served the Kazakstan Communist Party as a central publication changed its name to *Egemen Qazaqstan* (Independent Kazakstan). *Leninshil Jas*, the komsomol (youth organization) journal, followed it with the new name *Jas Alash* (Young Alash) indicating the national awakening early in the 20th Century. The word "soldat" was replaced with its Kazak counterpart "ulan" despite its long-term service within the Red Army. Cities such as Tselinograd (city of grain), Pavlodar (gift for Pavel, Russian Tsar), Panfilov (Russian general who lost his life during the Second World War), Petropavlovsk (Petr and Pavel, Russian Tsars), and many others changed their names to Kazak ones: Aqmola (later Astana), Kereku, Jarkent, and Kiziljar respectively. The names of Stalin's victims such as Magjan JUMABAYEV, Turar RİSKULOV, Jusipbek AYMAVİTOV, and so on were given to cities, villages, streets, and schools making them immortal. In Semey one of the universities was named after SHAKARİM who was exiled during the Stalin period. Names like LENİN, KİROV, MARX, DZERJİNSKİY, and the like began to disappear from everywhere including history books.[32] This Kazak researcher went even further pointing out the fact that since the beginning of independence, Kazaks started naming children Beybars, Kabanbay, Bogenbay, and Tomiris to show respect to their past.

Between 1953 and 1980, after about a thousand Kazak schools had been closed, some began to reopen after 1991. Along with Kazak schools, books that had been waiting underneath the desks for some seventy years have also begun to reappear in print. Despite these rapid changes, however, it would be unrealistic to expect things to turn around right away. The results of change have been in evidence in recent years. It has been this hope that has kept the spirit of Kazak

---

32 Almagül ISINA: Sovyetler sonrası Kazakistan leksikolojisindeki değişiklikler. *Bağımsızlıklarının 10. Yılında Türk Cumhuriyetleri*. Ed. by Emine Gürsoy-Naskali and Erdal Şahin. Haarlem, NL: SOTA, 2003, pp. 91–104.

identity alive among the Kazak people, allowing the Kazak language to survive the alphabet shifts and harsh restrictions.

Forging a new alphabet
Having certain visual script symbols is very important for the development of a group identity. In this respect, the Kazak language has shared with other Turkic languages of Central Asia, as well as languages of the former Soviet Union other than Russian, the common fate of alphabet shift one after another.[33]

The replacement of the Arabic alphabet, first with a Roman script and then with a Cyrillic alphabet, made its impact upon the people of the region by restricting the use of their native languages to certain limited functions. Thus, they could use Kazak only at home, at rituals, or to greet one another. The imposition of what is called the "alphabet revolution" meant compelling the Central Asian nationalities "to abandon their ancient cultural tradition dating back through centuries and symbolically expressed in their alphabets."[34] The Arabic alphabet was a link between people and their religion, Islam. Thus, by abandoning the Arabic alphabet, this policy cut ties between the people and their faith. Over the decades it also helped the former Soviet ideologists to administer an anti-religious or anti-Islamic education for Central Asians in general. One scholar, after interviewing ordinary people in the region, reports the willingness of the people to return to one of the previous alphabets:

The effect of the replacement of the Arabic script with Latin (i. e. Roman) was to limit the use of Kazak to homes and the streets, making the Kazaks functionally illiterate in their own language. [...] Only in 1989 did the balance of power begin to change significantly. Besides the freedom-of-conscience law, which reconnected the republics to the roots of Central Asian culture, another new law allowed them to use their own language again. Now Kazak, Uzbek,

---

33 Orhan Cem BABAKURBAN: "The symbolism of ABC, ABV, or ALIFBE in the quest for group identity in Central Asia." Preliminary Research Report for the Seminar in Central Asian Studies, supervised by Prof. Edward Allworth at Columbia University of New York City, April 7, 1991, p. 4. (Unpublished)
34 Walter KOLARZ: *Russia and her colonies.* New York: Frederick A. Praeger, 1952, p. 34.

Kirgiz, Tajik, and Turkmen are all gradually replacing Russian as the official government languages; in Kazakstan, certain jobs are restricted to speakers of Kazak. All five republics also have plans to revert eventually either to the Latin or the Arabic alphabet.[35]

The sentiments concerning these alphabet changes were bitter. Like other Central Asian peoples, the Kazak people had lost touch with their written history, literature, language, and therefore, with their culture prior to the twentieth century. The introduction of a new alphabet after abandoning the Arabic one, "was an excellent means of weeding out all books of the existing literature of the peoples of the U.S.S.R. which were imbued with the spirit of the past."[36]

Recent script reforms in Kazakstan, as well as in other Central Asian republics, began during the *perestroika* and *glasnost'* period. Since then, the intellectuals have been openly discussing the alphabet issue. In response to President Mikhail GORBACHEV's new policies, many Kazak intellectuals have increasingly asserted their right to gain greater access to their literary and cultural heritage. Several Kazak writers, philologists, and literary experts advocate expanding the study of the Arabic script in higher educational institutions and introducing it as a subject in secondary schools. The same kind of concern appeared among the intellectuals in the independent Central Asian states after the disintegration of the Soviet Union in 1991.[37]

An editorial article entitled "A Joint Alphabet Is Necessary" concerned with adopting a joint alphabet among the Turkic speaking peoples appeared in 1992.[38] This revolves around the Kazak saying "Türki tildi – tügel bol" which translates as "You, Turkic speaking people, unite!", and begins by telling a little story about an ailing man giving advice to his sons. Before he passes away, he wants to teach

---

35 Robin WRIGHT: Report from Turkestan. *The New Yorker*, April 6, 1992, p. 64.
36 Kolarz, p. 35.
37 Dissatisfaction on this score is by no means limited to Kazakstan. To examine the same sort of development in Uzbekistan, see John SOPER: Classical Central Asian language to be taught in Uzbek schools? *RL* 259/88, May 18, 1988; and *Saodat*, no. 10, 1988, p. 34, cited in "Restoring the Uzbek cultural heritage: Uzbek literary journal proposes study of ancient Turkic script" by Annette BOHR. *Radio Liberty Research*, RL 554/88, Dec. 5, 1988, pp. 1–3.
38 Ortaq alipbi kerek. (Editorial). *Ana Tili*, no. 38 (130), September 24, 1992, pp. 1, 6.

them a lesson in order to keep them together and strong in their life. He calls them around him. After giving each of them one or two small twigs of birch, he asks each to break the twigs. This they do easily. Then he wraps a handful of twigs and asks them to do the same thing again. This time, the boys cannot break the bundle. The father concludes by saying "if you walk one by one, you can be readily broken up. But, if you always keep together and do not separate, no enemy can break you."

Although this story is commonly known around the world, the time at which it was printed in Kazakstan makes it even more important there. For at the beginning of the process of building a new nation, it served to make an impact on the Kazak people, teaching them a good lesson. In addition to its lesson on the necessity of the unification among Kazaks, this article gives historical accounts of the alphabets which Kazaks have used. The reason that the past Soviet government introduced the Cyrillic alphabet is no longer good enough for the Kazak intellectuals. According to Soviet officials, the Romanized alphabet for Kazak was not well suited to the loan words from the Russian language and from other languages. When it comes to the present situation, this article mentions the Kazak Diaspora's using three different alphabets: those who live in East Turkistan, Iran, Saudi Arabia, and other Muslim countries use the Arabic script, but have recently switched to the Roman script; those who live in Turkey use the Roman alphabet, and those who live in Kazakstan use a modified Cyrillic alphabet.

Recently, particularly after 1991, some intellectuals in Central Asia have been reiterating their complaint that ignorance of the Arabic script has made the literary past all but inaccessible to the reading public. As a result, some Kazak literary journals have already begun to introduce the Arabic script to their readers.

It is stated that "the very arbitrariness of any system of signs for sounds facilitated the assembling process."[39] Accordingly, intellectuals in all of the Turkic republics believe that a common alphabet can eventually bring the peoples of these republics closer together culturally and help them develop a close relationship on every level of

---

39 Benedict ANDERSON: *Imagined Communities. Reflections on the Origin and Spread of Nationalism*. London-New York: Verso, rev. ed., 1991, p. 43.

society. Scholars from the Central Asian republics, along with Azerbaijan and Turkey, gathered in 1991 in Istanbul for a symposium organized by the Institute of Turkic Studies at Marmara University. As a result of their deliberations they agreed to develop a joint alphabet based on the Modern Turkish alphabet, with five additions.[40] As yet it is not in use.

During this symposium, in addition to plans for a common alphabet for all Turkic peoples, Kazak scholars discussed the future of the Kazak language. Their opinions showed that there are three basic trends among intellectuals in Kazakstan in regard to developing a new alphabet or continuing with the Cyrillic alphabet. One of the five Kazak linguists who took part pointed out that "changing an alphabet is not a scholarly matter... the Kazak language has two or three unique letters. This is a matter of technology and organization. It is necessary to reach a common opinion." Meanwhile, another Kazak academician was concerned about Kazaks who live in East Turkistan. He makes his points by saying that:

The Uyghurs and Kazaks are using an Arabic alphabet. Despite the fact that they switched to the Latin alphabet fifteen years ago, and when after five or six years as they began to read the books and newspapers published in Turkey, the Chinese (Gov.) made them switch back to the Arabic alphabet. [...] If other Turkic peoples accept the Latin alphabet, they may be able to do the same thing. It is necessary to have a common alphabet.[41]

Since the fall of the former Soviet Union, different lines of thought have developed among intellectuals in Kazakstan; 1) Writers and historians over sixty years old want to reintroduce the Arabic alphabet. This is because most of the older Kazaks do not know their history; 2) After the 1917 Revolution, the masterpieces of Kazak civilization (culture) were printed in Cyrillic. Therefore, some of the intellectuals prefer the Cyrillic alphabet; 3) Around October 1991, the

---

40 For the signatories see Orhan SÖYLEMEZ: Final circular of the symposium on the contemporary Turkic alphabets (November 18–20, 1991). *UmidHope*, vol. 1, no. 1, Spring 1992, p. 21.

41 *Milletlerarası Çağdaş Türk Alfabeleri Sempozyumu, 18–20 Kasım 1991* (Symposium on the Contemporary Turkic Alphabets (November 18–20, 1991). İstanbul: M.Ü. Türkiyat Araştırmaları Enstitüsü, 1992, p. 32.

journal *Ana Tili* published an article which discussed the necessity of adopting the Roman alphabet from academic, political, and economic perspectives, and debates about the Roman alphabet also began. In the Kazak Cyrillic alphabet there are forty-two letters, which makes it more difficult for Kazak children to learn their language. Russian children learn their alphabet in two or three months, whereas the Kazak children learn it only after four or five months; 4) One Kazak professor argues for an alphabet based upon the medieval seventeen-letter Orhun-Yenisei alphabet.[42] This alphabet is the earliest surviving alphabet used by the Turkic peoples.

Despite all these Roman alphabet tendencies, another participant raised the political aspects of the alphabet issue. According to him, there is propaganda strongly in favor of the use of the Arabic alphabet in journals, magazines, and on television. In some schools, he says, children even get their education in the Arabic alphabet. The Roman alphabet needs to be propagated. He suggests that instead of teaching different Turkic languages in the schools it would be more appropriate to teach the old language of the Orhun inscriptions.[43]

Some of the Turkic-speaking republics have already begun using the Roman script for writing. For example, the Parliament of Azerbaijan has already passed a law on the use of the Roman script instead of the Cyrillic. The Parliament of the Republic of Uzbekistan did the same thing on September 3, 1993. Uzbekistan began using the new alphabet in 1995, and planned to complete the transition by the year 1999. Kazakstan's *Ana Tili* printed the headline of issue number 39, dated October 1, 1992, in three different alphabets, modified Cyrillic, modified Roman, and modified Arabic.

Alphabet change has not been the only preoccupation of Kazak intellectuals, however. Despite all these efforts by scholars and intellectuals of Kazakstan, those holding high-ranking positions in the administration of the Republic do not give priority to the alphabet issue. A Kazak official made it clear that priority goes to economy and political stability rather than to the alphabet issue.[44] He also mentioned

---

42 Ibid., p. 34.
43 Ibid., p. 53.
44 One of the People's Deputies of the Republic of Kazakstan and academician, Orazaly Sabdenovich SABDENOV, Chairman of the Supreme Soviet Committee on

that in the course of a gradual democratic process, the alphabet issue will eventually draw attention.

In contrast, some intellectuals want to get a more immediate result from these debates over the alphabet issue. For example, a Kazak specialist discusses the alphabet issue from a different perspective in an article entitled "Why are we thinking too much?" As an academician, he looks at the alphabetic graphics which were accepted for Kazaks and, in his opinion, there is no doubt that the Roman script would play an important role in the development of his country in the fields of economics, sociology, and politics. He presses his point saying that "nowadays, all of the Turkic peoples have awakened and seen that they are branches of the same tree. However, because of the variety of their writing systems in the Cyrillic alphabet, they are not able to see their common heritage and think accordingly." He continues:

Starting this year [1992], our Azerbaijani brothers switched to the Latin [i.e., Roman] script. For example, recently in Baku I bought a journal called Yurt (*Jurt*). The Gagauz people, who also gained their autonomy are also debating their alphabet problem in the journal *Ana Sözü*. But we Kazaks, why are we thinking so much about this? Having become an independent country, we need to take our fate into our own hands. We must think carefully about the detail, then make a decision.

After making his point, he introduces his own project for a joint alphabet for Kazaks as well as other Turkic-speaking peoples. His projected alphabet consists of thirty-one letters.

Even more important than the number of vowels in these alphabet plans is the exclusion of the Russian characters. An equally important point is the decrease in the number of letters. As discussed earlier, using fewer letters makes it easier for children to learn.[45] However, in recent years the alphabet issue seems to have been shelved and overshadowed by other important economic and social problems. A

Science and Education, talked to a group of scholars and students of Central Asian Studies during his visit to Columbia University in New York City on September 28, 1993.

45 Ghali NYTÏSHÛLÏ (from Enotaevka Village, Astrakhan State, Russian Federation): Nege sonsha köp oylanamïz? *Ana Tili*, no. 46 (158). November 19, 1992, p. 7.

recent article by a Kazak scholar seems to have ended this discussion. Articulating on the alphabet issue early in the 1920's, Dihan Qamzabekuli says "since we are to shift to the Latin scripts, let us keep in mind three important points; 1. Not to have many letters, 2. Not to accept any foreign (unidentified) letters, and 3. It should be not far away from the alphabet system used in the 1930s."[46] Following this article during the early days of the year 2003 through Internet, a new Latinized alphabet for Kazakstan was circulated, but nothing else came out in the matter.

President Nursultan Abishuli NAZARBAYEV attended the Kurultay of the World Kazaks in Almatï and delivered a speech in which he slightly touched upon the language issue but not the alphabet. However, the way that the latest language law describes the requirements for becoming a president is very important to keep in mind. To become a president for Kazakstan one should have been born in Kazakstan, be no less than thirty-five years old, one ought to have lived no less than fifteen years in Kazakstan, and, the most important, be able to speak the State language freely.[47]

As a last statement one should mention that there is a saying widely spread among the Kazaks, especially intellectuals. They ironically mock the situation of the Kazak language issue by saying "we talk and discuss about the condition of our own language using Russian!" This makes them laugh as well as consider the issue deeply.

---

46 Dihan QAMZABEKULI: Qazaq ziyalilarining alipbi aytisi. *Qazaq Ädebieti* no. 50 (2732). December 14, 2001, p. 11.

47 Article 42/2, cited in Bilgehan Atsız GÖKDAĞ: Kazakistan Cumhuriyetinin dil siyasetine sosyo-linguistik bir yaklaşım. *Türkler,* vol. 19. Ankara: Yeni Türkiye Yayınları, 2003, p. 415.

Lalitavajra as a Promoter of Manchu and Mongol Buddhist Literature

Hartmut WALRAVENS (Berlin)

The album

In 1976 a magnificent album of the pre-existences of the lCaṅ-skya Qutuɣtu was shown at a Cologne exhibit of *Buddhist Art from the Himalaya*, mainly from the collections of Werner SCHULEMANN[1] (1888–1975), professor of pharmacology at Bonn University. The name may ring a bell – the collector was a brother of the celebrated author of the *History of the Dalai Lamas*, Günther SCHULEMANN (1889–June 15, 1964). The album attracted some attention as the brilliant colourful miniatures were accompanied by quadrilingual captions (Tibetan, Mongolian, Chinese, Manchu) with the Mongol and Manchu ones rhyming in alliteration. It was soon pointed out that this treasure might be identical with a similar album formerly in the possession of the Berlin Museum of Ethnology and unaccountably lost after WWII. It was not removed to the Soviet Union like so many "trophies" from German collections but had found its way into the art trade. The collector kindly restituted it to the Berlin Museum as soon as the provenance was proven. Fortunately, it was already described by Albert GRÜNWEDEL as early as in 1885 – still the most detailed investigation.[2] Later on it was briefly mentioned by Klaus SAGASTER und Karl-Heinz EVERDING.

The album is entitled:

bstan-pa'i rtsa-lag-byams-brtse-kun-gyis spyi-bo-nas dbaṅ-bskur-ba rgyal-srid-chen-po'i slop-dpon-lCaṅ-skya-hu-thog-thu'i 'khruṅs-rabs bco-lṅa-la gsol-ba 'debs-pa

---

1   See R. O. MEISEZAHL: In memoriam Dr. Werner Schulemann (1888–1975). *Tribus* 26.1977, 7–9, Portr.
2   Notizen zur Ikonographie des Lamaismus. *Original-Mittheilungen aus der ethnologischen Abtheilung der Königlichen Museen zu Berlin* 1.1885, 38–45, 103–131, 1 ill.

Guanding pushan guang ci da guoshi Zhangjia Hutuketu shiwu shi xiang zan
灌頂普善廣慈大國師章嘉胡圖克圖十五世像讚
Šajin-i ündüsülügči tükemel sain tangsuk nigülesküi-tu yeke olon-un bakši Jangja Qutuɣtu-yin arban tabun türül-ün jalbaril maɣtaɣal
Śajin ba ulara bireme sain ambula jilangga amba gurun-i baksi janggiya hôtuktu-i tofohon jalan-i nirugan maktacun

Grünwedel translated the Tibetan title as "A plea[3] to the fifteen generations of the august teacher lCaṅ-skya Qutuɣtu, the powerful victorious, who received the consecration (abhiṣeka) on his head by all the teachers who investigated the root of the religion" which is supported also by the Mongol version while the Chinese and Manchu versions slightly differ: *xiang zan – nirugan maktacun* means just "pictures and eulogies".

The descendancy line as explained by Grünwedel is:

Gr 46: Ñan-thos dgra-bcom-pa Cunda
Gr 11: Grub-dbaṅ Śakya-bśes-gñen
Gr 50: Darpanâcârya
Gr 90: Lo-chen Ka-ba-dpal-brtsegs
Gr 66: dPal-ldan Rig-'dsin-sgro-phug
Gr 28: 'Gro-mgon Si-si-ri-pa
Gr 56: 'Dul-'dsin rDo-rje-seṅ-ge
Gr 74: 'Phags-pa bLo-gros-rgyal-mthsan
Gr 42: rJe-btsun bsod-nams-rgyal-mthsan
Gr 75: Byam chen chos-rje
Gr 40: rJe-btsun chos-kyi rgyal-mthsan
Gr 6: mKhas-grub dpal-'byor-lhun-grub
Gr 29: lCaṅ-skya ṅag-dbaṅ blo-bzaṅ chos-ldan
Gr 8: mKhyen-rab grags-pa-od-zer
Gr 30: lCaṅ-skya rol-pa'i rdo-rje

The last plate shows Lalitavajra (ill. 1–3) who is praised as follows:

---

3   *gsol-ba 'debs-pa* – to make a request.

Nenehe nenehei sain tacin forobun-i hôsun de.
Ne geren mergese ci colgorofi amba soorin de.
Nememe nomun-i baitangga sebjen be sebjeleme selgiyebuhe.
Nesuken śakgiya-i doin iśi danjun-i genggiyen:

With the power of the vow of the good teaching of antiquity,
on the seat of honour as he excels all sages of the present time
he makes the enjoyment in the application of the law spread more,
The priest of the gentle Śâkya, the light of divine wisdom and
religion[4], the Enlightened One.

Here is a description of the miniature, following Grünwedel:
This splendid miniature shows in its middle piece a portrait of the
religious dignitary on a red cushion, richly gold embroidered, with
blue, red and green borders, its back is light blue and surrounds the
figure like an aureole. A magnificent throne made of animals standing
on each other, and a back of dragons, Nâgî and Garuḍas, forms the
basis of it all. The great lama is sitting in the position of Tsoṅ-kha-pa,
only his left hand is in his lap. It is covered by a white cloth and holds
a golden Amṛta vessel, which sits in a dark blue bowl. The right hand
is held up and keeps with thumb and index, forming a mudrâ, the stem
of a lotus blossom; on both sides rose-red lotus flowers excel the
figure; they bear the attributes of TSOṄ-KHA-PA or MAÑJUGHOSHA.
The underrobe is purple, the vest purple with light yellow lining, a
rich, with golden beams and golden stars, fire-red robe flows around
the body. His right arm is bare. On his head he wears a round lemon-
yellow hat with three tall turned-up pointed flaps. The face – certainly
a portrait – shows a slight beard and lean, intelligent features.

The side figures include, upper middle: RGYAL-VA BSKAL-BZAṄ
RGYA-MTHSO; then follow in one row: 'JIGS-BYED, 'JAM-PA'I RDO-
RJE, GSAṄ-'DUS BDE-MCHOG; on the sides, left: TSHE-DPAG-MED,
below: PHYAG-RDOR 'KHOR-CHEN, on the right: SGROL-DKAR,

---

4   Here ROL-PA'I RDO-RJE's dharma name is quoted: ye-śes bstan-pa'i sgron-me
     which looks at first slightly puzzling in its Manchu garb: *iśi danjun*.

below: PHYAG-RDOR GOS-SÑON-CAN; below left: CHOS-RGYAL-GYI SGRUB YUM-BCAS, middle: MGON-PO PHYAG-DRUG-PA, right: LHA-MO.

During his visit to Jehol in Qianlong 45 (1780) the Panchen BLO-BZAÑ DPAL-LDAN YE-ŠES composed a rhymed eulogy on the 14 pre-existences of the lCaṅ-skya Qutuɣtu ROL-PA'I RDO-RJE. The Tibetan booklet was translated into Mongolian and published as *Getülgegči uɣuɣata tegüsügsen šasin-i geyigülügči degedü blama ɣuvan ding puu šan zi da gu srigi lcang sgya rin bo ce degedü qubilɣan beye tü-yin töröl-ün üyes-ece erkilen toɣurbiju jalbarin batu-da orusiɣulqu ünen üges-i ügülegsen süsüg-ün lingqua-yi delgeregülügči jögelen qura kemekü orusiba* (The mild rain which opens the lotus blossom of piety, by beginning, with true words most determinately describing in respectful prayer the personal preexistences of the liberator, the high lama who explains the perfect teaching, the august incarnation, the Guanding pushan guangci daguoshi 灌頂普善廣慈大國師 lCaṅ-skya the teacher jewel).[5]

UNKRIG's translation follows another, less preferable version, which was published as a folding booklet with illustrations.[6] The eulogy was apparently occasioned by a description of the emperor's descendancy line prepared by the Panchen in the VIIIth month of 1780.

While there are some factors to indicate a relationship between the Panchen's work and the palace album the matter seems to be more complex:
– The original Tibetan text of the descendancy line is not available for comparison for the album. Therefore only the text translated by Unkrig and a further trilingual text described by Heissig *PLB* (no. 153) which are at hand may be used for this purpose. The colophon of the

5   Walther HEISSIG: *Die Pekinger lamaistischen Blockdrucke* (abbrev. *PLB*) 152: Staatsbibliothek zu Berlin: Libri mong. 111; see also: W. A. Unkrig: Der Regen, der den Lotosblütenmund der Frommen voll erschließt. Ein Andachtsbüchlein aus der Feder des Taschi-Lama Blo-bzaṅ dPal-ldan Ye-śes. In mongolischer Fassung mitgeteilt und übersetzt. *Ethnos* 15.1950, 131–165.
6   Cf. Staatsbibliothek zu Berlin: Libri mong. 5; Heissig *PLB* 153.

former indicates that it was intended to prepare a popularized version of the Panchen's work – how close it may be to the original remains unclear. A preliminary comparison shows that

— the album gives 15 preexistences which are clearly identified and are described by eulogies (*maktacun*)

— the Mongol text gives 18 preexistences which are (at least partly) not clearly identified even if accompanied by woodcut illustrations. The texts are in the form of prayers (*gsol-ba 'debs-pa – jalbaril*), and thus each verse ends in *jalbarimui*. The last lines of the verses of the album, however, give the names of the incarnations.

— The first eulogy of the album and the fourth prayer of the Mongol text refer to Cunda, eulogy 15 finds a parallel in prayer 18. Subject to further investigation it seems as if the corpus of 15 incarnations was prefixed by another three deities, according to Unkrig's assumption, Sâkya T'ub-pa, Mañjusrî, and Târâ.

— The contents of the eulogies and the prayers are different, and also the alliteration schemes for corresponding verses are different.

At this point, one can only speculate that either the album is an independent creation by Buddhist court dignitaries, or that it is based on the Panchen's text and the Mongol version turned the descendancy line into a devotional popular prayer book. The latter view would be supported by the additional argument that the available sources credit the Panchen with establishing the descendancy line, not a booklet of prayers. In this context one may remember that the album uses in its title the terms *gsol-ba 'debs-pa – jalbaril* (prayer) for the Tibetan and Mongol version, but *xiang zan – maktacun* for the Chinese and Manchu versions. (s. above)

The portrait
Looking back at the portrait of Rol-pa'i rdo-rje (ill. 2), it seems to be quite different from the usual line of portraits that are extant in the form of thangkas. A number of them were made available through the Himalayan Art Centre on its website: portraits in the Ashmolean Museum, Oxford, the American Museum of Natural History (New York), Yonghegong, Peking, Field Museum of Natural History,

Chicago, etc. These thangkas (with the exception of one in a private collection, cf. ill. 4) present an elderly man whose face shows slight shadowing in the European fashion. It may be doubtful whether a pupil of the Jesuit Giuseppe CASTIGLIONE (†1766) was involved in painting it (as suggested in a description of one such portrait by Christie's) but there is surely Western influence. One would assume that the portraits show the lCań-skya in the 1780s.

The album, however, offers the portrait in a different setting, the lCań-skya looks much younger, no shadowing was applied to the face. Nevertheless it seems to have been taken from life as already Grünwedel assumed. The swelling on the right cheek is more pronounced than in the thangkas.

If we take into account that the portrait is part of an album of preexistences it comes to mind that the Panchen provided a descendancy line for Rol-pa'i rdo-rje. Also, as K.-H. Everding pointed out[7] the descendancy line was modified in 1794, so we have a date *ante quem*. Considering the supposed similarity to life, we might say before 1786.

In addition, the original collector of the album was the German ambassador to China, Max von Brandt[8] who reported that the album originated in the palace. This would make perfect sense looking at the careful and expensive style of both texts and miniatures. So does the text in four languages which points to the Qianlong emperor.

There is no indication what the immediate purpose of the album may have been – it might have been destined to become one of the imperial presents for the Panchen who alas! passed away in Peking in 1780.

Summing up, the album *might* have some connection with the establishing of the descendancy line by the Panchen in 1780; and we have the statement that it came from the palace – and it looks like

---

7   Karl-Heinz EVERDING: *Die Präexistenzen der lCań skya Qutuγtus*. Wiesbaden: Harrassowitz 1988. (Asiatische Forschungen 104.), p. 29.
8   Max von BRANDT, 1835–1920, see his: *Dreiunddreissig Jahre in Ostasien. Erinnerungen eines deutschen Diplomaten*. Leipzig: Wigand 1901. 3 vols.

work of the imperial workshops. So it *might* very tentatively be dated around 1781.

As mentioned, there is a major flaw in these arguments – the lCaṅ-skya looks younger than in the thangkas ...

Baron Alexander von Staël-Holstein described a document accompanied by the portrait of Rol-pa'i rdo-rje accompanied by five deities, in colour, dated 1770. Whether this might have any connection with the present picture remains unclear as there is no reproduction of the Peking copy available.[9]

The STAËL-HOLSTEIN document seems to confirm, however, that the descendancy line as we see it was not a creation of the Panchen but had been current earlier. Therefore the album may have originated much earlier as well, e.g. as a tribute to the lCaṅ-skya on the completion of one of his major projects, e.g. the Mongol Tanjur in 1749, the Dhâraṇî Collection 1759, or the printing of the trilingual Dhâraṇî Collection in 1767 ... It would still be a work of the palace artists and express the emperor's esteem of his friend and spiritual mentor.

Rolpa'i rdo-rje's literary work

There are several biographies of Rol-pa'i rdo-rje which are also available in Western languages.[10] For this reason it may suffice here to say that the Yongzheng Emperor saw to it that he was invited in 1724 as a "guest" to the imperial court where the eight year old boy was educated and became a lifelong friend of Prince HONGLI, the later Qianlong Emperor. He undertook several political missions and became the Emperor's spiritual mentor and adviser in religious mat-

---

9   Alexander von STAËL-HOLSTEIN: Remarks on an eighteenth century Lamaist document. *Guoxue jikan* 國學季刊 1.1923, 401–412.

10 E. Gene SMITH: *'The Life of Lcang skya Rol pa'i rdo rje'* in *Among Tibetan texts* Boston, Somerville: Wisdom Publications 2001, pp. 133–146. – Hans-Rainer KÄMPFE: *Die soziale Rolle des 2. Pekinger lCaṅ skya Qutuqtu Rol pa'i rdo rje (1717–1786).* (Beiträge zu einer Analyse anhand tibetischer und mongolischer Biographien). Diss. Bonn 1974. 394 p.
Xiangyun WANG: The Qing Court's Tibet Connection: Lcang skya Rol pa'i rdo rje and the Qianlong Emperor. *Harvard Journal of Asiatic Studies* 60.2000, 125 ff.

ters. While his original language was Tibetan, he was well versed in Chinese, Mongolian, Manchu and Sanskrit, and therefore the Emperor asked him to supervise Buddhist publication projects.

The first time the lCaṅ-skya became involved in major translation work seems to have been the case of the Mongolian Tanjur. According to the chronicle *Altan erike*[11]: "When in Qianlong 6 (1741), the Iron-Chicken year, he [Rol-pa'i rdo-rje] arrived, on account of a scheduled chanting of the Golden Kanjur, to pay his respects to the emperor he asked whether there were printing-blocks of the Kanjur and Tanjur?

As this remark made it clear that this would increase the well-being and benefit of the Teaching and the living beings, (the emperor) decreed that it was necessary to translate the Tanjur into Mongolian and ordered the Reverend [Rol-pa'i rdo-rje] to see to it."

Abbots, incarnations, qutuɣtus, dka'-bcu [དཀའ་བཅུ][12], doctors and güüsi [國師] who were proficient in Tibetan, Mongolian and theology were invited to Peking, from Tibet, the 49 Mongol Banners, and the 7 Khalkha and 8 Tsakhar Banners as well, and as of 1742, unter the supervision of both dignitaries, the Tanjur was "newly translated, the translations corrected and collated with the original". The translation work started in Dec./Jan. 1741/42.

The biography of the BLO-BZAṄ BSTAN-PA'I ÑI-MA (1689–1762) emphasizes as a special contribution of Rol-pa'i rdo-rje towards this work, that "His Holiness the knowledgeable lCaṅ-skya" had created "a vocabulary useful for the purpose of text collation". This *Merged ɣarqu-yin orun neretü toɣtaɣaɣsan dagyig* [*Dag-yig mkhas-pa'i 'byuṅ-gnas*] ("Die Bedeutungen festlegendes Wörterbuch, genannt Ort der Gelegenheit zur Hervorbringung von Gelehrten" [Heissig]), a Tibetan-Mongolian biglot, was compiled by Rol-pa'i rdo-rje in the short period from Qianlong 6, 1741, October-November to November-December 1742, Qianlong 7, with the cooperation of a large team of scholars.[13]

---

11 HEISSIG *PLB* 83.

12 Sarat Chandra DAS: *Tibetan-English dictionary*, p. 50: a Buddhist scholar who has acquired such great proficiency in sacred literature as to be able to interpret the meanings of a term in ten different ways.

13 HEISSIG *PLB* 85.

This terminological dictionary was of decisive importance for the development of a classical translation language. ...[14]

After the passing of the dGa'-ldan siregetü BLO-BZAŇ BSTAN-PA'I ÑI-MA the lCaň-skya Qutuγtu Rol-pa'i rdo-rje gradually moved forward to take the leading position in translation work. Thus, in 1748, he checked the critical *Bodhîcaryâvatâra* translation which was made for the Mongol Tanjur.

One year later, in 1749, the work on the Mongol Tanjur was completed. The imperial postface, dated 27.IV.1749 says:

"... to translate the Tibetan Tanjur into Mongolian, the execution of this work started from the last winter month of the Whitish Chicken year, Qianlong 6 (1741/2) onwards. It needed more than 8 years and came to an end by the first summer month of the yellow snake year, IV.1749. The 225 volumes of the complete Tibetan Tanjur with altogether 80.059 folios (resulted) in 108.016 folios in Mongol translation ...."[15]

In the same year, Qianlong 14, 1749 work started on a major new translation enterprise, namely the large collection of Dhâraṇî in four languages, *Dazang quanzhou* 大藏全咒.

Rol-pa'i rdo-rje also translated (around 1749) the Tibetan work *bslab-bya sñiň-po* into Mongolian as *Surtayun-u jirüken quriyaγsan* (Concise essence of teaching)[16].

He wrote by himself, using old guidelines like the personal instruction by his former teacher BLO-BZAŇ CHOS-'JIN a guidance called *Siditen-ü erketü zamboba-yin yosun-u qomšim bodisung-un ulayan kötelbüri rasiyan-u jici qayilumal kemekü ubadis orusiba* ("Red thread of Qomšim Bodhisattva for the ritual of the teaching of the powerful magician Zamboba, called the Purest of the Drink of Immortality").[17]

He also compiled a "Description of the White Pagoda, which is situated within the west gate of the imperial capital and evokes

---

14 HEISSIG *PLB* 87.
15 HEISSIG *PLB* 89.
16 HEISSIG *PLB* 99.
17 HEISSIG *PLB* 108.

devotion": *Qaɣan-u yeke balɣasun-u örüne-yin qaɣalɣa-daki čaɣan suburɣan-u ɣarcaɣ süsüg-i nemegülükči kemekü orusiba.*[18]

By the end of 1770 Rol-pa'i rdo-rje compiled the history of the famous Buddha statue made of sandalwood in the Candan juu monastery in Peking, *Candan joro-yin domoɣ ergiküi kemjiye aci tusa-luɣa qamtu tobčilan quriyaɣsan erdeni erike neretü orusiba* (The story of the sandalwood Buddha, narrated in brief, with the degree of its veneration and the merits [to be achieved], entitled Necklace of Jewels).[19]

In Qianlong 38 (1773) the printing of the large quadrilingual Dhâraṇî collection *Manju kitad mongɣol töbed kelen qabsuruɣsan bügüli ganjur-un tarni – Han-i araha Manju nikan monggo tanggôt hergen-i kamciha amba g'anjur nomun–i uheri tarni* (The Dhâraṇî of the whole Kanjur collected in Manchu, Chinese, Mongol and Tibetan) was completed (ill. 5–6). The large work comprises 10.302 Dhâraṇî and 451 Sutras; ... HEISSIG assumes that the translation work had started already in Qianlong 13 (1748) as several imperial decrees of that date are quoted in the *Tongwen yuntong* 同文韻統, a work that was appended to the Dhâraṇi Collection (preface 1750). That may well be. In his preface to the completed work dated 17.XI.1758 the Emperor emphasizes the principle of correct transcription of the Sanskrit sounds because otherwise the dhâraṇîs would lose their power. He continued: "Thus we have decreed to assemble many officials for proofreading the whole and these extracted the promulgated dhâraṇîs from the sutras and compiled them after receiving instruction from the national preceptor, the lCaṅ-skya Qutuɣtu. In this way the incomparably great work was completed, the dhâraṇî of the whole Kanjur collected in Manchu, Chinese, Mongolian and Tibetan."

Judging from this introduction the compilation was already finished in 1758. The imperial quadrilingual poem (ill. 7) which is repeated in each fascicle is dated 4th day of the summer intercalary month Qianlong 24 (1759) [i.e. 27 July 1759]. The work contains an index

---

18 HEISSIG *PLB* 116.
19 HEISSIG *PLB* 135.

and in addition imperially commissioned treatises on the transcription of the Sanskrit alphabet[20] and the pronunciation of the dhâranî.[21] The discussion of such issues is a consistent continuation of thoughts which had been investigated already during emperor SHENGZU's times by TOB ČIN WANG, the head of the Tibetan School GOMBOJAB and others. GAOZONG's intense interest in these philological and religious issues may be partly explained by his earlier studies of Sanskrit, together with the lCaṅ-skya Qutuɣtu Rol-pa'i rdo-rje, and his study of Buddhist-Lamaist fundamental works, as he himself said: "In my leisure time I studied also the whole religion of Buddha."[22]

There is also an edition of this work in three languages; it contains the same dated imperial poem like the quadrilingual version.[23]

Until lCaṅ-skya's time there were few translations of Buddhist texts into Manchu. Ch'ien-lung now suggested that lCaṅ-skya undertake the supervision of the translation of the entire Bka'-'gyur into Manchu. Working from 1772 through the late 1770's, the process went very slowly because lCaṅ-skya made final corrections and passed each volume on to the emperor for his personal approval, after which the colophons were prepared.[24]

The pentaglot *Sayin galab-un minggan burqan-u nere*[25], with colophon by Rol-pa'i rdo-rje, is sometimes credited to him but it was compiled by a certain DEM-CHI BSTAN-PA.[26]

---

20 *Han-i araha Manju nikan monggo tanggôt hergen-i kamciha ali g'ali.*

21 *Han-i araha Manju nikan monggo tanggôt hergen-i kamciha tarni hôlara arga.*

22 HEISSIG *PLB* 136.

23 H. WALRAVENS: *Buddhist literature of the Manchus.* New Delhi: International Academy of Indian Culture 1981, 8–9. – It is said that 200 copies of this version were printed in 1767. The Mongol transcription was added later on. See also H. Walravens: Eine unbeachtete dreisprachige Dhâranî-Sammlung in der Library of Congress. *Über Himmel und Erde.* Festschrift für Erling von MENDE. Hrsg. v. Raimund Th. Kolb und Martina Siebert. Wiesbaden: Harrassowitz 2006 (Abhandlungen für die Kunde des Morgenlandes 57,3), 475–489.

24 E. Gene SMITH: *Among Tibetan texts.* History and literature of the Himalayan plateau. Edited by Kurtis R. Schaeffer, with a foreword by Jeffrey Hopkins. p. 143.

25 Friedrich WELLER: *Tausend Buddhanamen des Bhadrakalpa.* Leipzig: Asia Major 1928. XXV, 268 p.

Rol-pa'i rdo-rje also wrote an introduction to a collection of 300 images, *ɣurban jaɣun burqan tu*; the artist, however, is unknown.[27]

The lCaṅ-skya Qutuɣtu also wrote a prayer to the tutelary deity of China: *Guan looye-yin öčig takil orusiba – kvan lha'i gsol mchod bžugs-so – guwan looye-i bokda be bolgomire nomun toktoho.*[28]

In 1784 he composed eulogies of Avalokiteśvara, and the Green and White Târâ: *Qomšim bodisadu-a noyuyan dâra eke cayan dâra eke-yin maytayal orusiba.*[29]

Also due to him was *Ariyuluyci jang üile üljei qutuy-un gamadani kemegdekü orusiba* (Exorcistic ritual, called the miraculous cow of affluence, Kâmadhâni). no d.

The Manchu Kanjur[30]

The lCaṅ-skya's last major publication project was the compilation of a Manchu Kanjur, by imperial command (ill. 7–9). Work started in 1773 after the emperor had thought about the undertaking already in 1772. It meant not only translating but also weeding out material which had crept into the Kanjur section of the Tripiṭaka but did not belong there. For the emperor it was not primarily a religious project as almost all Manchus knew Chinese by that time; for him it was in the first place a matter of national importance. Only a small number of copies was printed – we definitely know about 12 which were distributed to the imperial monasteries where Manchu was the liturgical language. One was given to the Panchen but at that time only

---

26 Heissig *PLB* 141.

27 *Lalitavajra's manual of Buddhist iconography* [ed. by] Sushama LOHIA. New Delhi: International Academy of Indian Culture 1994. 283 p.

28 Heissig *PLB* 149.

29 Drei Hymnen auf Guan-schï-yin, die Grüne und die Weisse Târâ. In mongolischer Fassung mitgeteilt, ins Deutsche übertragen und mit Anmerkungen versehen von W. A. UNKRIG. *Sinica* 17.1942, 266–274, 1 Falttaf. See also Heissig *PLB* 154.

30 See H. WALRAVENS: Der Mandjurische Kandjur. *Central Asiatic Journal* 51.2007, 77–153.

14 volumes were ready.[31] Later on part of the printing blocks and the printed folios were destroyed by fire. Nevertheless the emperor had the pleasure to see this important work finished during his lifetime. The editorial process had taken its time as the lCaṅ-skya was to do the final proofreading, and then each volume had to be approved by the emperor himself who tended to be particularly painstaking when his native tongue was concerned, and he certainly had a number of last minute corrections.

For many years the Kanjur was the least known Manchu text, and after WWII it seemed doubtful whether a complete copy had survived. Fortunately, a large number of the original printing blocks was found in the palace, and a complete printed copy surfaced at the Potala in Lhasa, so that in 2002, the Manchu Kanjur was printed again – partly from the original blocks.[32]

Like the Mongol Kanjur, the heavy wooden book covers of each volume were decorated with coloured miniatures (ill. 9–10) showing appr. 500 (different) deities. The captions are in Manchu and Tibetan; unfortunately they are not free of mistakes and inconsistencies. Also, much use was made of the Aligali letters, often in cases when they were not absolutely necessary, at least from a layman's point of view.[33] Just by applying the regular Manchu alphabet many Sanskrit names could perhaps have been rendered more closely to the original than was actually done. LUO Wenhua assumes that is probably due to the fact that the main supervisor, the lCaṅ-skya Qutuɣtu did not live to see the work completed[34], and the book covers were certainly at the end of the production line.

---

31 On October 28 Qianlong sent Panchen the printed Manchu translation of the Buddhist canon in fourteen cases, delivered by the Sixth Prince and Manchu officials.

32 *Manju hergen-i ubaliyambuha Amba Gʻanjur nomun.* Peking: Zijincheng chuban-she 2002. 108 Bde.

33 For a general discussion of the issue see G. STARY: An unknown chapter in the history of Indian writing: The "Indian Letters" (tianzhu zi 天竺字). *Central Asiatic Journal* 48.2004, 280–291.

34 *Qianlong Manwen dazangjing huihua Zang chuan fojiao zhongshen* 乾隆滿文大藏經繪畫藏傳佛教眾神. Peking: Zijincheng chubanshe 2003. 2 vols.

The passing of Rol-pa'i rdo-rje put an end to a period of busy translation and printing of works in Mongolian and Manchu which was never to be repeated.

Appendix: The Manchu eulogies of the album

Manchu is not a widely known language, and therefore it may be useful to make the texts of the *maktacun* (eulogies) of the album available. They are also nice examples of Manchu poetry – the alliteration is obvious. Practically all the specimens of this kind of court poetry that are known were composed by the emperor himself or some of the highest court officials.

Šajin ba ulara bireme sain ambula jilangga amba gurun-i baksi janggiya hôtuktu-i tofohon jalan-i nirugan maktacun

1
Enduringge šajin-i ejen Šigiyamuni fucihi-i
Eldengge hesei rasiyan be gingguleme wehiyefi.
Enteheme ilan jalan-i suingga bata be gidaha.
Erdemungge Šarwag'e-i bongko zunda-i genggiyen.

2
Amba Nagenzuna-i oyonggo šajin-i namun be.
Alifi jafame šajin de tusa arafi.
Akômbume jurulame dosire weesihun hafun be yongkiyaha.
Ambula sidi doro baha toosengge šakgiya šeniyen-i genggiyen:

3
Geren fuchi-i da fulehe oho baturu Manjusiri-i.
Genggiyen be dauhai bargašabume dahame ejelefi.
Getuken-i juwe jergi jurgan be hafu ulhihe.
Geren ci colgoroko sidi baha bancen darban azarya:

4

Fucihi-i nomun be jafara forobun-i hôsun.
Fulehe yongkiyangga nimanggi noho ba na de.
Fucihi-i hesei genggiyen be bireme akôname eldembuhe.
Fulu taciha amba lozawa g'awa balzik-i genggiyen:

5

Jakôn hacin heolen ula nomun be yooni ashôfi waliyame.
Jalandarakô cio sere bolgoi bade mutebun-i durun be tukiyefi.
Ja akô amba somishôn tarni cargi dalin de akônaha.
Japan-i wesihun ulhicun tarni be ejelehe ropukba-i genggiyen:

6

Amba gosingga jilangga bodi mujilen be deribufi.
Anan-i ninggun hacin-i ergengge be doobure ujen be alime.
Amba jilan-i bulekuśere fusa-i genggiyen be hargaśaha.
Akdacun oho ergengge-i ujui miyamigan sisiriba-i genggiyen:

7

Abida fucihi-i dosholome gosiha oyonggo fusa.
Akarakô beyei weri be gosire bodi mujilengge.
Amba fusa-i yabun cargi dalin de akônaha.
Akdacun wembure nomun be jafara dorji sengge-i genggiyen:

8

Ba na be uherilere han-i ujui miyamigan.
Ba bade fucihi śajin be ambarame badarambuha.
Baturulame fucihi-i ulan be sirara nomun toosengge.
Badarakô fusai yabungga enduringge lorui jiyalzan-i genggiyen:

9

Eiten fulehe aiman-i mederi cargi dalin de akônaha.
Elhe untuhun sasa banjire hafun be bahafi.
Ede tangkari yongkiyangga jakôn aiman be takôrśara.
Enduringge aitubure akdacun Sonom jilzan-i genggiyen:

10
Nesuken horonggo akdacun Zungk'aba fucihi-i nomulaha.
Nememe śumin narhôn hesei namun be ejelefi.
Ne amaga-i weilen be bireme akônaha.
Nemeyen mergen doro baha jamcin corji-i genggiyen:

11
Imata nikenjere holbohon-i jecen dalin akô doro.
Ineku doroi akômbume hafu ulhifi weri de.
Icihi akô sure ulhisu-i nomun be nomulaha.
Iletu ferguwecuke akdacun coiji jiyalz'an-i genggiyen:

12
Eiten suduri tarni-i oyonggo jurgan de ulhisu badarafi.
Ele śumin narhôn tarni ulhicun be iletulehe.
Ede tangkari-i tuwakiyangga sebe ahacilame takôrara.
Erdemungge mergen sidi baha baljur lunjub-i genggiyen:

13
Enteheme icihi akô ulhicun-i doro be sithôfi.
Eiten suduri tarni-i ubadis mujilen de fulhureme.
Ele urebume mutebuhe wesihun bodi de isinaha.
Enduringge hafu sure yongkiyaha jakba otser-i genggiyen:

14
Yaya tacin fonjin-i erdemu cargi dalin de akônaha.
Yayadame nomulara giyangnara banjibume arara de toosengge.
Yala tanggô tumen erdemungge mergesei ujui miyamigan oho.
Yargiyan nesuken horonggo fusa lobzang coidan-i genggiyen:

15
Nenehe nenehei sain tacin forobun-i hôsun de.
Ne geren mergese ci colgorofi amba soorin de.
Nememe nomun-i baitangga sebjen be sebjeleme selgiyebuhe.
Nesuken śakgiya-i doin isi danjun-i genggiyen:

UNKRIG translated the corresponding *jalbaril* of the Mongol text (Sven Hedin Collection, Stockholm) to no. 15, the maktacun for Rol-pa'i rdo-rje, as follows:

> Wiewohl am Ende der Zeit in Ansehn der Glaubenslehre des (Mannes) vom Zuckerrohr(hain)
> Finsternis herrscht. ist doch aus der Rüstung anderer Siegreicher
> Ja dank der Barmherzigkeit ein Trost erstanden – eine einz'ge Rettung:
> Ihr – meinem heiligen erlösenden Lama – gilt mein Fleh'n.

The translation of the corrsponding *maktacun* at the beginning of the article shows that both texts are completely different – another argument for an early dating of the album.

List of miniatures of the Manchu Kanjur

The following is an index to the Manchu names of the deities represented in the miniatures; the Tibetan names which also accompany each picture are not included. The Sanskrit identifications were provided on the basis of the Tibetan and Manchu names and the iconography by the editors of *Qianlong Manwen dazangjing huihua Zang chuan fojiao zhongshen* 乾隆滿文大藏經繪畫藏傳佛教眾神. Peking: Zijincheng chubanshe 2003. 2 vols.

The alphabetical listing makes it obvious that the same name was occasionally transcribed / translated in different ways. Especially the second part of the Kanjur makes much use of the aligali letters: unfortunately, this does not make the reading easier. Sanskrit k is represented by "g": Agṣobya fucihi but also by "g'": Ag'aśa garbha, and by "k": Akcubi fucihi; on the other hand, Sanskrit "g" is occasionally rendered "k": Aknebid'abhug'a. The situation with t and d is similar. Long vowels are sometimes represented in the transcription: A śle ṣaa, Aa radraa, often not: Ag'aśa garbha, Anurat.

"rāja" usually becomes "ranza".[35] Many more examples for these and other peculiarities can be found by going through the index.

This listing was mainly provided to prove that there is indeed a change in the transcription system somewhere in the middle of the huge work, no doubt connected with the lCaṅ-skya's passing.

In a number of cases translations were adopted or preferred, like Aisin mutehe fucihi, and Akdun yabungga. They were probably names already established earlier, and we know about the lCaṅ-skya's interest in the issue of proper rendering of names and terms. Thus he promoted the publication of the Thousand Buddha names.

For the purpose of this brief survey of the lCaṅ-skya's publication project no effort has been made to investigate the transcription method and to compare the miniatures (of which also a blockprinted version in red print exists) with the other extant Buddhist pantheons.

A samgaranza (Asaṅgarāja) 067-6
A śle ṣaa (Aśleṣā) 046-5
A t'amg'arama p'atma fucihi (Viśvakarmapadma) 070-2
Aa radraa (Ārdrā) 100-6
Abhi bodi fucihi (Vairocanābhisambodhi) 038-1
Abhi z'aniya ranza (Abhijñārāja) 108-2
Abida d'em dhare fucihi (Pīta-Tārā) 055-2
Abiz'ida (Abhijit) 105-3
Abizida (Abhijit) 013-6
Abkai aiman fusa (Ākāśagarbha) 024-2
Ad'ambihaya (Atāmāvihāya) 065-2
Ad'ayamasi (Atyantamasi?) 095-3
Ag'ara (Saṁbhava) 053-4
Ag'aśa garbha (Ākāśagarbha) 069-5
Agṣobya fucihi (Akṣobhya) 091-1
Aisin boconggo marz'yei (Kanakavarṇa-Tārā) 066-2
Aisin eldengge eme (Kanakāprabha-Prajñāpāramitā) 021-1

---

35 As W. A. UNKRIG pointed out earlier, this goes probably back to a misreading of "aa" – the second a was mistaken for an "n" (even if the diacritical dot in Manchu was missing).

Aisin mutehe fucihi (Kanakamuni) 084-1, 085-1
Akcubi fucihi (Akṣobhya) 025-1
Akdun yabungga (Vajrīputra) 088-2
Aknebid'abhug'a (Agni-Bhayatrāṇa) 073-3
Aligan wacir eme (Vajrasparśā) 064-7
Alin-i toosengge han fucihi (Śailendrarāja) 019-2
Alo (Vartālī) 099-3
Amba surengge eme fucihi (Prajñāpāramitā) 052-2
Amoghan amguśa homsima bodisado (Amoghāṅkuśa-Avalokiteśvara)
    060-2
Amoghap'aśa homsima bodisado (Caturbhuja-amoghapāśa-
    Avalokiteśvara) 060-1
Amtan-i wacir eme (Vajragandhā) 064-6
Amug'a darhini (Amoghadarśin) 006-2
Amugsidi (Amoghasiddhī) 093-2
Amuha fucihi (Amoghadarśin) 094-1
Ananda (Ananta-Nāgarāja) 007-6
Anggidan akdun yabungga (Aṅgaja) 086-2
Anila (Manila-Yakṣasenāpati)   077-5
Anurat (Anurādhā) 012-3
Anurdha (Anurādhā) 103-5
Ardir (Ārdrā) 009-7
Arg'amasi (Arkamasi) 094-3
Arya balo (Avalokiteśvara) 040-2
Aryadewa baksi (Āryadeva) 047-2
Aśfinii (Aśvinī) 047-5
Aslis (Aślesā) 010-6
Aśofinii (Aśvinī) 106-5
Aśog'a siri (Aśokaśrī) 012-2
Aśuwani (Aśvinī) 014-7
Atbasa śiri (Samantāvabhāsavyūhaśrī) 018-2
Atimugdibaśid'ii (Adhimukti-Vaśitā) 066-4
Ayurdhara beiśarwaṇa (Āyurvardhara-Vaiśravaṇa) 054-4
Az'ala (Acala) 067-5
Az'alaa eme (Acalā) 091-5

Bazra raga (Vajrarāga) 056-5
Bazra ranza 056-4
Bazra uṣniṣa fucihi (Vajroṣṇīṣa) 063-1
Beiḍuorya ranza (Vaiḍūryaprabhārāja) 107-2
Beiruz'ana (Vairocana) 064-2
Beiśarwana (Vaiśravana) 041-6, 058-6, 077-6, 078-6, 079-6, 080-6,
    081-6, 083-6, 084-6, 085-6, 086-6, 087-6, 088-6
Beiśarwani (Vaiśravaṇa) 001-6
Bharaṇii (Bharaṇī) 106-6
Bheikanfi (Bhairavī) 017-7
Bheirawa (Bhairava) 015-6
Bheirawa badi (Bhairavapati) 015-3
Bheirawa baramida (Bhairavapāramitā) 015-4
Bhikanda (Bhiṣanta-Bhairava) 016-4
Bhumi garbha (Kṣitigarbha) 069-6
Bi akô eme fucihi (Nairātmyā) 019-3, 072-2
Bida nata (Pīta-Mahākāla) 008-5
Bida nata (Vaśaṁkara-pīta-caturmukha-Mahākāla) 012-5
Bidi (Pīti-Bhairava) 016-6
Big'rnad'a śirigama (Vikrāntagāmiśrī) 104-1
Bikranda (Suvikrāntaśrī) 107-1
Bikranda g'amini (Vikrāntagāmiśrī) 018-1
Bimala (Vimala) 007-2
Bip'aṣyain fucihi (Vipaśyin) 082-1
Bira nandi (Vīranandin) 005-1
Bira sena (Vîrasena) 004-2
Birdazaya (Yuddhajaya) 103-2
Biringgirdi (Bhīṅgīriti) 005-3
Biro bakca abka (Virūpākṣa) 020-6
Biro rag'a abka (Virūḍhaka) 020-4
Birobakca (Virūpākṣa) 001-7
Birodaki (Virūḍhaka) 001-3
Biroo rag'a (Vaiśravaṇa) 075-4
Birtifi dewei (Pṛthivī) 004-3, 092-6
Biru bakca (Vaiśravaṇa) 074-6, 075-6, 076-6

Birubakca (Virūpākṣa) 041-3, 058-3, 077-7, 078-7, 079-7, 080-7,
    081-7, 083-7, 084-7, 085-7, 086-6, 087-7, 088-7
Birujag'a (Virūḍhaka) 041-4, 058-4, 077-3, 078-3, 079-3, 080-3, 081-
    3, 083-3, 084-3, 085-3, 086-3, 087-3, 088-3
Biruo rag'a (Dhṛtarāṣṭra) 074-4, 076-4
Birya gedu fucihi (Vīryaketu) 036-1
Biryap'aramid'ii eme (Kṣānti-Pāramitā) 082-5
Biśag'aa (Viśākhā) 103-4
Biśala beiśarwaṇa (Śyāmapīta-Vaiśravaṇa) 054-3
Biśarmana (Virūpākṣa) 074-7, 075-7, 076-7
Biśarmana abka (Vaiśravaṇa) 020-7
Biṣazai fucihi (Bhaiṣjyaguru) 034-3
Bisnu (Viṣṇu) 005-7
Biśowa uṣṇiṣa fucihi (Viśvoṣṇīṣa) 069-1
Biśowabhug'a fucihi (Viśvabhū) 089-1
Biśuwanara (Agni) 002-4
Bizayani (Vijayā) 018-3
Bolori eme (Śaraddevī) 021-5
Bolori-i okin tenggeri (Śaraddevī) 072-6
Boobai biyangga fucihi (Ratnacandra) 046-2
Boobai dengjan eme fucihi (Ratnadīpā) 023-1
Boobai elden badarara fucihi (Ratnārcis) 044-2
Boobai giyolonggo fucihi (Ratnaśikhin) 077-1
Boobai śu ilha fucihi (Ratnapadmavikrāmin) 019-1
Bornawaśo (Punarvasu) 010-3
Bośa (Puṣya) 010-4
Brabasa-śiri (Prabhāsaśrī) 012-1
Brad'ibanagui ḍam (Pratibhānakūṭam) 063-6
Brahama (Brahman) 004-5; 005-6, 008-2
Brahama dada (Brahmadatta) 009-6
Brahama p'arap'ha (Brahmajyotirvikrīḍitābhijña) 100-2
Brahama wabasa (Brahmajyotirvikrīḍitābhijña) 014-1
Bud'id'hi ud'gariṣta (Bodhyutkariṣṭa) 057-5
Budara bara zida (Jinarṣabha-Vaiśravaṇa) 084-5
Bunarbasu (Punarvasu) 046-3

Dayanap'aramid'ii eme (Dhyāna-Pāramitā) 089-3
Dengjan eldengge fucihi (Dīpaṅkara) 092-2
Dengjan-i eme (Dīpā) 045-7
Deza nandi (Anantaujas) 011-2
Dhaniṣza (Śatabhiṣā) 105-5
Dharma dhowaza (Dharmadhvaja) 062-3
Dharmabana fucihi (Dharmakīrtisāgaraghoṣa) 108-1
Dibamg'ara (Dīpaṅkara) 079-1
Dibangg'ara (Dīpaṅkara) 002-1, 080-1
Dibangg'ara fucihi (Dīpaṅkara) 051-2
Dig'ṣanoṣṇiṣa fucihi (Tikṣṇoṣṇīṣa) 050-1
Dirda rasda abka (Dhṛtarāṣṭra) 020-3
Dirdarasda (Virūḍhaka) 074-3
Dirdirasda (Dhṛtarāṣṭra) 041-5
Dirdirasta (Dhṛtarāṣṭra) 077-4, 078-4, 079-4, 080-4, 081-4, 083-4,
     084-4, 085-4, 086-4, 087-4, 088-4
Dirdirasta (Virūḍhaka) 076-3
Dirdisdiri (Dhṛtarāṣṭra) 001-4
Dirdista (Virūḍhaka) 075-3
Dirlogi banda (Trailokabandha) 017-5
Dirlogi baśa (Trailokavaśā) 015-5
Dirlogi naśa (Trailokanaśā) 018-5
Dirlogi tanma (Trailokadama) 016-5
Doksin eme fucihi (Caṇḍadevī) 023-6
Dorgi erlig han (Antarasādhana-Dharmarāja) 071-5
Du-i ragamaa eme (Dūraṅgamā) 091-6
Duin galangga z'onda (Sita-caturbhuja-Cundā) 061-1
Duwaz'adewei (Dhvajā) 108-5
Duwei di gusuma fucihi (Dvitīya-Kusuma) 035-2
Elabure fucihi (Cintamaṇi ?)) 075-1
Elhe obure fucihi (Subhakara) 081-1
Erihangge eme (Mālyā) 045-4
Esrun (Brahman) 024-4, 025-4, 026-4, 027-4, 028-4, 029-4
Esurun abka (Brahman) 019-4
Ferguwecuke jilgangga eme (Sarasvatī) 022-1

Gôlmamasi (Kulamasi) 095-4
Gômira (Kaumira) 050-3
Gôta garbha (Guṇagarbha) 065-5
Gubera (Kubera) 003-5
Gubheira (Guhya-Bhairava) 015-7
Gugud'sund'a (Krakucchanda) 089-2
Gulagumarii (Kula-Kumārī) 059-6
Gumba (Kumbha) 047-6
Gumbhadewei (Kalasī) 107-5
Gurdun jafaha eme (Cakradharā) 051-7
Gusuma fucihi (Kusuma) 035-1
Gusuma śiri (Kusumaśrī) 013-2
Haa syam eme (Hāsyā) 042-7
Hafu bulekuśere fucihi (Vipaśyin) 086-1
Hari fucihi (Śākyasiṁha) 033-1
Haritabasudhara (Manoharā-Vasudhārā) 054-5
Hasada (Hastā) 011-6
Hasd'aa (Hastā) 102-5
Hasd'abid'abhug'a (Hasti-Bhayatrāṇa) 073-6
Hiyan-i eme (Dhūpā) 045-6
Hiyan-i toosengge han fucihi (Gandheśvararāja) 029-1
Hondor mahag'ala (Caṇḍa-Mahākāla) 080-5
Hormosda (Śatakratu) 001-5, 026-6, 027-6, 028-6, 029-6
Hormosda abka (Śatakratu) 019-6
Hormosta (Śatakratu) 024-6, 025-6
Horon gidaśara fucihi (Vikrāntagāmiśrī?) 076-1
Hôturi fulehungge fucihi (Śūradatta) 047-1
Hôturingga okin tenggeri (Kālīdevī) 072-5
Hôturingga urgungga fucihi (Vīranandin) 044-1
I śuwara (Maheśvara) 005-4
Icihi akô fucihi (Vimala) 046-1
Icihi geterembure fusa (Sarvanivaraṇaviṣkambin) =26-2
Id'ibig'rnad'a (Suvikrāntaśrī) 103-1
Ig'ṣobhya (Akṣobhya) 056-1
Ilan tangkari mayamigan fucihi (Trisamayavyūha) 092-1

Indara g'ad'u (Indraketudhvajarāja) 102-2
Indara ged'u (Indraketudhvajarāja) 016-2
Indrabard'i fucihi (Indrarāja) 068-2
Inṣagumarii (Īrṣyā-Kumārī) 059-5
Iśana (Iśvara) 003-6
Iśowara (Iśvara) 068-3
Iśowara ranza (Iśvararāja) 062-4
Iwalogid'a (Avalokiteśvara) 069-4
Jalumbure fucihi (Pūrṇa) 074-1
Jana bheira (Jñāna-Bhairava) 016-3
Jemengge-i eme (Naividye) 042-4
Jilan-i bulekuśere fusa (Avalokiteśvara) 025-2, 043-2
Jilgan-i wacir eme (Vajraśabdā) 064-4
Juwan emu cirangga fusa (Ekādaśamukha-Avalokiteśvara) 045-2
Juwan emu cirangga homsima Bodisado (Ekādaśamukha-
    Avalokiteśvara) 073-1
Juwari eme (Varṣādevī) 021-4
Juwari-i okin tenggeri (Varṣādevī) 072-3
Kara zambala (Kṛṣṇa-Jambhala) 024-7, 025-7, 026-7, 027-7, 028-7,
    029-7
Kinsarbawa Homsima Bodisado (Ḍāk-Lokeśvara) 073-2
Kulig'a (Kulika-Nāgarāja) 007-7
Kulungge eme (Vādya) 044-3, 048-3
Kz'atibid'ibhug'a (Ḍāk-Bhayatrāṇa) 060-5
La sya eme (Lāsyā) 042-6
Labdu boobai serengge (Ratnāgni) 039-1
Laśleṣa (Aśleṣā) 101-5
Logi śuwara fucihi (Lokeśvara) 026-1
Lohô jafaha eme (Rahūdharā) 051-4
Maga bid'ibhug'a (Nāga-Bhayatrāṇa) 060-4
Maghaa (Maghā) 046-6
Maha bala fucihi (Mahābala) 032-2, 039-5
Maha g'asib (Mahākāśyapa) 023-2
Maha hma sag'ara fucihi (Mahāhimāsāgara (?)) 037-1
Maha siri dewei eme (Mahāśrīdevī) 085-5

Maha z'awara masi (Mahācīvaramasi) 096-3
Mahaa stanap'rasd'a (Mahāsādhanaprāpta) 065-3
Mahaa zana id'ri fucihi (Prajñāpāramitā) 057-1
Mahabala fucihi (Mahābala) 031-2, 032-4
Mahag'ala fucihi (Mahākāla) 031-4; 033-4, 034-4, 035-4, 036-4, 037-4, 038-4
Mahi śuwara (Maheśvara) 092-4
Maidari (Maitreya) 002-2
Maidari fusa (Maitreya) 027-2
Manjusiri (Mañjuśrī) 001-2, 054-2
Manjusiri fusa (Mañjuśrī) 028-2
Mansire eme (Nṛtya) 044-4, 048-4
Manutbhafi (Manudbhavī) 018-7
Mara dewei (Māradevī) 049-7
Marg'asar (Mṛgaśirā) 009-6
Margamasi (Markamasi) 094-4
Marigasira (Mṛgaśirā) 047-7
Marigasiraa (Mṛgaśirā) 100-5
Mazniyuśirii (Mañjuśrī) 070-4
Med're fucihi (Maitreya) 091-2
Med'ri (Maitreya) 070-6
Mek (?) (Mūlā) 012-6
Mek (Maghā) 010-7
Miha (Maghā) 101-6
Minadewei (Mīnā) 107-4
Mirdi śiri (Smṛtiśrī) 015-2
Mohagumarii (Moha-Kumārī) 059-3
Moo lam (Mūlā) 104-3
Morin-i bilhangga (Hayagrīva) 040-5
Mudara ranza (Mudrārāja) 063-4
Mukśan jafaha eme (Daṇḍadharā) 051-6
Nag'aranza iśora (Nageśvararāja) 004-1
Nama dewaśiri (Suparikīrtitanāmaśrī) 016-1
Nand'eramasi (Antardhānamasi) 094-5
Nandeward'i śiri fucihi (Nandivartiśrī?) 053-2

Narayana (Nārāyaṇa) 013-1, 099-2
Nayoorda bid'ibhug'a (Cora-Bhayatrāṇa) 060-6
Nesuken eme fucihi (Śāntidevī) 023-3
Nibara dambradont (Sarvanivaraṇaviṣkambhin) 070-5
Nila danṭa (Nīladaṇḍa) 039-4
Ninggun galangga (Ṣaḍbhuja-mahākāla) 030-4
Niyamangga fucihi (Vajragarbha) 042-1
Niyengniyeri eme (Vasantadevī) 021-3
Niyengniyeri-i okin tenggeri (Vasantadevī) 072-4
O sayoṣca (Jyeṣṭhā) 103-6
Okin tenggeri (Kālīdevī, Śrīdevī) 049-5
Okin tenggri (Kālīdevī, Śrīdevī) 030-5
Oṣadhi ranza (Oṣadhirāja) 065-4
P'ad'ag'ra masi (Padâkramamasi) 096-5
P'adali (Padali) 097-4
P'adme p'arap'ha (Padmajyotirvikrīḍitābhijña) 101-1
P'ala p'aramid'ii eme (Bala-Pāramitā) 089-6
P'amg'aza p'atma fucihi (Paṅkajapadma) 057-2
P'ara aśowag'a fucihi (Aśokottamaśrī) 106-2
P'aragra masi (Paragramasi?) 097-3
P'arilari nangird'i (Suparikīrtitanāmaśrī) 102-1
P'atma p'aṭa (Padmapattra) 067-4
P'atma ranza (Padmarāja) 067-3
P'atmadewei (Padma) 107-6
P'atmoṣṇiṣa fucihi (Padmoṣṇīṣa) 068-1
P'rabha wadi (Prabhavatī) 018-6
P'rahamidad'd'a fucihi (Brahmadatta) 095-2
P'raṇidhana p'aramid'ii eme (Praṇidhāna-Pāramitā) 089-5
P'ratid-habaśid'ii (Praṇidhāna-Vaśitā) 066-5
P'urwaṣaṭaa (Pūrvāṣāḍhā) 104-4
Poniyamo (Dūtī) 071-6
Pug'ana (Mekhila-Yakṣasenāpati) 075-5
Pukdadara (Anila-Yakṣasenāpati) 076-5
Rad'ana sadofi (Ratnasattvī) 052-4
Rad'ana sambhawa (Ratnasaṁbhava) 064-1

Rad'nap'atma big'rnad'a fucihi (Ratnapadmavikrāmin) 105-1
Rad'nosṇiṣa (Ratnoṣṇīṣa) 067-1
Rad'na jagi (Ratna-Ḍākinī) 043-4
Rad'na sambawa fucihi (Ratnasambhava) 055-1
Radna zandra fucihi (Ratnacandra) 094-2
Rag'anata (Rakta-Mahakāla) 007-5
Rahôla (Rāhula) 079-2, 080-2
Rakcasa (Nairṛti) 002-6
Rakda nata (Rakta-caturmukha-Mahākāla) 013-5
Rakdagumarii (Rakta-kāmarāja-Kumārī) 059-4
Ratna akni (Ratnāgni) 005-2
Ratna braba (Ratnaprabha) 003-2
Ratna sambawa (Ratnasaṁhava) 088-1
Ratna siki fucihi (Ratnaśikhin) 037-2
Ratna sparta (Ratnārcis) 062-6
Ratna zandara (Ratnacandra) 007-1
Ratna zandara brapa (Ratnacandraprabha) 006-1
Rebad'ii (Revatī) 047-4
Rewad'ii (Revatī) 106-4
Rid'ibaśid'ii (Ṛddhi-Vaśitā) 066-3
Rohiṇii (Rohiṇī) 100-4
Rowakini (Rohiṇī) 009-4
Sad'abhiṣaa (Dhaniṣṭhā) 105-4
Sada g'arma ubadiśag'a dhara (Ṣaḍaṅga-upadeśaka-Tārā) 054-6
Sadabis (Dhaniṣṭhā) 013-7
Sag'are nag'a ranza (Sāgara-Nāgarāja) 092-5
Śag'ya simha fucihi (Śākyasimha) 062-1
Sahaliyan Maṇjusiri fucihi (Kṛṣṇa-Mañjughoṣa) 059-2
Sain bihangga eme (Sukhaṇṭhī) 022-5
Sain cirangga eme (Sumukhī) 022-3
Sain dursungge (Rūpadhārin) 039-2
Sain funiyahangge eme (Sumatī) 022-4
Sain wa-i eme (Gandhā) 045-3
Sain yabungga eme (Sugatī) 022-6, 086-5
Saledara fucihi (Jinendra) 031-1

Samanda badara fusa (Samantabhadra) 029-2
Samnad'abathra (Samantabhadra) 070-3
Samsaradyod'a fucihi (Krakucchanda) 050-2
Śandi dewei (Śāntidevī) 049-3
Śangg'abala (Śaṅkhapala-Nāgarāja) 008-4
Sanggida (Saṇṭhila-Yakṣasenāpati)   078-5
Saniyana g'adu (Jñānaketu) 057-3
Saniyana p'arabha (Jñānaprabha) 057-6
Śanyan mahag'ala (Sita-Mahākāla) 043-5
Śanyan Manjusiri (Sita-Mañjughoṣa) 071-1
Śanyan manjusiri fucihi (Sita-Mañjughoṣa) 059-1
Śanyan sarangga fucihi (Sitātapatrā) 061-2
Śanyan śu ilha fucihi (Sitapadma) 043-1
Śanyan śu ilhangga (Sitapadma) 030-1
Śaradewei (Śaṅkhā) 108-3
Śaribudari (Śāriputra) 022-2, 081-2
Sarwa eme (Samantaprabhā) 090-6
Sarwa śeg'a ghad'ig'a (Sarvaśokaghātika) 057-4
Śarwan (Śravaṇā) 013-4
Śarwaṇa (Śravaṇā) 104-6
Sarwaruzi śiribyuha (Samantāvabhāsavyūhaśrī) 104-2
Satz'alo (Varahī) 099-6
Śayama nata (Kṣati-tāraka-nīla-caturmukha-Mahākāla) 014-5
Sengguwecun ci aljaha (Abhayaṁkara) 040-2
Sid'a iyoṣe fucihi (Sita-Amitāyus) 056-2
Sid'abaramid'a fucihi (Sita-Prajñāpāramitā) 063-2
Sid'ad'abad're fucihi (Sitāpatrā) 053-1
Śida beiśarwani (Sita-āyurbardhana-Vaiśravaṇa) 006-5
Sida nata (Sita-caturmukha-āyurvardhana-Mahākāla) 011-5
Śigiya singha fucihi (Śākyasiṁha) 038-2
Śigiyamuni (Śākyamuni) 001-1, 069-2, 093-1
Śigiyamuni fucihi (Śākyamuni) 024-1, 040-1, 042-2, 045-1, 051-1,
    052-1, 054-1, 058-1
Śilap'aramid'ii eme (Śīla-Pāramitā) 082-4
Simhabid'abhug'a (Siṁha-Bhayatrṇa) 073-5

Simhanada (Siṁhanāda) 050-5
Śiri buṣba (Kusumaśrī) 100-1
Śiri aśowag'a (Aśokaśrī) 099-1
Śiri barabha (Prabhāsaśrī) 098-2
Śiri bhadra fucihi (Bhadraśrī) 096-2
Siri dana (Śūradatta) 008-1
Śiri dewei (Kālīdevī, Śrīdevī) 017-4
Śiri samrid'yu (Smṛtiśrī) 101-2
Śiri z'andana (Candanaśrī) 097-2
Śiribarza dewei (Śrivatsā) 108-4
Śiridana fucihi (Śūradatta) 095-1
Śirii aśowag'a fucihi (Aśokottamaśrī) 062-2
Śirii fucihi (Śikhin) 082-2
Śirii zagd'a (Śrījagat) 067-2
Śirinariyana (Śrīnārāyaṇa) 042-5
Śirisuhasda (Bhagavan-Mahākāla) 044-5, 048-5
Sirwan za fucihi (Amoghadarśana) 027-1
Sniyanabaśid'ii (Jñāna-Vaśitā) 066-6
Somishôn erlig han (Guhyasādhana-Dharmarāja) 071-7
Soorya dewei (Ādityā) 092-3
Śu targama (Śūraṁgama) 053-5
Śubawadi (Subhadra?) 076-2
Subra disḍa fucihi (Supratiṣṭhita) 034-1
Subudi (Subhūti) 021-2
Śukla nata (Sita-cintāmaṇi-Mahākāla) 005-5
Sulag'ṣa nam (Suparikīrtitanāmaśrī) 107-1
Sumeru indaranza fucihi (Śailendrarāja) 105-2
Sumidii eme (Sādhumatī) 091-4
Suorya fucihi (Sūryaketu) 049-1
Surya (Ādityā) 004-4
Suwaraghoṣa fucihi (Svaraghoṣa) 106-1
Śuwari (Śvātī) 103-3
Suwayan boconggo mariz'yei (Pīta-Mārīcī) 066-1
Suwayan manjusiri (Pīta-Mañjughoṣa) 071-2
Ṭagi ranza (Ṭakkirāja) 039-3

Tarni śuwara fusa (Dhāraṇivaśita) 030-2
Toosengge eme fucihi (Īśvaradevī) 023-5
Tulergi erlig han (Bāhyasādhana-Dharmarāja) 071-3
Turśungga wacir eme (Vajrarupā) 064-3
Tuweri eme (Hemantadevī) 021-6
Tuweri-i okin tenggeri (Hemantadevī) 072-7
Ubap'adhibaśidii (Upapatti-Vaśitā) 061-6
Ubaya p'aramid'ii eme (Upāya-Pāramitā) 089-4
Ubendara (Upendra) 002-5
Ucun-i eme (Gītā) 044-7, 048-7
Ud'd'ara bhadrabadaa [Schreibfehler] (Uttarabhādrapadā) 047-3
Ud'd'ara p'hadrap'adaa (Uttarabhādrapadā) 106-3
Ud'd'ara pilgônii (Uttaraphālgunī) 102-4
Ud'd'arṣada (Uttarāṣāḍhā) 104-5
Udarabadarabat (Uttarabhādrapadā) 014-6
Udarapalguni (Uttaraphālgunī) 011-4
Udarasat (Uttarāṣāḍhā) 013-3
Urama (Uramasi?) 097-5
Usei eme (Phalā) 042-3
Uṣṇiṣa dhofiza fucihi (Uṣṇīṣadhvaja) 065-1
Utbala niyag'a fucihi (Nilotpala) 028-1
Wa-i wacir eme (Vajrarasā) 064-5
Wacir banangga (Vajrapātāla) 040-6
Wacir bani (Vajrapaṇi) 020-5, 069-3
Wacir cinggilakô eme (Vajraghaṇṭā) 051-3
Wacir dara (Vajradhara) 048-1
Wacir funiyehengge (Uṣṇīṣcakravartin) 040-3
Wacir g'ilaya (Vajrakīla) 093-4
Wacir g'rud'a (Vajrakrodha) 093-3
Wacir jafarangge (Vajra-Yakṣasenāpati) 074-5
Wacir jagi (Vajra-Ḍākinī) 043-3
Wacir mutgara (Vajramudgara) 093-6
Wacir sadofi (Vajrasattvī) 052-3
Wacir sadowa (Vajrasattva) 056-3
Wacir sosna (Vajragadā) 093-5

Wacirbani fucihi (Vajrapaṇi) 031-5, 032-5, 033-5, 034-5, 035-5, 036-
     5, 037-5, 038-5
Warahamuki (Varahamukhī) 098-6
Warahi eme fucihi (Vajravarahī) 019-7
Warali (Varālī) 097-6
Warni (Tejovatī) 018-4
Waruna (Varuṇa-Nāgarāja) 008-3
Waruna (Varuṇa) 002-7, 009-2
Waruna dada (Varuṇadeva) 010-1
Waśi dewei (Īśvaradevī) 049-6
Wasoki (Vāsuki-Nāgarāja) 008-6
Wesihun śu ilha fuchi (Agrapadma) 078-1
Yakca abarazida (Aparājita-Yakṣasenāpati) 087-5
Yama (Dharmarāja) 002-3
Yawadi (Yavati) 071-4
Yayade anaburakô (Aparājita) 040-4
Z'agradewei (Cakrā) 108-6
Z'andrig'a (Candaraprabha) 053-6
Z'ed'iśure (Sattva) 050-6
Z'edasiddhi (Sattvasiddhi) 068-4
Z'id'd'abaśid'ii (Citta-Vaśitā) 061-4
Z'zad'd'ridewei (Chattrā) 107-3
Zadi gusuma (Jātīkusuma?) 077-2
Zadur buza (Caturbhuja-Mahākāla) 010-5
Zadurbuza (Caturmukha-Mahākāla) 009-5
Zala bid'abhug'a (Jala-Bhayatrāṇa) 073-4
Zala indara fucihi (Jinendra) 032-1
Zambala (Jambhala) 030-6
Zambala fucihi (Jambhala) 031-3, 032-3, 033-3, 034-3, 035-3, 036-3,
     037-3, 038-3
Zandan śiri (Candanaśrī) 011-1
Zandara (Candrā) 004-6
Zandara dewei (Candrā) 092-7
Zandara fucihi (Candraketu) 049-2
Zaniyana (Jñāna-Pāramitā) 090-3

Zid'raa (Citrā) 102-6
Ziwara masi (Cīvaramasi) 095-6

The Mongol Kanjur[36] which was translated much earlier, also contains
representations of deities, in this case accompanied by their names in
Mongol and Manchu; the latter are only transliterations of the Mongol
names, and therefore a comparison with the Manchu names of the
Manchu Kanjur would not be useful.

---

36 *Mengguwen Ganzhuer foxiang daquan* 蒙古文甘珠尔佛像大全. Köke qota: Nei
   Menggu renmin chubanshe 2002. 2 vols.

1. Berlin Album (Ethnologisches Museum, Staatliche Museen zu
Berlin, Preußischer Kulturbesitz, I D 7524, fol. 15. Courtesy (ill. 1–3)
Dr. Wang Ching-ling

2. Berlin Album, fol. 15, portrait of Lalitavajra

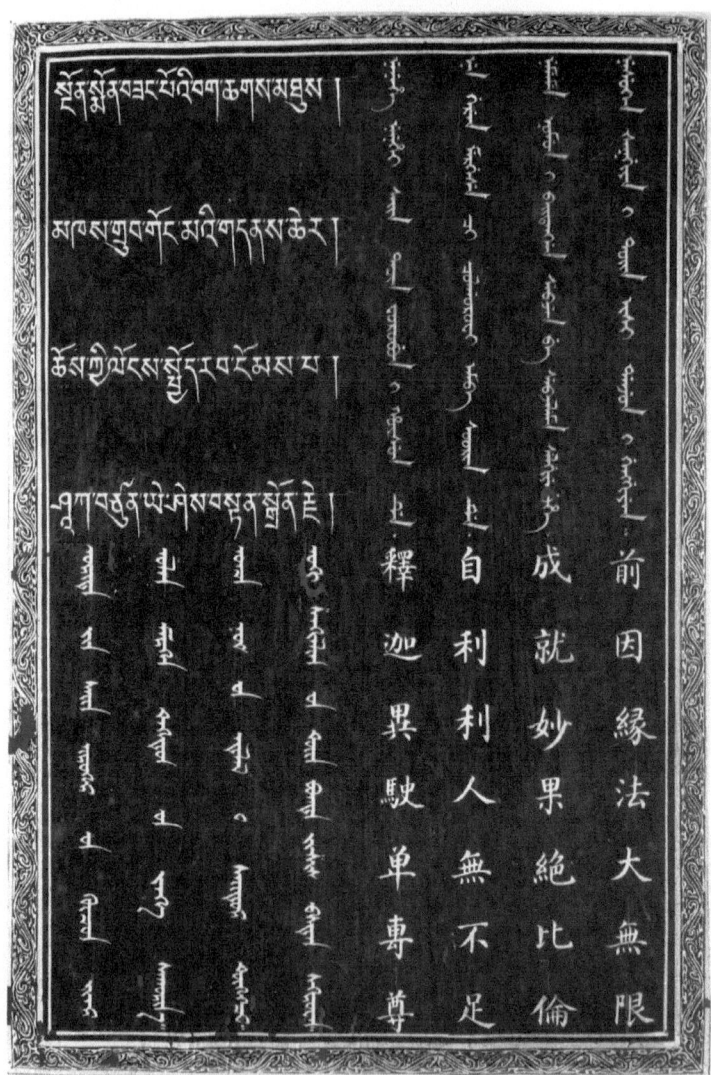

3. Berlin Album (Ethnologisches Museum, I D 7524), fol. 15,
quadrilingual eulogy on Lalitavajra

4. Lalitavajra (thangka, private collection, quoted from *Himalayan Art* [website])

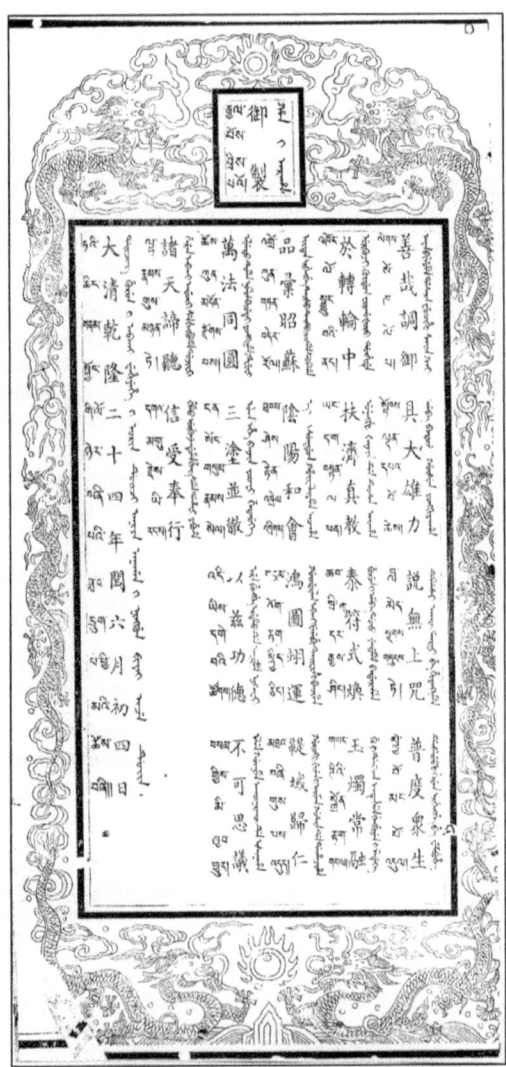

5. Imperial poem on the completion of the translation of the Complete
Dhâraṇî Collection (*Han-i araha Manju nikan monggo tanggôt
hergen-i kamciha amba g'anjur nomun-i uheri tarni*), Qianlong 24
(1749) (photo private)

6. Sample page of *Han-i araha Manju nikan monggo tanggôt hergen-i kamciha amba g'anjur nomun-i uheri tarni*
Text: Beginning of Fucihi nomulaha amba wacir hiyan sere gebungge toktobuha darani (read from right to left)

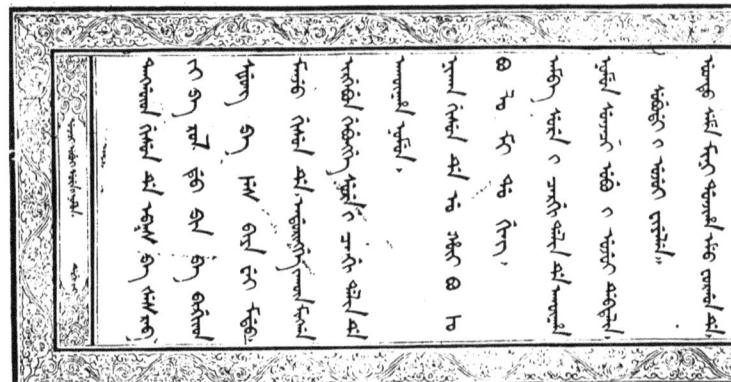

7. Beginning of fol. 1a of the Manchu Kanjur, vol. 22. (detail)
The text is *Amba sure-i cargi dalin de akônaha nomun. sunjaci ubui
ujui debtelin*

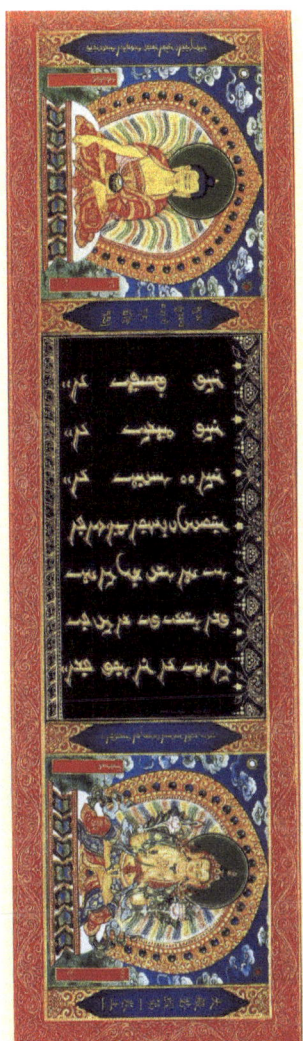 

8–9. Manchu Kanjur, top and bottom cover; the central panel gives the title of the sutra, the red slips the names of the deities in Tibetan and Manchu.

The Role of the Ancestor Cult in the Turks' Statehood Conception

Münevver Ebru ZEREN[1] (Istanbul)

In presenting my paper about the role of the ancestor cult in the Turks' statehood conception, I will be picking some specific examples from different periods of the history of the Turks. These are mainly: Ancestor cult definition, state ceremonies, representations of ancestors and the ruling clan and state related symbols.

The ancestor cult, encountered in many ancient cultures in the world, is based on the belief that the ancestors could interfere with their descendants' lives, to help, inspire, protect, punish and bring fortune or misfortune. The related material culture consists of cult objects like idols, relics, portraits, statues, masks, tablets or inscriptions, altars, ancestor halls, shrines to make sacrifices, food offerings, prayers, or simply to commemorate them. The ancestor cult also has strong links with a society's death and mourning rites, afterlife conception, burial practices (i.e. embalmment) and tomb building. Thus, among Turks this cult should first be positioned within the Old Turkic religion.

The textual evidence testifies that the old national religion of the Turks, called either Sky God Religion or Tengrism, provides a faith system composed of the belief in a Sky God, a belief in natural powers called "water-land spirits", and the veneration of the ancestors[2]. The ancestor cult was practiced for heroic, legendary Turkish rulers like *Oghuz Kaghan*, *Alp Er Tunga* (*Afrasiab*), previous rulers and mighty warriors (*alp*). As this religion defined God-man-

---

1 Ass. Prof. Dr., Haliç University, Faculty of Sciences and Letters, History Department, *ebruzeren@yahoo.com*.
2 Harun GÜNGÖR: "Eski Türk Dini." *Yaşayan dünya dinleri.* Ed. Ş. Gündüz, 2nd edition. İstanbul: Diyanet İşleri Başkanlığı Yayınları, 2007, pp. 529–535.

universe relationships in an integrated and harmonious way, it was also referred to as "universalism", a system defining both the religion and state fundamentals, initiated earlier by the Chou dynasty[3], probably having been established by proto-Turks in China at the end of the second millennium B.C[4]. It seems to have shaped in its turn God-ruler-state relationships, the Turks' conception of statehood and their idealism on world sovereignty. In line with the "Sacred Kingship" concept, popular among many ancient nations, state and religion were two entities supporting each other based on the common leadership of the Turkic ruler. Thus, the religious services for the Sky God, water-land spirits and ancestors were celebrated as state ceremonies.

Turks have an amazing heritage related to their ancient rulers' direct messages, inscribed in several *bengü taş* ("eternal stone") beginning in the 8th century and onward. These inscriptions contain the words *apa* and *äçü*[5] describing "ancestor", which were used in hendiadyoin. Other words meaning father, *ata* and *kaŋ,* were frequently used to refer to the previous father kaghan, such as *(k(a)ŋ(ı)m k(a)g(a)n*. The remote past, shedding light on how they established the state (*il*), how they united and ensured the wealth of their people (*bodun*) and finally legislated to extend the state law (*törü*), found voice in these eternal stones so lively and intimately. The relationship of land (country) and ancestors was clearly highlighted in the expression *apamız eçümüz tutmış Yer Sub* ("water-land governed by our ancestors")[6].

---

3 Emel ESIN: *İslâmiyetten önceki Türk kültür tarihi ve İslâma giriş (Türk Kültürü El Kitabı, II, Cild I/b'den Ayrı Basım)*. İstanbul: Edebiyat Fakültesi Matbaası, 1978, p. 43.

4 Wolfram EBERHARD: *A history of China*. London: Routledge & Kegan Paul, Reprinted 1977, p. 23.

5 Hatice ŞIRIN USER: *Köktürk ve Ötüken Uygur Kağanlığı yazıtları sözvarlığı incelemesi,* 2nd edition. Konya: Kömen Yayınları, 2010, pp. 248–249.

6 Költigin Inscription East Side 19th line and Bilge Kağan Inscription East Side 16th line. Bkz. Şirin User, *ibid,* p. 248.

Ancestors called out to their descendants as virtuous rulers, wise statemen, powerful commanders, history teachers, and most importantly, as fathers caring for their children. They also listed their wishes from their descendants for the continuity of their state and identity. Inscriptions also testify that this heritage was carefully protected by their heirs, who often mentioned the forefathers of their ruling clan, or even the historical events about the previous Turkic state founders. So, as it turns out, the Old Turkic inscriptions become the primary organic connection between the Turks and their ancestors. This precious heritage was highly supported by a strong oral tradition, including epics and elegies of heroic, legendary Turkish rulers and *alp*s (i.e. *Manas*). The wolf appears as the ancestor of the Turks, either as a father, a mother or a guide, leading the way to a new homeland where a new state becomes established.

State ceremonies executed by Turks generally have a dual character, having both sacred and secular functions. It is noted in the Han Shu, that the Huns were making sacrifices for their ancestors, Heaven, Earth and spirits in the big meeting held in Lung-cheng in the fifth month of the year[7]. The Northern Wei emperors, of Turkic origin, continued suburban sacrifices called *jiao* for Heaven and Earth, accompanied by ancestor emperor and empress[8]. The typical material culture of the Northern Wei ancestral cult consists of the cavern shrines built on mountain tops to venerate the ancestors, as the continuation of the steppe peoples' tradition of the ancestor cave. The emperor would personally undertake the ceremony of shooting the sacrificial animals – horses, oxen and sheep – and offer them. Chinese chronicles recorded the ancestor ceremonies of the period of the Turkic Kaghanate: The Turk kaghan gathered the tribal leaders each

---

7   Ayşe ONAT, Sema ORSOY, Konuralp ERCILASUN: *Han hanedanlığı tarihi bölüm 94 A/B, Hsiung-nu (Hun) monografisi (açıklamalı metin neşri).* Ankara: Türk Tarih Kurumu Basımevi, 2004, p. 8.

8   Shuguo CHEN: "State religious ceremonies." *Early Chinese religion. Part Two: The Period of Division (220–589 AD),* Vol. I, Ed. John Lagerwey, Lü Pengzi. Leiden, Boston: Brill 2010, pp. 82, 91.

year to make sacrifices in the ancestors cave (*sien-k'u*)[9]. The Western
Turks of the Turkic Khaganate sent a high-ranking officer to the
ancestors' cave in the fifth month of the year[10].

During the Orhun Uygur period, when Manichaeism was the state
religion, the enthronization prayers held a syncretic character covering
both ancient Turkic beliefs and the Manichaean faith. A striking
example of the ancestors having divine ruling authority, *kut,* to bring
fortune to the new kaghan, is evident in a Manichaean text, TM III,
34, 16–22: "*The fortune (qut) of the land Ötükän, the fortune of the
first wise kings, of the fathers of the kings, the fortune of the holy
throne may rest upon our heavenly iduq-qut.*"[11]

The sacred value of ancestor tombs for state administration and
important state declarations are seen in a few, but significant
examples. In the Tariat Inscription left by Moyun Çor, based on O.
Mert's suggested reading, different tribes gathered at the ancestors'
tomb in 748 and declared that the Uygurs had the right to rule from
then on, the ancestors' tomb being under their protection[12]. Visiting
father and ancestor tombs was a tradition of the enthronization in the
Seldjukid [13] and Ottoman [14] states.   In the latter, this ceremony
happened after the new sultan girded himself with a sword in the
mausoleum of Hz. Eyyub Sultan, a companion of the Prophet
Muhammad (S.A.V.).   During this ceremony, sacrifices were made

---

9 LIU Mau-Tsai: *Çin kaynaklarına göre Doğu Türkleri.* Çev. Ersel
   Kayaoğlu, Deniz Banoğlu. İstanbul: Selenge Yayınları, 2006, p. 23.
10 Édouard CHAVANNES: *Documents sur les Tou-Kiue (Turcs) Occidentaux.*
   Saint Petersburg 1903, p. 15.
11 Hans J. KLIMKEIT: "Manichaean kingship: Gnosis at home in the world".
   Numen, Vol. 29, Fasc. 1, July 1982, p. 25.
12 Tariat Inscription South Side 5th line, see Osman MERT: *Ötüken Uygur
   dönemi yazıtlarından Tes - Tariat - Şine Us.* Ankara: Belen Yayıncılık
   Matbaacılık, 2009, p. 171.
13 İsmail Hakkı UZUNÇARŞILI: *Osmanlı devleti teşkilatına medhal.* 4th
   edition. Ankara: Türk Tarih Kurumu Basımevi, 1988, p. 64.
14 Abdülkadir ÖZCAN: "Cülûs". *Türkiye Diyanet Vakfı İslâm ansiklopedisi,*
   C. VIII, 1993, p. 111.

and also at the tomb of Fatih Sultan MEHMED II, the prominent ancestor who initiated this ceremony[15]. Another common ritual in Ottoman military history was that the tomb of BARBAROS HAYR-EDDIN PASHA was visited by the Ottoman navy before serious sea campaigns. The modern Uygurs in Eastern Turkestan still celebrate annual mazar festivals such as *Ordam* at the tombs of the rulers who fought a holy war to bring and expand Islam in the region, like SATUK BUGHRA KHAN and his son ALI ARSLAN KHAN of the Qarakhanid State and other martyrs[16].

Regarding the representation of deceased ancestors, there are several words in Old Turkic, depicting the artistic statues or bas-reliefs from stones erected near the graves: *bediz*[17], *sin, taş baba*. Respectable deceased could also be depicted in the form of a wooden statue, such as Manas' wooden double or dummy made from his clothes, as a temporary substitute, called *tul*, in Kirghiz tradition[18]. G. Kubarev suggests that the Ancient Turkic statues represented specific individuals as hero or warrior to commemorate them. Some widely known statues have even specific names in the Altai, Mongolia and Tuva. The statue cult includes feeding, binding with kerchiefs or belts, and painting them. A golden statue found in the palace of HUI-T'O, the leader of the Huns in 121 B.C. was interpreted either as a Buddha statue or an ancestor statue inspired by twelve gigantic metal human statues of Shih-huang-ti symbolizing *Ursa Major*[19]. Kubarev high-

---

15 Arzu TOZDUMAN TERZI: "Sultan Abdülaziz'in kılıç kuşanma merasimi." *Osmanlı'nın izinde. Prof. Dr. Mehmet İpşirli armağan.* İstanbul 2013, p. 470.

16 Rachel HARRIS, Rahilä DAWUT: "Mazar festivals of the Uyghurs: Music, Islam and the Chinese State." *British Journal of Ethnomusicology,* Vol. 11, No. 1 (2002), pp. 101–103.

17 Gleb KUBAREV: "Ancient Turkic statues: Epic hero or warrior ancestor?" *Archaeology, Ethnology and Anthropology of Eurasia,* 1 (29), 2007, p. 142.

18 *ibid.,* p. 143.

19 K. SHIRATORI: "On the territory of the Hsiung-nu prince Hsiu-t'u Wang and his metal statues for heaven-worship." *Memoirs of the Research*

lights that this statue tradition continues among modern Turkic peoples, who call the statues *batır* (hero) and make large and artistic sculptures named *kos-alp, alyp-tas, tumyktyn-alyby*[20].

The main beliefs related to ancestors in Buddhism were shaped around Buddha images, statues, cave shrines, *stupa* and *tijandi*[21]. The iconic phase of Buddhist art started with Mahāyāna Buddhism, probably flourishing in Northern India or Turkestan during the Kushan period. The Northern Liang dynasty established by Turks was the initiator of building Buddhist cave shrines in China and gigantic stone statues representing Buddha, mainly Buddha Maitreya. The Northern Wei dynasty enriched Chinese Buddhist art with the gigantic emperor statues imitating Buddha or bodhisattva iconography. Among the other monumental Buddha statues in Central Asia, one needs to list the two colossal Buddha statues in Bamiyan, built during the Turkic Khaganate. This magnification of Buddha images seems to be highly related with the ancestor cult of the Turks. It was also demonstrated by evidence that *pañcavārṣika* (*môksha*) was being celebrated by the Bamiyan ruler as a state ceremony in an area between *Mahāparanirvāna* and *Shakyamuni Buddha* statues[22].

Department of the Toyo Bunko, V. Tokyo, 1930, p. 30–54; Emel ESIN: "Burkan ve Mani dinleri çevresinde Türk san'atı (Doğu Türkistan ve Kansu'da)." *Türk kültürü el kitabı Cild II, Kısım Ia. İslâmiyetten önceki Türk san'atı hakkında araştırmalar.* Ed. H. İnalcık, v.d. İstanbul: Milli Eğitim Basımevi, 1972, p. 359.

20 KUBAREV, *ibid.*, p. 143.
21 Dietrich SECKEL: *The art of Buddhism.* Trans. A. E. Keep. New York: Crown Publishers, 1964, pp. 138–139. Seckel indicates explicitly that *tiandji*, which is a kind of *sanctuary holding Buddha and other deities images* was related with "ancestor veneration" and "sacred kingship" concepts.
22 Deborah KLIMBURG-SALTER: *The Kingdom of Bamiyan: Buddhist art and culture of the Hindu Kush.* Naples: Istituto Universitario Orientale, Rome: Istituto Italiano per Il Medio ed Estremo Oriente, 1989, p. 123.

The ancestor cult seems to have a strong link with the determination and manipulation of family lineage, especially for ruling and high-rank elite classes. It is typical for a ruler to base his lineage on a widely known (i.e. *Chengis Khan*), a heroic (*Oghuz Khan*) or a mythological king to legitimate his sovereignity. The hierarchical ranking of the elites around the ruler is determined by the nobility of their family lineages, or the services given by them and/or their ancestors. Old Turkic terminology regarding this ranking includes *orun* (place), *ülüş* (share) and *kuram* (hierarchic alignments of beys around the ruler). The distribution of the hunted meat by Kün Han in a festive banquet among the 24 grandsons of Oghuz Khan, based on state hierarchy, is a good example[23]. The *tamgas* and *onguns,* like the birds of prey of these 24 Oghuz tribes, are the lineage symbols of the tribes or ruling clans as an emblematic connection with their ancestors. A couplet from Kutadgu Bilig indicates the significance of the heritage of rank and name from father to son: *ata ornı atı ogulka kalır* ("the rank and name of the father are left to the son")[24].

Another ancestor related symbol related to the state is the genealogical tree of the ruling dynasty. In fact, ancestor veneration generally seems to have some links with the water-land cult including the mountain, tree and fire cults of the ancient Turks. Each Turkic leader and clan had a sacred mountain and mountains are mostly called *han* or *ata*[25]. The hearth cult, practiced among Altai and Yakut Turks who made sacrifices and food offerings to the fire was probably related to the ancestor cult[26]. There are some lively scenes in Varahsha and Pandjikand from the Turkic Kaghanate period, depicting a festive banquet held around the hearth. The beech tree was considered a sacred cult object in order to build a forest after the mourning cere-

---

23 EBULGAZI BAHADIR HAN: *Şecere-i Terakime (Türkmenlerin Soykütüğü),* Haz. Zuhal Kargı ÖLMEZ. Ankara: Simurg Kitapçılık, 1996, p. 246.
24 Yusuf HAS HACIB: *Kutadgu Bilig,* Trans. Reşid Rahmeti Arat. 2nd edition. İstanbul: Kabalcı Yayınevi, 2008, p. 108, Couplet nr. 110.
25 Ünver GÜNAY, Harun GÜNGÖR: *Başlangıçtan günümüze Türklerin dini tarihi,* 5th edition. İstanbul: Rağbet Yayınları, 2009, p. 73.
26 *Ibid,* p. 77.

mony for the ruler's family had been held, especially during the Northern Wei dynasty. Uygurs and Kipchaks believed that they originated from a tree[27]. TUQAQ, the father of the eponymous *Seldjuk* of the *Seldjukids,* was said to have dreamed prophetically of the dynasties founded by his issue, symbolized by the giant tree grown out of his navel, reaching the heavens. This surprisingly matches with the famous story of Osman Bey's dream in which a plane tree emerged from his navel as a prophecy of the Ottoman State's foundation[28].

It seems that the Turks' ancestor cult left traces on the most important state symbol, the flag (*tug*). The wolf as mythical progenitor, symbolizing the Turks' power and freedom, took its place on the Turks' flag. The wolf attached on top of the flag during the period of the Turks and Uygurs was another cult object. J.-P. ROUX suggested that the *yak* tails attached to the Ottoman flags were the remote reflections of an ancestor cult[29]. Astrological emblems like sun, moon and stars, which appeared since the Chou dynasty could be explained by the importance of the astral cult among the Huns and the Hunnic Shan-yü, being the "offspring of sun and moon" as mentioned by Shiratori. Additionally, the forefather of the Turks, the first Turk or perhaps the first Turkish ruler[30], called *Ay-Atam* ("My Moon-ancestor") was made known through the famous story narrated by AY-BEK ÜD-DEVADARÎ in the Mamluk period[31].

---

27 *Ibid*, p. 75–76.

28 Regarding these and similar dreams in Turkic statehood tradition, cf. Abdullah TEMIZKAN, Erhan AKTAŞ: "Türk devlet geleneğinde iktidarın meşrulaştırılmasında rüyanın kullanımı." *Karadeniz Araştırmaları*, 33, Bahar 2012, pp. 13–22.

29 Jean-Paul ROUX: *Eski Türk mitolojisi.* Trans. Musa Yaşar Sağlam. Ankara: Bilge Su Yayıncılık, 2011, p. 39.

30 Pertev Naili BORATAV: *Türk mitolojisi. Oğuzların – Anadolu, Azerbaycan ve Türkmenistan Türklerinin mitolojisi.* Ankara: Bilge Su Yayıncılık, 2012, pp. 35–36.

31 Bahaeddin ÖGEL: *Türk mitolojisi,* Türk Tarih Kurumu. Vol. 1. 5th Edition, Ankara: Türk Tarih Kurumu Basımevi, 2010, p. 483-485.

Finally, why were the ancestors venerated and prayed to? The common expectation from ancestors for the sake of different Turkic dynasties and states, seems to be receiving their blessings. One important prayer from the Chou period was made for *King Wu* and other kings of ancient times, for long rulership and continuous governmental power.

After the adoption of Mahāyāna Buddhism by the Uygurs in the Turfan and Kansu regions, the ancestor veneration continued with the "merit transfer" practices based on the belief that the deceased people might still receive merits after death by means of their descendants' donations. There are many colophons and stone tablets, showing prayers in detail for the wellbeing of their deceased family members via listing their names specifically[32]. At the very beginning of the prayers there were always good wishes for the state and the rulers. *Kutadgu Bilig* includes a nice couplet told by *Ödgülmiş* regarding the benefit granted by the blessing of the father:

Atam kıldı erdi kör edgü dua / Dua birle tegdim bu yirke aga[33]
(My father made a good prayer/ I reached that position with prayer)

Today, Muslim Turks still pray for the sake of the state, deceased state leaders, especially Atatürk, heroes and martyrs, deceased family members, especially parents. They believe that their parents' blessings are very important for their fortune in daily life and afterlife.

Bibliography

BORATAV, Pertev Naili: *Türk mitolojisi. Oğuzların – Anadolu, Azerbaycan ve Türkmenistan Türklerinin mitolojisi.* Ankara: Bilge Su Yayıncılık, 2012.

CHAVANNES, Édouard: *Documents sur les Tou-Kiue (Turcs) Occidentaux,* Saint Pétersbourg 1903.

CHEN, Shuguo: "State religious ceremonies". *Early Chinese religion,*

---

32 Yukiyo KASAI: *Die uigurischen buddhistischen Kolophone.* Turnhout: Brepols 2008 (Berliner Turfantexte XXVI.), p. 38.
33 Yusuf HAS HACIB: *Kutadgu Bilig,* pp. 376–377; Couplet nr. 1803.

Part Two: The Period of Division (220–589 AD), Ed. John Lagerwey, Lü Pengzi. Volume One. Leiden, Boston: Brill 2010, pp. 53–142.

COOK, Constance A.: "Ancestor worship during the Eastern Zhou", *Early Chinese Religion, Part One: Shang Through Han (1250 BC– 220 AD),* Ed. John Lagerwey, Marc Kalinowski. Leiden: Brill 2009, pp. 237–279.

EBERHARD, Wolfram: *A history of China.* London: Routledge & Kegan Paul, Reprinted 1977.

EBULGAZI BAHADIR HAN: *Şecere-i Terakime (Türkmenlerin Soykütüğü).* Haz. Zuhal Kargı Ölmez. Ankara: Simurg Kitapçılık, 1996.

ESIN, Emel: *İslâmiyetten önceki Türk kültür tarihi ve İslâma giriş (Türk kültürü el-kitabı, II, Cild I/b'den ayrı basım).* İstanbul: Edebiyat Fakültesi Matbaası, 1978.

GRÜNWEDEL, Albert: *Altbuddhistische Kultstätten in Chinesisch-Turkistan. Berichte über archäologische Arbeiten von 1906 bis 1907 bei Kuča, Karašahr und in der Oase Turfan,* Königlich-Preussische Turfan-Expeditionen. Berlin: Georg Reimer, 1912.

GÜNAY, Ünver; Harun GÜNGÖR: *Başlangıçtan günümüze Türklerin dini tarihi,* 5th edition. İstanbul: Rağbet Yayınları, 2009.

GÜNGÖR, Harun: "Eski Türk dini". *Yaşayan dünya dinleri.* Ed. Ş. Gündüz. 2nd Edition. İstanbul: Diyanet İşleri Başkanlığı Yayınları, 2007, pp. 529–539.

HARRIS, Rachel; Rahilä DAWUT: "Mazar festivals of the Uyghurs: Music, Islam and the Chinese State". *British Journal of Ethno-musicology,* Vol. 11, No. 1, 2002, pp. 101–118.

HAS HACIB, Yusuf: *Kutadgu Bilig.* Trans. Reşid Rahmeti Arat. 2nd edition. İstanbul: Kabalcı Yayınevi, 2008.

KASAI, Yukiyo: *Die uigurischen buddhistischen Kolophone.* Turnhout: Brepols 2008. (Berliner Turfantexte XXVI.)

KLIMBURG-SALTER, Deborah: *The Kingdom of Bamiyan: Buddhist art and culture of the Hindu Kush.* Naples: Istituto Universitario Orientale, Rome: Istituto Italiano per Il Medio ed Estremo Oriente, 1989.

KLIMKEIT, Hans J.: "Manichaean kingship: Gnosis at home in the world". *Numen,* Vol. 29, Fasc. 1, July 1982, pp. 17–32.

KUBAREV, Gleb: "Ancient Turkic statues: Epic hero or warrior ancestor?" *Archaeology, Ethnology and Anthropology of Eurasia,* 1 (29), 2007, pp. 136–144.

LIU Mau-Tsai: *Çin kaynaklarına göre Doğu Türkleri.* Trans. Ersel Kayaoğlu, Deniz Banoğlu. İstanbul: Selenge Yayınları, 2006.

MERT, Osman: *Ötüken Uygur dönemi yazıtlarından Tes - Tariat - Şine Us.* Ankara: Belen Yayıncılık Matbaacılık, 2009.

ONAT, Ayşe, Sema ORSOY, Konuralp ERCILASUN: *Han hanedanlığı tarihi bölüm 94 A/B, Hsiung-nu (Hun) monografisi (açıklamalı metin neşri).* Ankara: Türk Tarih Kurumu Basımevi, 2004.

ÖGEL, Bahaeddin: *Türk mitolojisi.* Vol. 1. 5th edition. Ankara: Türk Tarih Kurumu Basımevi, 2010.

ÖZCAN, Abdülkadir: "Cülûs". *Türkiye Diyanet Vakfı İslâm ansiklopedisi,* Vol. VIII, 1993, pp. 108–114.

ROUX, Jean-Paul: *Eski Türk mitolojisi.* Trans. Musa Yaşar Sağlam. Ankara: Bilge Su Yayıncılık, 2011.

SECKEL, Dietrich: *The art of Buddhism.* Trans. A. E. Keep. New York: Crown Publishers, 1964.

ŞIRIN USER, Hatice: *Köktürk ve Ötüken Uygur Kağanlığı yazıtları sözvarlığı incelemesi.* 2nd Edition. Konya: Kömen Yayınları, 2010.

TEMIZKAN, Abdullah; Erhan AKTAŞ: "Türk devlet geleneğinde iktidarın meşrulaştırılmasında rüyanın kullanımı". *Karadeniz Araştırmaları,* 33, Spring 2012, pp. 13–22.

TOZDUMAN TERZI, Arzu: "Sultan Abdülaziz'in kılıç kuşanma merasimi". *Osmanlı'nın izinde, Prof. Dr. Mehmet İpşirli armağanı.* İstanbul: Timaş Yayınları, 2013, pp. 465–484.

UZUNÇARŞILI, İsmail Hakkı: *Osmanlı devleti teşkilatına medhal.* 4th edition. Ankara: Türk Tarih Kurumu Basımevi, 1988.

Poetic Travels in Mongolia
Literary Fiction by Travellers[1]

Hartmut WALRAVENS (Berlin)

Travelogues are often of great interest as historical source material. Explorers, like POTANIN[2] (1835–1920), PRŽEVAL'SKIJ[3] (1839–1888) and Sven HEDIN[4] (1865–1952) in the case of Central Asia, to name just a few, presented facts and figures of the region for the first time. Their collections of ethnographical and natural history objects enriched the museums and gave reliable information on fauna, flora, mineral resources and the material culture. The lifestyle, the customs and habits, the economy were described in more detail by other travellers, like missionaries, merchants and scholars. The languages were explored, vocabularies collected, and books assembled.

---

1   This paper was originally read at the Bucharest PIAC Conference in 2008 of which no proceedings could be published, owing to unfortunate circumstances. As it directs the attention to two interesting books which might not easily come to most scholars' knowledge it is given here as an appendix. – The author likes to express his gratitude to Christine BELL for kindly polishing his translations from those books.

2   Grigorij Nikolaevič POTANIN: *Vospominanija.* Novosibirsk: Zapadno-Sibirsk. Kn. Izd. 1983. 332 p.; Conclusion: 1986. 339 p.; Potanin: *Pis'ma.* 1–5. Irkutsk: Univ. 1987–1992.

3   PRŽEVAL'SKIJ, Nikolaj Michajlovič. *Russkie voennye vostokovedy. Biobibliografičeskij slovař.* Moskva 2005, 193–196; Vasilij Michajlovič GAVRILENKO: *Russkij putešestvennik N. M. Prževal'skij.* Moskva: Mosk. Rabočij 1974. 142 p.; Donald RAYFIELD: *The life of Nikolay Przhevalsky (1839–1888) explorer of Central Asia.* London: P. Elek 1976. XII, 221 p.

4   *Die Werke Sven Hedins.* Versuch eines vollständigen Verzeichnisses von Willy HESS. Stockholm: Sven Hedins Stiftelse, Statens Etnografiska Museum 1962. 131 S. (The Sven Hedin Foundation. Sven Hedin – Life and Letters.1.) – Willy HESS: *Die Werke Sven Hedins. Ein Nachtrag.* Stockholm: Sven Hedins Stiftelse, Etnografiska museet 1980. 24 S. (The Sven Hedin Foundation, Sven Hedin – Life and Letters.3.)

Only occasionally the work of writers is appreciated as a contribution to the knowledge of the respective cultures as often fictional
elements are more predominant than the actual familiarity with the
people and the region. We do have instances, however, where the
writers were intimately acquainted with what they wrote about, at the
same time either gifted writers or accomplished scholars. The latter
sometimes used pseudonyms in order not to be identified at first
glance. And the motivation to write fiction about the regions they
knew well was certainly in part the preoccupation with the country
and the people, but also simply the need for an additional income.

A good example is a writer by the name of Peter ZUCKMANTL who
did not make it to the bestseller lists. One of his books is listed as
"Mongolisches Intermezzo. Darmstadt: Leske, 1953. 174 p." by
YUAN T'ung-li in his *China in Western literature.*[5] The book relates
the story of a young German woman who went to Peking to visit her
uncle around 1940 and who got stuck when the Pacific War broke out.
So she decided to take up work at the German Hospital. In company
she met a young man from Alsace, Renee [apparently phonetic
rendering of René] with whom she becomes friends but it remains
unclear till the end of the book whether this acquaintenceship will turn
into a more serious relationship. The two young people decide to
spend a weekend in the Western Hills but as the political and military
situation around Peking becomes critical they are advised by a
friendly Father with whom they are staying to seek refuge with a
Mongolian tribe not very far away. There, to their amazement, they
meet Chingbator again, a Mongolian journalist, whom they know
from Peking parties, only that here he seems to be a commanding
figure. They also meet his sister who used to live in Europe and get
acquainted with her life history. Both young people gain a lot from the
experience of their kind hosts, and when they are finally rescued by
American forces they realize that it was not just an adventure but
something that changed their lives ...

---

5   New Haven: Yale University Press, 1958, 458.

CHINGBATOR comments on his fellow-countrymen

"Wir Mongolen denken noch so, wie wir vor einigen hundert Jahren gedacht haben. Selbst mir fällt der Wechsel immer schwer, wenn ich aus Peking hierher komme. Jetzt aber ist mein Platz bei meinem Stamme, wo doch nicht nur vielleicht, sondern wahrscheinlich bald der sehr schmerzhafte Schritt ins Heute kommt. Sie werden sehen, daß meine Leute moderne Waffen und Ausrüstung haben und zu bedienen verstehen, aber im Herzen sind sie noch genau so einfach, wie ihre Vorfahren es vor Jahrhunderten waren." [We Mongols still think the same way as we did several hundred years ago. Even I find the transition difficult when I come here from Peking. But now my place is with my tribe where not only possibly but probably soon the painful step into today will come. You will notice that my people have modern weapons and equipment and know to handle them but in their hearts are as simple as their ancestors were centuries ago.] (p. 107–108)

The author gives a little colophon, disclaiming any similarity with existing people:

"Es läßt sich nicht leugnen, daß es China, die schöne Stadt Peking und die kahlen Berge in ihrem Westen tatsächlich gibt. Aber alles sonst in diesem Roman Erzählte entspringt lediglich der Phantasie des Verfassers, und es liegen ihm keinerlei wahre Begebenheiten zugrunde. Sollte jemand aber doch eine Ähnlichkeit zwischen sich oder einem seiner Freunde mit einer der Gestalten dieses Buches entdecken glauben, so sei ihm versichert, daß es sich natürlich auch nicht leugnen läßt, daß alle Menschen Arme und Beine, einen Kopf und oftmals auch Gefühle haben. Alle weiteren Ähnlichkeiten zwischen den Gestalten dieses Buches und Personen unserer Zeit aber sind rein zufällige. Und das ist ja auch viel schöner so." [It cannot be denied that China, the beautiful city of Peking and the barren mountains in its West really exist. But everything else told in this novel sprang exclusively from the author's imagination, and it is not based on any real events. If somebody discovers similarity between himself or one of his friends and one of the figures of this book, he may be assured that it can not be denied that all humans have arms and legs, a head and often also emotions. All further similarities between the characters in this book and persons in our times are however purely coincidental – and that is much nicer so.]

The same author is responsible for two children's books that deal with Mongolia:

Dschingis-Khan erobert sich ein Weltreich (Göttingen: W. Fischer [1956]. 126 p.) [Chinggis-Khan conquers himself an empire]

Marco Polo. Abenteuerliche Entdeckungsfahrt nach China (Göttingen: W. Fischer [1956]. 111 p.) [Marco Polo. Adventurous exploration trip to China]

They are aimed at boys, 12–16 years old and make good reading. It becomes clear that the author either read the standard history books carefully, or was himself knowledgeable because of his professional studies. The present writer had the good fortune of receiving the two books as a present – from an orientalist bookseller, with the argument: "I cannot sell these to my customers. Would you accept them." The conversation went on: "Yes, thank you. I am very happy to have them!" "Really?" "Yes! Did you not realize the author's name is a pseudonym?" "Who is it?" "Walther HEISSIG!" – "I am sorry, I really could have sold them!!" The standard reference works do not explain the pseudonym; it was taken from a little town in Austrian Silesia where Heissig's mother's family came from – Zuckmantel.[6] Heissig had been involved in the so-called Shanghai Trial in 1946 when he and a number of of the German citizens (like Herbert Mueller[7]) were accused of having worked for the Japanese Intelligence *after* the end

---

6   *Meyers Konversationslexikon*, 5th ed. Vol. 17. Leipzig, Wien 1897, 1095 reports that Zuckmantel (spelt with an "e") is 416 m above sea-level, close to the Prussian border, had almost to 5,000 German inhabitants (in 1890), a linen and silk industry, a brewery and a brick factory.

7   See H. WALRAVENS: *Herbert Muellers (1885–1966) Forschungsreise nach China 1912–1913*. Aus den Akten und Korrespondenzen neu bearbeitet und durch historische Fotos ergänzt. Wiesbaden: Harrassowitz 2017. 219 p. (Asien- und Afrika-Studien der Humboldt-Universität 49.)

of the European war. All accused were sentenced to years of imprisonment; a few years later the juridical validity of the sentence was in doubt and the prisoners were released without another word. Heissig had to start his career from scratch as a Privatdozent at Göttingen University, and a small honorarium from publications was more than welcome ... *Mongolisches Intermezzo*, by the way, should not be confused with *Ostmongolische Reise*, Heissig's book on his travels in Eastern Mongolia, published by the same publisher.[8]

While Heissig[9] proves himself a skilled writer he would not have claimed for himself to be a poet or artist. He was above all and foremost a scholar.

The opposite is true for an author who as a young man was a participant of Sven HEDIN's Sino-Swedish Expedition. Later on he studied art and started writing. His major book that is based on his personal experiences in Mongolia was published in 1950 under the title of *In geheimer Mission durch die Wüste Gobi* (On a secret mission through the Gobi desert). It is the story of two boys, Christian, son of a surgeon at the German Hospital in Peking, and his school friend Big Tiger. They are looking for a suitable place to fly their kites, and friendly soldiers take them on to a transport train for this purpose. The train and the passengers get into a battle zone, quite unexpectedly, and this makes it impossible for the boys to return to their families right away. So General WU Peifu (吳佩孚 1874–1939) sends them with a soldier on a trip to Urumči to forward a letter to the provincial governor, assuming that nobody will suspect the schoolboys to carry an offical document. The boys make interesting acquaintances during their travel, with Chinese and Mongolian children, adolescents and adults, getting glimpses of Mongolian life and collecting experience. They also get into a series of adventures which

---

8   Darmstadt: Leske, 1956. 169 p.
9   Walther HEISSIG (1913–2005) as one of the world's foremost Mongolists does not need an introduction here. See H. WALRAVENS: *Walther Heissig (1913–2005), Mongolist, Zentralasienwissenschaftler, Literaturwissenschaftler und Folklorist: Leben und Werk – Würdigungen, Dokumente, Forschungsberichte und Rundfunkprogramme auf Audio-CD.* Wiesbaden: Harrassowitz 2012. 460 S.

are carefully constructed by the author to form a logical development and leading to a climax, unravelling the identity of an unscrupulous villain. The story is always within the boundaries of probability and the intellectual level of the heroes. The language is simple but well chosen and reminds the German reader a bit of the narrative style of Erich KÄSTNER (1899–1974). At first reading it seems just a simple story; following the leads and overtones of the language, one detects hints and associations that make the book pleasant and entertaining even for adults. Mongolia around 1930 is depicted through the eyes of the unprejudiced boys – the Mongols are represented like usually honest and likeable people, and their lifestyle while different from the Chinese and European ways is shown with sympathy.

The author uses several stylistic means of captivating the readers' attention:

– Chinese and Mongolian words are translated often in a very literal way to make them special and convey a bit of the ambience of a far away country. Thus good night is rendered "Schlafen, gut schlafen!", the robbers are Honghuzi 紅鬍子, i.e. "red beards", a person is "ein Stück Mensch", by translating the Chinese numeral. Thus more distance is created for the reader who will not quickly follow just the narrative thread but will have to rest here and there for a moment to take in the uncommon phrases. "Keine Bedenken deswegen" and "Es gibt keine Hilfe" (*meiyou fazi* 沒有法子) are easily remembered.

– Peoples' names are usually translated. The soldier Fu 福 who is in charge of the trip, is referred to as "Glück" (Good Fortune), one soldier is called "Ungemach" (Affliction), and he justifies his name by his pessimistic outlook and his not encouraging life experience. A Mongolian girl is named Siebenstern (Seven Star). There are also Ohnezehen (Toeless) and Nicht-Gibt-Es-Nicht (translated in the English version as "Nowhere-at-all").

– There is some philosophy in the book to support the interpretation, or understanding, of events. As the boys could hardly come up with such, the author lets Big Tiger quote from the sayings of his grandfather, which might be considered proverbial.

– Habits and customs of the Mongols are explained in conversation, thus not lecturing the reader but confronting him with them – he learns by asking and listening:

"Als ich die Mongolen kennenlernte" sagte er [Glück], "dachte ich zuerst, sie wären Kinder und keine vernünftigen Menschen, denn sie gaben mir zu essen, ohne daß sie dafür was haben wollten. Dabei war ich ihnen fremd, und keiner kannte mich." – "Man nennt das Gastfreundschaft", sagte Christian, "Gastfreundschaft ist etwas Schönes, aber weiter nicht verwunderlich". "Sie waren aber selbst nicht reich", gab Glück zu bedenken, "und allmählich erfuhr ich, daß alle so sind. Die Mogolen sind sonderbare Leute, sie sind anders als wir Chinesen, und sie schenken Sachen weg. Für die sie höchstens einen Haddak haben wollen." – "Dann", sagte Großer Tiger nachdenklich, "sind sie bessere Menschen als wir."– "Besser oder nicht", erwiderte Glück achselzuckend, "sie sind eben anders. Wenn sie einen Handel machen, feilschen sie genau so wie wir, und Rotbärte gibt es auch bei ihnen eine ganze Menge." ["When I got to know the Mongols", he (Good Fortune) said, "I thought at first they were children and not reasonable people as they fed me without asking for anything in return. And that although I was strange to them and no one knew me." – "That is considered hospitality", said Christian, "hospitality is something beautiful but otherwise not unusual." – "But they were not well-to-do themselves," Good Fortune objected, "and gradually I learned that they are all this way. The Mongols are peculiar people, they are different than us Chinese, and they give things away and only want a haddak for them." – "Then", Big Tiger said thoughtfully, "they are better people than we are." – "Better or not", replied Good Fortune, shrugging his shoulders, "they are just different. When they make a deal, they haggle the same way as we do, and there are also a lot of Redbeards among them."](p. 378)

This example shows another feature of the book: The author tries to depict real life – he emphasizes the value or advantage of a situation, or behaviour, but avoids painting in black and white.

Small wonder, the book won a prize when it was published and was subsequently translated into a number of languages, unfortunately not in its complete form. The original publisher had the book abridged, assuming that it was too bulky, and thus some of the subtleties had to be sacrificed. And it is this abridged version that served as the basis for translation. The original edition was only republished in 1993.

A few quotations may give more insight into the author's way of presenting Mongolia to the reader:

From: *Fremde* [see Bibliography]: "Du und ich" erklärte er, "wir beide waren verschiedenen Sinnes, und was wir voneinander wußten, war von weit her. Jetzt siehst du mich an, und mein Denken ist dir offenbar; und ich weiß, was du sagen willst, ohne daß davon gesprochen werden muß.

Also bist du ein Mongole geworden, denn bei uns ist das so: Man redet nicht viel, aber man weiß." [You and I, he explained, we both were of different minds, and what we knew of one another was very removed. Now you look at me, and my way of thinking is known to you, and I know what you want to say, without having to talk about it.

Thus you have become a Mongol, as with us things are such: one does not talk so much but one.]

From: *In geheimer Mission*
"Im Westen schwebte die Sonne über den Zackenrändern ferner Berge. Sie war groß und rot wie eine feurige Kugel, die über eine Welt rollten, von der man nicht glauben konnte, daß sie schon fertig sei. Es gab Bodenwellen und niedere Hügel, die aussahen, als ob sie morgen ebenso gut irgendwoanders sein könnten. Risse zogen durch die Erde, von denen man nicht sicher war, ob sie sich nicht über Nacht schließen würden, um tausend Meilen weiter wieder aufzubrechen. Der magere

Graswuchs erschien als der sinnlose Versuch, Leben in eine Gegend zu bringen, die kein Leben duldete. Wahrscheinlich war morgen das Gras verdorrt, und man erwachte zwischen Blöcken von Urgestein und rieselndem Sand, wenn es überhaupt ein Erwachen gab." [In the West the sun was suspended over the zigzag rims of distant mountains. It was large and red like a fiery ball which rolled over a world that one could not believe is already finished. There were ridges and low hills which looked as if they might as well be somewhere else tomorrow. Rifts ran through the ground, of which one could not be sure whether they might close overnight only to open again a thousand miles away. The sparse growth of grass seemed like a senseless attempt to bring life into an area which did not permit life. Probably the grass would be dried up tomorrow, and one awakes between boulders of ancient rock and trickling sand, if there was an awakening at all.]

"Man war schnell daheim in der Wüste, weil alle schwierigen Dinge fehlten. Es gab überhaupt nichts als harten Boden zum Darauftreten und den Himmel zum Anschauen. Am Himmel glänzten die Sterne, und weil der Mond gerade irgendwo anders schien und erst spät aufging, mußte Glück achtgeben, damit er den Weg nicht verlor. Wieder einmal hatte er keinen anderen Wegweiser als den schmalen Trampelpfad der Kamele, an den er sich halten mußte. Aber Glück war getrost. Er kannte diesen Weg aus Erzählungen anderer, als habe er ihn selbst begangen." [One was quickly at home in the desert because all difficult things are wanting. There was nothing but hard ground to step on and the sky to look at. The stars glittered in the sky, and as the moon was just then shining elsewhere and rose late, Good Fortune had to pay close attention as to not lose his way. Once again he did not have any other lead than to keep to the narrow track of the camels. But Good Fortune was confident. He knew this path from the stories of other people like he had trodden it himself.]

"Nachdem eine Weile ausgiebig geschwiegen worden war, begann der alte Mongole zu reden. Er sprach mit tiefer Stimme, ohne sie zu heben oder zu senken, und er wandte sich an Christian: ‹Bist du schon lange im Mongolenland?› fragte er. Glück mußte einspringen: ‹Der armselige Ausländer› sagte er, ‹kennt das Grasland erst seit vier Tagen.› ‹Ich bedauere ihn aufrichtig›, erwiderte der Alte. ‹Wie traurig muß es sein›, sagte die Frau, ‹nicht als Mongole geboren zu sein!› ‹Gewiß› bestätigte der Alte, ‹es ist ein Unglück; aber welch ein Glück für ihn, daß er den Weg zu uns gefunden hat!›" [After a time of extended silence, the old Mongol began to speak. He spoke in a deep voice, without raising or lowering it, and he turned to Christian: "Have you been long in the Mongol land?" he asked. Good Fortune had to step in: "This miserable foreigner", he said, "knows the grass land for only four days." – "I com- miserate with him sincerely", replied the old man. – "How sad it must be", said the woman, "not to be born as a Mongol!" – "Certainly", confirmed the old man, "it is a misfortune; but how lucky for him that he found the way to us!"]

"Dieser Mensch [the Mongolian prince Dampignak]" sagte er, "wandert jenseits der herkömmlichen Regeln, das ist sein Hochmut.
Silber und Gold achtet er gering wie den Stein am Wege, das ist seine Sicherheit.
Er spricht lieber mit Pferden und Hunden als mit Menschen, das ist seine Traurigkeit." ["This person", he said, "wanders yonder of customary rules, that is his pride.
Silver and gold he despises like a stone in the way; that is his security.
He prefers to talk to horses and dogs than to people, that is his sorrow."]

These examples give an impression of the author's sensitive approach and his exceptional handling of a rather simple-looking language.

Who then was the author of this both delightful and informative novel?

Fritz MÜHLENWEG[10] (1989–1961) was the son of a Constance drug-store owner; he learned the same trade but was interested to get away. Through Lufthansa who were planning an airlines connection with China he got in contact with Sven Hedin and served the Expedition in various capacities (mostly administrative) between 1927 and 1932. After his return he studied art in Vienna, married a fellow student and the couple settled on Lake Constance. They were friends of the painter Otto DIX and kept a low profile during the Nazi period, painting and illustrating. Stimulated by their seven children who wanted to hear stories, Mühlenweg started writing ... His work was not only appreciated. An influential critic blamed him for not being more political in his novels. The only analysis from the East Asian point of view that we have so far focuses on Mühlenweg's poetic rendering of songs from the *Shijing* (Book of Songs).[11]

For about 30 years Mühlenweg's great novel had fallen into oblivion, in spite also of its translation into other languages. Now it is available again, also in paperback editions, in unabridged form, and it continues charming readers and presenting them with life in traditional Mongolia – a world that does no longer exist any more.

Bibliography

Fritz Mühlenweg: *In geheimer Mission durch die Wüste Gobi.*
(Lengwil:) Libelle (1993). 776 p.
The complete version of the novel.

Fritz Mühlenweg: *Großer Tiger und Christian.*
München: dtv (1983). 621 p.
Abridged version.

---

10 See Ekkehard FAUDE: *Fritz Mühlenweg – vom Bodensee in die Mongolei.* Lengwil: Libelle Verlag 2005. 201 p.

11 Gabriele GOLDFUß: Tausendjähriger Bambus: Lyrik und Prosa Fritz Mühlenwegs (1898–1961). *Chinawissenschaften. Deutschsprachige Entwicklungen. Geschichte, Personen, Perspektiven.* Hamburg: Institut für Asienkunde 1999, 505–527.

The original was published in two volumes in 1950–51 (Freiburg: Herder) as *Großer Tiger und Kompaß-Berg* and *Null Uhr fünf in Urumtschi*.

Mühlenweg's own travel account was published as:
Fritz Mühlenweg: *Fremde auf dem Pfad der Nachdenklichkeit*.
(Lengwil:) Libelle (1992). 301 p.
Original: *Das Tal ohne Wiederkehr*. 1952.
Big Tiger and Christian. By Fritz Mühlenweg. With an introduction by Peter Fleming. Illustrated by Rafaello Busoni. Translated by Isabel and Florence MacHugh.
London: Jonathan Cape (1954). 558 p.
Also: New York: Pantheon Books. 1954.

I hemmelig mission gennem Gobi-ørkenen.
København: Borgen 1963. 3 vols.

Attraverso il deserto di Gobi.
Milano: Fabbri 1955. 2 vols.

Kompas-Berg en Grote-Tijger.
Gent: Vanmelle 1954. 2 vol.

En misión secreta a travès del desierto de Gobi.
Barcelona: Herder 1956. 4 vols.

L'heure du dragon.
Paris: Alsatia 1959. 575 p.

På hemligt uppdrag / Gobiöknen. Förord av Sven Hedin.
Stockholm: Natur och kultur 1955. 437 p.

PETER ZUCKMANTL

MONGOLISCHES INTERMEZZO

C · W · LESKE VERLAG
DARMSTADT

Walther Heissig's novel *Mongolian Intermezzo*, published in 1955.

Walther Heissig's children's book on Marco Polo, published
appr. in 1956

Walther Heissig's children's book on Chingis Khan, published
appr. in 1956

Big Tiger and Christian

by

Fritz Mühlenweg

With an Introduction by
Peter Fleming

Illustrated by Rafaello Busoni

Translated by Isabel and Florence MacHugh

LONDON

JONATHAN CAPE THIRTY BEDFORD SQUARE

Translation of the condensed version of Mühlenweg's
In geheimer Mission durch die Wüste Gobi

Fritz Mühlenweg
In geheimer Mission
durch die Wüste Gobi

Libelle

Modern republication of the full text of Mühlenweg's book

Mühlenweg's travelogue (modern republication)

Name Index

The names of Buddhist deities are not included as they are given in alphabetical order in the article

'Abdu'llah 46
'Abdu'sh-Shahîd (Khwâja) 42
'Alî-Shîr Beg 20
'Dul-'dsin rDo-rje-seṅ-ge 184
'Gro-mgon Si-si-ri-pa 184
'Jam-pa'i rdo-rje 185
'Jigs-byed 185
'Phags-pa bLo-gros-rgyal-
    mthsan 184
Aalto, Pentti (1917–1998) 89,
    91
Abdrahmanov, Savitbek 169
Abû-Sa'id (Auzbeg) 42
Abu'l-Ghâzî Bahâdur Khân
    135, 146, 233, 236
Ahmad Mirza 33
Aîsân-Daulat Begîm 20
Aisin Gioro Ulhicun 125
Akanova, Dana K. 168, 172
Akbar (1556–1605) 22
Aktaş, Erhan 234, 237
Ali Arslan Khan 231
Alici, Didem Mersin 157
Alpatov, V. M. 94
Altinsarin, Ibray 160
Amanjolov, Qorghanbek 158
An Shuangcheng 125
Anderson, Benedict 177
Aoki Kazuo 110, 125

Arat, Reşit Rahmeti (1900–
    1964) 89, 91
Atasoy, Nurhan 58
Aûlûgh Beg Mîrzâ 53, 55
Aymavitov, Jusipbek 174
Babakurban, Orhan Cem 175
Bâbur (Zahir-ud-Din Muham-
    mad Bâbur) (1483–1530)
    11 ff.
Bailey, Harold Walter (1899–
    1996) 88, 89, 92
Barbaros Hayreddin Pasha
    231
Baskakov, N. A. (1905–1995)
    143, 145
Bawden, Charles R. (1924–
    2016) 90, 91
Bayazid 34
Bazin, Louis (1920–2011) 89,
    94, 152
Bell, Christine 11, 239
Bellini, Gentile (ca. 1429–
    1507) 35, 60
Berdibaev, Rahmanqul 167,
    173
Beveridge, Annette Susannah
    11 ff., 58
Bihishti (Mullâ) 41, 50
Bira, Shagdaryn (1927–) 92
Biyarov, B. N. 144